# NAPOLEON'S DEATH: AN INQUEST

The author, Major-General Frank Richardson, CB, DSO, OBE, MD, joined the Royal Army Medical Corps in 1927 and from 1956 to 1961 he was Director of Medical Services of the British Army of the Rhine. This book and his previous volume, *Napoleon: Bisexual Emperor* are the fruit of twenty years of study of Napoleonic material.

# Napoleon's Death: An Inquest

FRANK RICHARDSON M.D.

*With a foreword by*
JAMES A. ROSS
*President of the Royal College of Surgeons,*
*Edinburgh*

WILLIAM KIMBER · LONDON

First published in 1974 by
WILLIAM KIMBER & CO. LIMITED
Godolphin House, 22a Queen Anne's Gate,
London, SW1H 9AE

© Frank Richardson, 1974
ISBN 07183 0383 0

Typeset by
Specialised Offset Services Ltd., Liverpool
and printed and bound in Great Britain by
Robert MacLehose & Co., Limited, Glasgow

# Contents

# List of Illustrations

# Foreword

### JAMES A. ROSS
*President of the Royal College of Surgeons, Edinburgh*

Napoleon's last phase, as Lord Rosebery called it, has been frequently described, including details of his final illness. Most of these writers have not been medical men, and like Sir Walter Scott, have accepted without question the diagnosis of a 'scirrhus of the pylorus', that is, cancer of the stomach.

This was the diagnosis which seemed most acceptable to Napoleon's custodians. It indicated that he died of an hereditary disease, and his death was unconnected with any of the factors produced by his captivity. The opinions of some of his doctors, O'Meara and Stokoe, that he might have been suffering from hepatitis, a disease brought on by the tropical climate of St. Helena, were simply discounted, and their reports actually altered to omit this aspect of affairs.

Now General Richardson in his *Napoleon's Death: An Inquest* re-examines the facts about Napoleon's last illness, bringing to bear his qualifications of being, in addition to an historian, a military man, and an expert physician.

In his work the evidence which is available to us is most carefully sifted, and scrutinised with a critical professional eye. While accepting that the terminal event may have been cancer of the stomach, he makes it clear that Napoleon almost certainly suffered from amoebic hepatitis, that is, disease of the liver, acquired by living in St. Helena.

The symptoms Napoleon suffered from strongly support the opinion expressed by Dr O'Meara in October 1817 and Dr John Stokoe, that he had hepatitis. Their views were unacceptable to Sir Hudson Lowe, who considered Napoleon's illness to be mere fabrication, and a sham right up till the time he was dying. No apologist for Sir Hudson can explain away the facts noted by General Richardson: Sir Hudson's callousness, his utterly unscrupulous behaviour in regard to O'Meara's reports on Napoleon's health, altering them, and suppressing the evidence of hepatitis, and later altering Dr Shortt's post-mortem report, quashing any mention of liver disease, to suit his own views; his tyrannical treatment, and dismissal of O'Meara and Stokoe, whose primary intention it was to help their patient.

Dr Arnott's behaviour is shown up as feeble and indeed incompetent, but Antommarchi's position, as the only properly trained, experienced pathologist at the autopsy is properly affirmed.

What a pity that microscopic examination of structures was not available at that time! The condition of the stomach, and the liver, would have been diagnosed without a doubt by modern histological methods. As it is, the only portion of tissue which was apparently preserved by Antommarchi was a small piece of the small intestine, not the prime centre of Napoleon's disease; and its histological examination in this century does not shed any more light on the problem.

The evidence of the condition of the liver and stomach rests solely on the appearances described by eye witnesses, and these are conflicting.

After a full review of all the evidence, General Richardson makes out a well-reasoned case for amoebic hepatitis as the cause of Napoleon's last illness and death. Though this view can neither be proved or refuted, it must receive serious consideration by the historian in the future.

James A. Ross
PRCS Ed.

# Acknowledgements

In this book I have had to deal severely with some doctors of the nineteenth century, mostly graduates of the University of Edinburgh, and it is appropriate that the chapters in which I do this should have been read by two prominent Edinburgh medical men — Sir Derrick Dunlop, a physician of international eminence, and Mr James Ross, the President of the Royal College of Surgeons of Edinburgh. I am deeply grateful to two such busy men for finding the time to do this and for encouraging me to believe that what I say has been worth saying. Mr Ross has set the stage for me with a fine Foreword, whilst the warm glow of encouragement which I derived from Sir Derrick's words in a personal letter, from which I quote below, can well be imagined, even if our very old friendship has led him to flatter me:

> Like your previous book it is a work of medical and historical scholarship. You have made out a good case for amoebic hepatitis and shown how very unlikely cancer was as a cause of death. Of course amoebiasis can't be *proved* but it seems very probable. I can hardly think that the British Government can be held at all responsible for Napoleon's premature death. They had surely to incarcerate safely this terribly dangerous man who had on so many occasions plunged the world into such horrors, and no one knew anything about the prevalence of the entamoeba histolytica in the island at the time.

Major-General Hugh Jeffrey, whilst Director of Pathology to the British Army, kindly read my chapter on the post-mortem examination of Napoleon's body.

Once again it is a pleasure to acknowledge the friendly help of the staffs of the National Library of Scotland and of the Wellcome Historical Medical Library, especially Mr Robin Price. I am grateful for permission to consult on a few occasions the libraries of The Royal College of Physicians of Edinburgh, the Royal Society of Medicine and the Royal Colleges of Surgeons of London and of Edinburgh.

Mr David Brown of the Naval Historical Branch, Ministry of Defence, kindly helped me with the case of Dr John Stokoe.

For information about Napoleon's death mask I am most grateful to Baron Eugène de Veauce, who has unravelled the fascinating and extremely complex history of the various casts, and expounded it in scholarly treatises, including his book 'Les Masques Mortuaires de Napoléon', Paris 1971. He is at present bringing the story up to date in a book in English, which is in preparation, to be entitled *Was this Napoleon? The Affair of the Mask*.

I hope I may be allowed to acknowledge my debt to my publishers; William Kimber himself, a formidable but always kind and helpful inquisitor, and Amy Howlett, no less vigilant but perhaps with a softer heart for the heretic.

Finally, if the achievement of a second book makes me a real author, I should perhaps do what many of them do, and dedicate this book to my wife — 'For Sylvia' — perhaps, or 'To my wife, without whose . . . etc etc'. I am sure she imagines that her contribution has been a negative one, in that love and patience have helped her not to obstruct the process. In fact, however, her unvarying commonsense, so much greater than my own, has helped much more than she can possibly know. Instead of the dedication she deserves I give her something she is sure to appreciate much more — a promise that this is positively my last book about Napoleon.

# Introduction

An entertaining pastime for an amateur student of history is the discovery that things learned at school as historical facts may not be true after all.

The story of Napoleon is a rich field for the challenging of traditional beliefs. For example, he was not really a particularly small man; he did not hate the British people, but admired, respected, even envied them. This is relatively safe ground; but, I admit, that when suggesting, as I did in my first book, *Napoleon: Bisexual Emperor*, that he was not a great lover and quite probably never a father, I did so in the spirit of Michel Leiris, a writer who likes to share the bullfighter's knowledge that he risks being gored.

Possibly I was then not so much a matador as a bull in the Bonapartist china-shop. This time the bulls before which I am trailing my cloak include the British Medical Profession. It is an article of faith to British doctors, and to the vast majority of all historians, that Napoleon died of cancer of the stomach. Suggestions, even in medical journals, that this may not be true, that an American author, who wrote in 1960 that 'Modern pathologists consider it practically certain that Napoleon did not die of cancer', might be right, are immediately denounced as a dangerous heresy.

To say with certainty whether Napoleon died of cancer, or from some other cause, one would have had to be present in St Helena in 1821, equipped with today's knowledge of pathology – and a microscope. However I hope that my examination of the case may be enough to convince fair-minded people that there are reasonable grounds for doubt; and that two British naval surgeons in St Helena who refused to toe the party line were most unfairly treated. Both of them were dismissed from the Royal Navy, one by sentence of a court martial. Their 'offence' was that they tried to do what they could for their patient. It was their misfortune that their patient, known to the world as the Emperor Napoleon, was the prisoner of a British Government which had decreed that he was to be known only as General Buonaparte, and that any ailments from which he might suffer must in no circumstances be capable of being attributed to the choice of place for his internment — the tropical island of St Helena.

The lengths to which His Majesty's Government and their obedient servants were prepared to go to maintain this fiction, if indeed it was fiction, may surprise some readers; but it is possible to feel some sympathy for the Government in their predicament. They were saddled with much more than the physical person of Napoleon. They were saddled with his Legend.

In France in 1815 the Legend, like the Sun of Austerlitz, was undergoing a partial eclipse. If Napoleon had any hope of recapturing some of his lost popularity he probably had a better chance of doing so in England than anywhere else in Europe. In later years it would be in Britain, as much as in any country including France, that the heroic image would be patched up, the Napoleonic Legend refurbished and cherished.

The recent tendency to denigration of the Emperor has been virtually confined to French writers. Owen Connelly of the University of South Carolina, in the Introduction to his book *The Epic of Napoleon*, 1972, refers to an exhibition in the French National Library in 1969, the bicentenary of Napoleon's birth, which was actually designed to expose how Napoleon had himself created the Napoleonic Legend, dramatising his own achievements. In contrast to this French presentation of the Emperor as a dissembler and manipulator, Mr Connelly describes the reaction of an acute American observer, Mr Hans. J. Morgenthau, who was left with an inescapable impression of Napoleon's incomparable greatness. Hitler, he wrote, if stripped of the parades, the fanaticism and the totalitarian re-integration of a disintegrating society was no more than a destructive maniac; but, 'Take away the artifices of the Napoleonic Legend and what is left is the greatest man of action the western world has seen.'

The latest major biography in English of Napoleon, by Vincent Cronin, is imbued with a spirit of adulation as glowing as any ever written. My own admiration of Napoleon falls far short of hero-worship. The shining pages of the wonderful saga seem to be too smudged with suffering and some dark deeds. I can hardly doubt that a considerable majority of people would agree that the world would have been a happier place if, on the 5th December, 1791, premature death had claimed Lieutenant Napoleone

Buonaparte, rather than Wolfgang Amadeus Mozart. True, we would have lost many thrilling pages in our history books; but countless hours of the purest pleasure would have been added to what we already have. Those who hint that Mozart had drained himself of invention and melody should remember that he had only just completed his great German opera, *The Magic Flute*; surely an ample promise of great developments to come.

In this book I examine the growth of the Napoleonic Legend; Napoleon's feelings for our countrymen and their feelings for him; and the varied factors which made it impossible for His Majesty's Government to grant his earnest request to be allowed to settle in our country, and ultimately edged them into a position which could be described as dishonest, even if it was not deliberately so intended. St Helena was so remote from the seat of Government that they had to depend upon their man on the spot, the Governor Sir Hudson Lowe, who was driven into playing an evil part, although he was by no means an evil man. Some British doctors tried to do their best for the exile; others, through ignorance or prejudice, failed him, and failed their country lamentably. Napoleon was granted some seventeen years more of life than Mozart, but he did not live as long as he had a right to expect. To what extent was our country's Government responsible?

Readers of my first book will know that I am an advanced case of what has been called 'foot and note disease'. Some people detest having to turn to notes at the end of a book. To them I can say that they will miss nothing really essential to the development of my thesis if they seal down pages 231 to 252. The notes are more or less asides, which I wanted to share with those who enjoy such things.

Finally, I am aware that nineteenth century practice has driven me into using the words 'English' and 'England' where a twentieth century Scottish Nationalist would prefer me to say 'British' and 'Britain'. Napoleon certainly knew the difference between the English and the Scots, but he almost habitually referred to us all as English, and thought of our country as England. I realise I shall just have to expose my book to furious pencillings, should it find its way into a Scottish public library. Some of these have to be seen to be believed. In a book on modern Scotland in an Edinburgh library, the word 'London' has been scored out wherever it occurs, and the name 'Quislington' substituted.

# CHAPTER I

# The Napoleonic Legend

In all the amazing story of Napoleon Bonaparte nothing is more amazing than the rapid growth of what soon came to be called the Napoleonic Legend. It continued to grow despite set-backs which would have eclipsed the reputation of a less superbly self-confident hero, or perhaps one should say of a less inspired practitioner of the art of mass hypnosis. It has survived almost undimmed to the present day, although bitter experience of lesser but more evil dictators has sharpened our perception of what lay behind its glittering facade. Behind that facade, which lends to the imposing edifice the appearance of the soaring temple of a new religion, lay a charnel house.

Napoleon himself was the chief architect and the most industrious builder of his Legend, and we may confidently accept his own statement about when he laid its foundations. It was at the Battle of Lodi in 1796, where he is said to have led the final charge across the bridge. His rise to military fame began, of course, at the Siege of Toulon where his assertive self-confidence based on his professional skill as an artillery officer, and the authoritative ring of his views on tactics, made him a marked man to the Directors, especially to the shrewd and influential Lazare Carnot. The ruthlessness with which he dealt with the Royalists after the town surrendered made him the natural choice when the vile and intriguing Paul Barras needed a soldier to suppress, with a 'whiff of grapeshot', the Royalist rising in Paris in *Vendémiaire* of the Revolutionary Year IV – October 1795.

Generals of the Revolution had to tread warily and, if they were unsuccessful, or failed to make war pay for itself and for as much else as possible, they found themselves in disgrace, or even under the guillotine. It was for military failure more than for being a member of the old aristocracy that young General Alexandre Beauharnais, whose widow, Josephine, Napoleon was to marry, perished by the guillotine.

General Bonaparte kept his ears cocked in the political jungle of Paris, but when his great opportunity came with his selection to command the Army of Italy there was no failure, no lack of loot sent home to his greedy Revolutionary masters. On his new command the impact of the Italian-speaking, Italian-looking young Corsican general, lean and hungry like his troops, fierce and hawk-like with untidy spaniel ears of hair hanging over the high collar of his coat, was considerable.

It was soon reinforced by something which speaks most warmly to soldiers — victories. His sweeping successes may have been helped by the poor quality of the generals who opposed him and the enthusiasm with which many Italians welcomed him as the conqueror who would liberate them from Austrian rule; but the flame of his genius which was to shake the world had been kindled and he was vividly aware of it himself.

In St Helena, looking back over his great career, he said to Las Cases, '*Vendémiaire*, even Montenotte, had not yet led me to consider myself a being apart. Not till after Lodi did I feel that I was destined to play a foremost part on our political stage, that kindled the spark of boundless ambition in me.' He told General Gourgaud, that at Lodi 'I felt the world spin away beneath me as if I was borne up into the air.' In fact he had become aware of his own great powers of leadership.

Soon after this profound spiritual experience and his triumphal entry into Milan, he told Marmont, one of his earliest comrades-in-arms, that his success was nothing to what lay ahead. 'In our days,' he added, 'no one has conceived anything great; it falls to me to give the example.'

He was then only twenty six years old, but was already displaying that love of theatrical declamation which was to grow stronger, as he became more and more conscious of the place in history to which he aspired, as a compound of Alexander the Great, Hannibal, Caesar and Charlemagne. He staked his claim early with a ringing declaration of the objectives of his advance on Rome — 'To restore the Capitol, to replace the statues of the heroes who rendered it illustrious, to rouse the Roman people.'

If those Italians who had looked upon him as a liberator were disillusioned when many of their statues, along with other portable articles of value, found their way to Paris, it could only have been because they had not heard his promise to his army on arriving in their country. 'Soldiers. You are naked and ill-fed. I will lead you into the most fruitful plains in the world. Rich provinces, great cities will be in your power. There you will find honour, fame, and wealth.' Later when he had become Emperor, he said, 'The French require a prince to be active, enterprising and courageous, and above all to take them robbing abroad.'

That formidable voice, first heard during the Italian campaign, was to resound for twenty years throughout Europe with growing vehemence, admonishing, threatening. He spoke, indeed dictated, to crowned heads in tones of easy familiarity. But what really mattered was what he said to his soldiers, those splendid rugged men who were to follow him unquestioningly because he knew, as few generals have known, how to touch their hearts — French hearts.

He often spoke of the importance to a military commander of the use of words, which he used to say must be like music which speaks to the soul. 'The influence of words over men,' he explained, 'is astounding. But you must speak to the soul in order to electrify the man.'

It has been questioned if many soldiers in the Army of Egypt really heard Napoleon's famous exhortation before the Battle of the Pyramids: 'Soldiers. From the tops of those Pyramids forty centuries look down upon you.' But by this time they knew his worth as a man of deeds as well as of many words. In the fierce heat of the arid desert any scrap of shade from a lone palm tree or ruined hut was jealously reserved by his soldiers for Bonaparte. Twenty-two centuries before him Xenophon's Greeks abused and beat the mutinous Soteridas, to whom Xenophon had good-humouredly surrendered his horse. Men recognise a leader and will look after him, in their own interests, when danger threatens.

The great Corsican certainly knew how to strike the right note for Frenchmen, and struck it well and truly to the end. The unhappily wavering Marshal Ney, sent by Louis XVIII to fulfil his rash promise to bring his old master to his new one in a cage, was lost when he read the famous proclamation before the march on Paris, with the typically Napoleonic promise: 'Victory will advance at the charge; the eagle, with the national colours, will fly from spire to spire right up to the towers of Nôtre Dame.'

'This is how one talks to soldiers,' said Ney.

In fabricating his Legend Napoleon needed no Dr Goebbels, for he was himself the first and probably the greatest practitioner of the often fraudulent arts of publicity, propaganda and the use of a controlled Press — the prototype of the modern dictator. Many biographies and fat volumes recording Napoleon's sayings on

almost every conceivable subject, his frequent monologues and
pontifications, convey the impression of an imperial Dr Johnson
attended by a horde of sycophantic Boswells. He lacked the Great
Cham's sense of humour and wit, and was unwilling to let others
have their say, even for the pleasure of demolishing them with
shafts of repartee.

In the collections of his sayings can be found pronouncements
borrowed from others, and often much improved. It was not
Napoleon but the Corsican patriot Pasquale Paoli, who called
England 'a nation of shopkeepers'. It may have been Napoleon
who called Wellington 'a sepoy general', but it sounds much more
like a jealous tongue in the Horse Guards. Napoleon, arriving
weary and haggard in Poland from the Russian snows in which he
had abandoned his great army, repeatedly said, 'There is but one
step from the sublime to the ridiculous'. Tom Paine, an author
much esteemed in Revolutionary France, had said that before,
though less succinctly. But 'Sufficient unto the day is the evil
thereof' is surely going a bit too far. Without for one moment
suggesting that Napoleon would have connived at the attribution
to himself of St Matthew's version of part of the Sermon on the
Mount, it has to be said that he was himself guilty of graver
offences than Biblical plagiarism. It is not for nothing that the
collections of Napoleon's sayings smack of the sacred book of a
new religion — a Napoleonic Koran. Unable to claim divinity, like
his hero Alexander the Great, Napoleon went to astounding
lengths in that direction. He tried to have his birthday, August
15th, celebrated as Saint Napoleon's Day, but as that was the
Feast of the Assumption he had to settle for August 16th.

Pope Pius VII had been too late with his protest against the
replacement in the calendar of St Roch by St Napoleon, but he
steadfastly refused to authorise Napoleon's new Imperial Catechism, wherein the children of France were told that their
Emperor was the image of God on earth, and that those who were
'lacking in their duty towards our Emperor resist the order
established by God himself, and render themselves worthy of
eternal damnation.'[1] In France Napoleon set himself above the
Pope. The complaisant Papal Legate, Cardinal Caprara, authorised the use of this travesty of Christianity, in May 1806, and the
bishops weakly complied.

Has any other dictator ever dared to go so far as this?

As Napoleon's seat on the throne became firmer he saw to it
that there was only one great man in France, to whom all

successes were attributed, whilst any bad news was suppressed or a scapegoat found to take the blame. He claimed that the word 'impossible' was not in his vocabulary and he treated disaster as if it had not occurred. Sent to Egypt by a Government which probably hoped to see no more of a man in whose growing influence they sensed a threat of military dictatorship, he treated the destruction of his fleet by Nelson at the Battle of the Nile with remarkable detachment. With his life-line severed he pressed on with his bold invasion of Syria, hoping to march in the footsteps of Alexander the Great. Frustrated by Sir Sidney Smith's defence of Acre he pretended that he had decided not to take the town as plague was raging in it. Not man but Nature herself had defeated General Bonaparte. Soon he slipped off home, persuading his supporters that he was needed in France, where his great conquests had been dissipated by ineffective lawyers. With considerable daring he evaded the British fleet and brought his small convoy safely to France. He had handed over his Army of Egypt, and his mistress Pauline Fourès, to the splendid Republican general, Kléber, who, like many men in that army, had become disillusioned by Bonaparte's callous unconcern for the welfare of his soldiers, even of the sick and wounded; to say nothing of his inexcusable massacre of thousands of Turkish prisoners of war. Kléber, left to reap the harvest of ill-will, was soon assassinated by an Arab fanatic, and when Bonaparte heard of his death he is said to have commented: 'One rival the less.'

Napoleon knew that he was little loved by the soldiers in Egypt, where the popular leaders were Kléber and Desaix. Bonaparte's soldiers had even cried, 'Let us have Kléber for our leader. He is humane and gentle.' But by the time the disgruntled survivors of the Army of Egypt reached France Napoleon's Star was in the ascendant. He had prevailed over his enemies in France and, narrowly escaping failure in the *Coup de Brumaire* with the resolute help of his brother Lucien, had made himself First Consul and virtual master of France. On the day of Kléber's assassination Desaix was killed at Marengo, where he saved the day for Napoleon who had badly bungled the battle. J.C. Herold comments:

> The price for his future victories was . . . paid by Desaix; the price for his past ones by Kléber.

In Kléber and Desaix France lost two great men whom Napoleon described as his two best generals. He could afford to praise them for they were both dead.[2]

Napoleon encouraged his soldiers to feel that each one had a marshal's baton in his knapsack, but he did not intend to let his marshals reach for a sceptre. Norwood Young, in a chapter about Napoleon's luck, analysed the potentialities of many French soldiers who might have done as well as Napoleon. He concluded that if Napoleon had not been able to escape from Egypt at the critical moment he might well have found one of them in occupation of the seat of power.[3] The heroic death of Desaix, and the great cavalry charge led by General François Etienne Kellermann at Marengo, ensured for these two an honoured place in French history. Napoleon was not slow to honour his debt to Desaix, but, in grandiloquently decreeing that such a hero's tomb must have the Alps for its pedestal, he kept the dead warrior conveniently far from Paris — in the Hospice of St Bernard. Napoleon's personal failure at Marengo was never mentioned.

Suppression of unpleasant facts and of anything which could dim the lustre of his fame became habitual, and it continues to this day. Napoleon's deliberate burnishing of his Legend whilst he was in St Helena was undertaken not only to secure his own place in history, but to pave the way for a restoration of the Bonaparte dynasty. He had been profoundly shocked by the measure of success achieved by General Malet's conspiracy in 1812, when he himself was far away in Russia, chasing the fatal will o' the wisp which, luckily for Europe, was to lure Hitler on a similar self-destructive aggression. The false news that Napoleon had died in Moscow was not received with noticeable gloom by the hundreds who believed it, and no one thought of the King of Rome, except Malet, who referred to him in his proclamation as 'a bastard child'. Commenting acidly on the failure of anyone to cry 'Vive Napoleon II', the Emperor said, 'I am forced to admit that all I have built is fragile.' He had for too long lived in a self-centred world in which hardly anyone dared to hint that his thoughts and actions might be less than perfect; in which everything revolved around his ambitions for France, but still more for himself and his insatiable family.

Of course the Malet coup collapsed before the Emperor reached Paris. Napoleon was back in his capital. All was well with France. The ragged victims of his inability to recognise when he was beaten were tottering through the snow, relying on the heroic Michel Ney for what protection they could get from the pursuing Cossacks. Their God of War had deserted them, remarking that he now weighed more on his throne than at the head of the army. He ended his XXIXth Bulletin, announcing the loss of nearly half a million men, with the bland assurance that 'The Emperor's health has never been better.' If he had heard Chateaubriand's bitter comment — 'Families dry your tears. Napoleon is well' — it is quite possible that he would have barely comprehended it. His well-being and that of France were by now synonymous — in his own mind at least.

No great general has ever been more wasteful of men's lives. Kléber said that Napoleon was the sort of general who needs a reinforcement of ten thousand men a month. Napoleon's own estimate, though a trifle lower, was expressed with a cold callousness which must appal us today, though something equally horrifying was said by one of the petty Napoleons of our own time. Napoleon's statement, 'I can afford to expend a hundred thousand men a year', was parallelled by Mussolini, when he said to Badoglio, 'I need only a few thousand dead to sit at the conference table in the rôle of a co-belligerent.'[4]

But Napoleon, at least, could afford to be honest with his soldiers. So firm was his grip on their hearts and minds that he could say to them, 'Soldiers, I need your lives. You must give them to me.'

Soldiers on active service develop a curious detached attitude to the possibility of being killed or wounded — those who are not afflicted by premonitions of death. Many come to feel invulnerable — 'It can't happen to me'; and when it happens to friends their grief, though sharp enough, is often oddly transient. A close friend, who has seemed the centre of the life of a unit, may be almost forgotten in a few weeks. This is not hardness of heart but a kind of mental insulation which is almost essential if one is to carry on. But how different it has to be for those who must stay at home awaiting news of close relatives.

If the ghastly carnage of the Napoleonic battles had been projected into every home in Europe with the impact of modern television reporting would the statesmen and generals have been swept away or compelled to make peace? Surely Napoleon could hardly have survived the shock, felt in his day by only a few, if the staggering selfish complacency of his XXIXth Bulletin had been felt by thousands who had seen for themselves the horrors of the Retreat from Moscow, so movingly described by many eye-witnesses. Would the 350,000 conscripts voted by a cowed French Senate for his 1813 campaign then have been forthcoming?

If Napoleon's rigorous censorship had not suppressed every adverse report there were many incidents which, in the hands of a free press, would have cracked the image of the omnipotent Emperor, the Little Corporal who cared for his soldiers as a father for his children. No newspaper printed his comment 'Soldiers are made to be killed', or published pictures of him on the field of Eylau, turning over the bodies of men who had died for him, saying, 'Small change! Small change! A night of Paris will soon adjust all these losses.'

One of the most terrible stories would have been that of the sacrifice of many lives during a mere invasion practice. Admiral Bruix had refused to send ships to sea because of an impending storm, but Napoleon, after a terrible scene culminating in Bruix's dismissal, sent the ships out himself, only to see them overwhelmed with terrible loss of life. On that occasion bribery with money by Napoleon's agents had to be resorted to, in addition to the normal censorship, to keep the dreadful truth from the public.

When reverses could not be concealed from the people, Napoleon's gift for ignoring unpleasant facts and seeing things only as he wished them to be, enabled him to gloss things over or to lay the blame elsewhere.

The Egyptian campaign was his first failure, for military conquest was its principal object. But it would be unfair to overlook its results in other fields — fields which showed the world that General Bonaparte was much more than a simple soldier. He took with him an impressive body of sages and scientists, and two printing plants equipped to print in French, Arabic and Greek. Napoleon, like many Frenchmen, was intensely interested in the mysteries of Ancient Egypt, and the expedition appealed strongly to the romantic, mystic side of his nature. In his dealings with the wise men and sheikhs he persuaded them that he genuinely desired to become a convert to Islam; indeed he half convinced himself, but, realism regaining control, he remarked, 'I was a Mahommedan in Egypt; I shall be a Catholic in France.'

His own grasp of art and science was superficial but, by his encouragement of his team of experts and by the foundation of the Institute of Egypt under Gaspard Monge, he laid the foundations of Egyptology, and of a strong influence of French culture in Egypt which endured for a very long time. It was at a meeting of the Institute that the Rosetta stone was first described, though its inscriptions were not deciphered, by Jean François Champollion, for thirty-two years.

When writing the history of the unsuccessful military campaign Napoleon cooked the figures of casualties and contrived to make it all sound most creditable to himself. Kléber was dead, so he could not set that record straight; but General Sarrazin tried to do so in a book published in 1811, dedicated to the heroic Kléber, in which he called Bonaparte a treacherous Corsican.

General Bonaparte had contrived to blame Nature for his failure at Acre, and it was even easier for the Emperor to make Nature his scapegoat for the much more disastrous failure of his badly-planned invasion of Russia in 1812. It was not the Russians who had defeated him but General Janvier and Février. But it is now known, from statistical records, that the winter of 1812 was not an unusually severe one, for Russia. Napoleon had taken none of the normal precautions against its onset. Everything that was needed for the welfare of his troops — their pay, clothing, rations and medical care, always received scant attention from this military genius to whom they were not men so much as instruments of his will — 'Troops are made to be killed!' His minister of the Interior, Jean Chaptal, wrote:

> He regarded men as base coin, or as tools with which he was to gratify his whims and ambition.

In 1813 scapegoats abounded. He told Metternich, 'It's my generals who want peace. I have no generals now. The cold of Moscow demoralised them.' He did not exaggerate. His generals were indeed sick of war and, even more, they were sick of him. As Metternich went to his remarkable interview with Napoleon in the Marcolini Palace in Dresden, Marshal Berthier stopped him and urgently impressed upon him, 'Do not forget that Europe requires peace, and especially France, which will have nothing but peace.' Napoleon's own Chief of Staff, his invaluable Berthier, thus ranged himself beside the Emperor's enemies, for the Emperor was determined not to have peace. Almost alone in Europe he wanted war, if he could not have his way in everything.

Hostility to Napoleon had frequently erupted during the mismanaged Russian campaign of 1812. For example Ney had exploded about the Emperor commanding from *behind* his army, and had said that he should go back to the Tuileries and leave the fighting to generals.

After the disastrous Battle of Leipzig Marshal Macdonald, who for the rest of his life was to remember the despairing cries of his soldiers, abandoned on the wrong side of the prematurely blown bridge over the Elster, was sickened by Napoleon's unconcern and came as near to hatred as his calm and generous heart would allow. Rough old Augereau was less restrained, and asked Macdonald, 'Does the bugger know what he's doing?' He went on to denounce the Emperor as a coward who had lost his head and was deserting and sacrificing them all.

But by 1814 'the bugger' unquestionably knew what he was doing. There was no sign of cowardice, no loss of the great general's head in that campaign to save France. It has been said that Napoleon's genius had never blazed more brightly than when he was fighting to save his capital. The swiftness of his movements to parry first one thrust and then another brings to mind the agility of such film-star duellists as Douglas Fairbanks or Errol Flynn, leaping from staircase to table, despatching one swordsman after another. And, like the hero of a film, Napoleon seemed to be invulnerable. According to Berthier he was trying to find death in the field. Napoleon admitted that he had deliberately exposed himself to enemy fire, adding, 'I am condemned to live'.

Napoleon had touched the heights of generalship, and luckily the required scapegoat was handy — Marmont's so-called treachery provided Bonapartist France with a new verb for the act of betrayal — *raguser*, from his title Duke of Ragusa.[5]

But the marshals blamed Napoleon, and they refused his appeals to rally the country for one last fling. Their spokesman, a grim-faced Marshal Ney, demanded his abdication. Soon after he had signed the Treaty of Fontainebleau, accepting his exile to the island of Elba, Napoleon took poison which failed to kill him, but caused a severe attack of vomiting and prostration. The evidence of his close friend and confidant Caulaincourt, as well as that of his valet Constant, that this attempt to commit suicide really took place is generally accepted as conclusive.[6]

Napoleon had often denounced suicide as the resort of weaklings. His true voice was the one which said, '*La haute tragédie est l'école des grands hommes.*' An unsuccessful attempt at suicide is regarded as a cry for help, and Napoleon was the last man to utter such a cry. The only other plausible explanation of the condition in which Napoleon was found is that he was overcome by one of the severe digestive upsets to which he was prone when things were not going well. It is however a fact that it had for long been the duty of his valet to ensure that he had always about his person a small leather sachet containing poison supplied to him by Corvisart, his family physician, Yvan, the

doctor who accompanied him on his campaigns, or Dr Cabanis, a
toxicologist. It has been suggested that the poison was either too
weak and only made him sick, or too strong so that his stomach
rejected it. Dr Yvan was sent for and Napoleon demanded from
him a stronger dose of opium. Yvan refused, left the room and
disappeared from the pages of history.

That Napoleon had provided himself with the means to commit
suicide as a last resort, to avoid capture and humiliation, does not
by any means imply that he was a suicidal type. Even if he did, in
a moment of bleak despair, make the attempt, it is likely that he
regretted it, for he did not refer to it again. He was in fact less of a
suicidal type than an incurable optimist. His much-vaunted Star
could not be an autumnal shooting-star doomed to extinction. It
had to be a comet which would reappear in its due time. Hope
revived and the active brain began to prepare the scene for that
reappearance.

He determined to leave the stage of his Glory on a theatrical
note of high tragedy, embracing in front of a parade of his Old
Guard their colour on the staff topped by the imperial eagle, as a
symbol of each one of them. He solemnly adjured them never to
forget the Glory they had won together. Claiming to have
sacrificed his own interests to those of France, he said that he
consented to live only to complete his final task — 'to recount for
posterity the great things we have done together.'

This superbly Napoleonic performance, dignified and emotion-
ally satisfying, was to be followed by scenes so painful that many
historians avert their eyes from the events of the journey through
France to embark at Fréjus for the island of Elba. One of those
who described Napoleon's humiliation, Dr Paul Bartel, in
*Napoléon à l'isle d'Elbe*, aptly entitles his chapter *Calvaire*.

The most complete account of the terrible journey is that of the
Prussian Commissioner, Count Truchsess von Waldburg, who could
be relied upon to omit no denigrating detail; but his story is fully
corroborated by many eyewitnesses. The first encounter was with
old Augereau, who kept his hat on his head, treated Napoleon
with contempt and reproached him for the insatiable ambition to
which he had sacrificed France. As they drove southwards,
especially when Provence had to be traversed, the Commissioners
found that they really had the task of protecting their prisoner
from the fury of the population, especially from the women. Cries
of 'Down with the tyrant', horrible insults, demands that he
should be handed over to their vengeance, grew louder; knives

flashed, firearms were raised.

The Russian General, Count Schuvalov, pacified a violently hostile mob by reproaching them for insulting a defenceless man, inviting them to see for themselves how abject he now was, and that he deserved to be treated only with contempt. For this humiliating advocacy he was actually thanked by Napoleon, whose morale had completely slumped. He had set out quite jauntily, telling the Commissioners that after all he had not done too badly, having started out with a six franc piece in his pocket and being now, at the end of it all, very rich. But now he saw, for the first time, how deeply Frenchmen, and Frenchwomen with sons and husbands to mourn, could hate him; and he became more and more fearful for his life, not only at the hands of the terrible war-weary crowds, but from poison with which he was convinced that the French Government would try to get rid of him.

In the neighbourhood of Avignon a band under a man called Mollot tried to seize him, but was beaten off by General Bertrand and the burly Swiss groom Noverraz. At Orgon, where Napoleon saw his blood-smeared effigy hanged in front of the inn in which he was hiding, Mollot, joined by a peasant called Durel, had another try. Durel actually grabbed Napoleon's collar and made him cry 'Vive le Roi'. Napoleon, shaking and sobbing, cowered behind Bertrand, and for the rest of the journey was frequently seen to be in tears. He insisted on adopting various changes of disguise, always with the detested white cockade in his hat. He made a Russian aide-de-camp wear his clothes, hoping to divert upon him the hostility and execration of the mobs.

When his sister Pauline met him, dressed in a mixture of enemy uniforms, she refused to embrace him until he had put on his own clothes. The ineffaceable memory of these days of horrid humiliation, and probably the needling of the proud Pauline, may have helped to steel his mind to attempt his last bid to regain power.

In St Helena Napoleon once said:

> Misfortunes also have their heroism and their glory. My career lacked adversity. If I had died on the throne, in the clouds of my omnipotence, I would have remained incomplete for many people. Today, thanks to misfortune, I can be judged for what I really am.

These philosophical reflections were occasioned only by his last disaster at Waterloo. During his active career he had a remarkable capacity for erasing from his mind anything which might ruffle his serene self-satisfaction. In 1812 the Grand Army had perished; but the Emperor's health had never been better. In 1814, after his dreadful journey through France, the respectful admiration of British sailors on board *Undaunted*, taking him to Elba, applied the first balm to his battered spirit. The brief interlude in his tiny island kingdom was almost idyllic. He personally designed his new flag and bent his great powers to making Elba prosperous. Hopes of restoration to the throne of France were nourished by reports that many Frenchmen, soon sickened by Bourbon stupidity, were toasting Napoleon's return 'with the violets'. There were clandestine visits by French Bonapartists, and open ones by English admirers. One of the principal factors which drove Napoleon to stake everything on one last throw was the foolish and spiteful refusal of the Bourbons to pay the pension awarded to him by the Treaty of Fontainebleau; but the shame of Orgon had to be wiped out if the Legend were to survive.

We may well ask if the Napoleonic Legend would live as it does today without the magic of The Hundred Days, and above all of its wonderful first twenty-one days — the triumphant flight of the eagle with the national colours to its final perch in Paris. That dazzling and exciting flight was marked by a noticeable change in public opinion, summarised in a contemporary broadsheet in Paris:

The Tiger has broken out of his den.
The Ogre has been three days at sea.
The Wretch has landed at Fréjus.
The Brigand has reached Antibes.
The Invader has arrived at Grenoble.
The General has entered Lyons.
Napoleon slept at Fontainebleau last night.
The Emperor will proceed to the Tuileries today.
His Imperial Majesty will address his loyal subjects tomorrow.

One of the most powerful voices raised against Napoleon soon after the news of his landing in France was received, was that of Benjamin Constant, the Swiss-born French philosopher and writer. Urged by the society beauty Mme Récamier to declare himself against Napoleon, he wrote in an article on March 19th — the day before Napoleon reached Paris — that Napoleon was more terrible and odious than Attila or Genghis Khan, because he had the resources of civilisation; and he had drawn away 'to the ends of the world the élite of the nation, to abandon it there to the horrors of famine and rigours of frost; by his will twelve hundred thousand brave men perished on foreign soil without succour, without maintenance, without solace, deserted by him after defending him with their dying hands.'

Every word of this was true, indeed the casualty estimate was a conservative one, but, alas for brave words, Benjamin Constant was soon to be found helping to draft Napoleon's new constitution. It was another example of Napoleon's genius for getting even enemies to work for him; and no doubt Constant served Napoleon in the hope of serving France, and so salved his conscience.[7]

But the opinions of civilians, even of statesmen, meant little to Napoleon if he could count on the support of the Army. He expected little from his old marshals. They had been allowed by Louis to keep their titles and personal fortunes. But the more junior officers, many put on half pay, living on the memories of past glory and thirsting for new adventures; and above all the rank and file — on these Napoleon knew he could rely. Wellington was also sure about this, and when Creevey asked him if he expected any desertions from the French Army, he replied 'Not upon a man from the colonel to the private in the regiment — both inclusive. We may pick up a marshal or two, perhaps, but not worth a damn.'

Marshal Soult, a military Benjamin Constant, in his initial weathercock swing, denounced Napoleon's return as an act of lunacy, calling him an adventurer and a madman. As Louis' Minister of War he was highly embarrassed by Napoleon's return and had to make plans to oppose him. However, in due course we find him at Waterloo, as Napoleon's Chief of Staff, a very inadequate substitute for the irreplaceable Berthier, who had fitted Napoleon like a glove. Berthier had cast himself from a window to his death rather than take up again the old yoke. In the event the military preparations to resist the invader, hailed in Royalist circles with hysterical fanfares, proved as ineffective as 'a flight of dragon-flies over troubled waters', in M. Manceron's memorable words. The brilliant though unpredictable Marshal Ney, having boldly set out to redeem his rash promise to Louis to bring the Usurper to him in an iron cage (a promise not at all to the liking of the fat king, who murmured that he would not care to be presented with such a bird) soon succumbed to the magic of his master's voice.

Marshal Murat, prepared to redeem his treachery of 1814 and to support Napoleon, was too busy being King Joachim, and trying to salvage his tawdry Neapolitan kingdom, to serve under the

Emperor's direct command — and what a difference he might have made to all those desperate cavalry charges at Waterloo.

Marshal Macdonald was still brooding over the sacrifice of his soldiers, when the Emperor had bungled the disengagement of his army after its defeat at Leipzig. How could so fine a soldier forget the cries of his own men being butchered on the wrong side of the Elster? But it is not, I hope, stretching the imagination too far to suppose that he felt some inborn reverence for legitimate Royalty in distress, for he was the son of a Scottish Jacobite Neil MacEachain, a schoolmaster of South Uist, who had taken the name of Macdonald and fled to France, after sheltering and helping Prince Charles Edward Stuart in his flight from the Outer Hebrides — 'over the sea to Skye'. After striving to rally the Royalist troops and escorting the king to safety in Menin, Etienne Macdonald returned to Paris, where he enlisted in the National Guard as a simple grenadier. He deserves a large share of the credit for the avoidance of civil war in France. This had been a distinct possibility.

The thrilling story of 'The Twenty One Days' is told by M. Claude Manceron in one of the splendid books in which he examines in fascinating detail quite short periods of Napoleon's career. The title of this book, *Napoleon Recaptures Paris*, may serve to emphasise that it was no picnic. It was a time of the utmost confusion. The Tricolour and the white flag of the Bourbons sometimes flew on opposite sides of the same street. Mayors and officials who had sworn allegiance to Louis changed sides sometimes only when Napoleon with his little army, which quickly snowballed to over twenty thousand, was actually in their town. But Napoleon had to advance with caution. In his eagerness to show to history a good face and heroic motives for his return, to pose as a liberator and above all to avoid bloodshed, he spent hours haranguing, even pleading with, obdurate officials. They could and did point out that he himself, by his abdication, had freed them from their oath of allegiance — but who could now release them from their more recent oath to Louis XVIII? The mayor of one village went so far as to complain, 'We were just beginning to have a little peace. Now you come to spoil it all again.'

Near Grenoble occurred the first really tense confrontation with the Army. General Marchand, commanding the Seventh Division, doubted if his troops would support him in his determination to arrest Napoleon; and of course when the moment came they would not. What a wonderful scene as the familiar portly figure walked up to the troops drawn up to oppose him, and actually under orders to fire upon him. Smiling and confident — but with what innermost thoughts? What if a dozen, or only one, of the men behind those raised muskets cherished feelings towards him such as those of the Provençal peasants who, barely eleven months before, had howled for his blood? But he walks forward — 'Soldiers of the 5th! Do you recognise me?' — throwing open his coat, inviting them to shoot their Emperor. Superb. The battalion commander surrenders his sword. Napoleon shakes his hand and allows him to ride away. No bloodshed.

After this Napoleon feels little fear of Ney and his iron cage. Ney, to placate his conscience and naturally doubtful of his welcome, has prepared a long statement, justifying himself, warning Napoleon that he must safeguard the interests of the Motherland. Napoleon barely skims it through, throws it into the fire and sends a message to tell Ney that he loves him as ever and is waiting to embrace him.

Later on Napoleon was to enjoy telling the story of General Ameil, captured early in March whilst commanding the cavalry of Napoleon's advanced guard, having ventured too far ahead of the spreading tide of Bonapartism. Taken before King Louis he said, 'Sire, we military men are libertines; if you are our legitimate sovereign, the Emperor is our mistress.'

In his arguments with civilian officials and his harangues to the soldiers Napoleon, as usual, did not err on the side of complete honesty. He implied that he had been encouraged to return by leading members of the Government in Paris, that he had an understanding with some of the great powers of Europe. He came only to restore the liberty of the peasants, the honour of the Army, the best of what the Revolution had achieved; to see his son enthroned as ruler of a free and prosperous nation at peace with its neighbours. It would not be inconsistent with his enigmatic character if he was truly sincere in these noble professions. But the intoxication of his welcome, the ever-growing volume of the cries of 'Vive l'Empereur', which could hardly be raised in honour of a four year old child, soon dispelled any doubts about who was to occupy the throne. At last on March 20th, his son's fourth birthday, it was of course His Majesty who entered his Palace of the Tuileries — borne up the great stairway, tossing on the shoulders of a wildly cheering throng, his eyes half-closed in a daze, whilst Count de la Vallette went backwards

Napoleon at the Battle of Lodi

The new house at Longwood on St. Helena, intended for Napoleon

Longwood House, St. Helena. 1. Billiard Room. 2. Drawing Room. 3. Bedroom. 4. Bathroom. 4a. Marchand (valet)

before him to clear a path, repeating as if hypnotised, 'It is you. It is you. It is really you.'

At this sublime culmination of the high adventure, before the legendary Hundred Days turned sour, Napoleon must have known complete happiness, even elation comparable to his vision at Lodi. He certainly said himself that it was the happiest time in his life. The Bonaparte dynasty was restored. Surely now his wife must return to him, bringing with her the heir to the throne which he had reoccupied.

But for once the man of action had permitted himself to dream. Meditation, reflection, he had always liked to say, were the springs which fed what men called his genius. Reflection should have warned him that Europe would never tolerate him. All too soon the dream was to dissolve in harsh reality, when Europe declared war, not on France, but on Napoleon. It cannot really be said that the great adventure ended on a note of noble tragedy, for Napoleon's leadership at Waterloo was inept and inert. Even if this was to some extent due to ill-health it has to be said that it was also tainted by overconfidence and dishonesty. With a touch of the old mastery he had stolen a march on his enemies by the speed of his concentration and advance into Belgium. Confident that he had no more to fear from Blücher's Prussians after the drubbing he had given them at Ligny, and unable to believe that he could for long be resisted by the motley Anglo-Dutch army in the Mont St Jean position, he scoffed at Marshal Soult's fears. These were soundly rooted in the marshal's personal experience of that army's redoubtable commander, in whose presence he knew that a single false move could be fatal.

A younger and shrewder soldier supported Soult's caution. General Maximilien Sebastien Foy had served in the Peninsula, where the magic of Wellington's name had sometimes sufficed to delay a French attack. Now he dared to warn Napoleon, 'Wellington never shows his troops; but if he is out there, I must warn your Majesty that the English infantry, in close fighting, is the very devil.'

The Emperor airily dismissed their advice. 'Because you have been beaten by Wellington you think he is a great general. I tell you Wellington is a bad general, and the English are bad troops, and this affair will be a picnic. We will sleep in Brussels tonight.'

Napoleon may have assumed an air of overweening optimism in order to stiffen the backbone of his Chief of Staff. It is outside the scope of this book to discuss the undoubted soundness of

c

Wellington's dispositions or Napoleon's mistakes. What mattered on the field that day was his dishonesty and failure in personal leadership.

At the most critical moment, when a last determined thrust might have broken through Wellington's line, Napoleon, quite out of touch with 'the sharp end', testily refused Ney's urgent plea for reinforcements, asking if Ney thought he could 'make troops' — he actually used a very coarse expression, one of his failings when under stress. He was indeed under considerable stress, for he knew, as Ney did not, that the rear and right flank of his army was threatened. When the approach of the Prussians revealed the terrible flaw in his appreciation of the situation, he craftily spread a rumour that it was Grouchy's troops coming to support him. He hoped, by this unpardonable subterfuge, to sustain the wavering morale of his soldiers; but when the realisation of his deceit began to spread, a deep sense of betrayal overwhelmed many of them.

Even now he could have retrieved much of his old magnetism, as he set off down the road into the valley towards the ridge where his last and most resolute enemy lay concealed. Napoleon had ridden at the head of the Imperial Guard, crying, *'En avant, tout-le-monde!'* But, unlike 1814, this time he was not seeking death in battle. So when he reached that well-known feature of the battlefield, the quarry or gravel-pit on the left of the road some five hundred yards short of the farmhouse of La Haye Sainte, he stepped aside and throwing open his coat so that the soldiers could see his orders and decorations, he watched them pass, leaving to Ney the nonour of leading the very last advance of a Napoleonic army.

A surprising number of the soldiers had never seen Napoleon at such close quarters. Even to those who had he was somehow still the hawk-like young general storming across the bridges of Arcola and Lodi, reining back a fiery charger as he pointed the way across the Alps — that hero of so many paintings, their own uniquely personal God of War, their Little Corporal. And there he stood, podgy, unhealthy-looking, unwilling — perhaps unable, to lead them further; making it seem plain that *tout le monde* did not include his sacred person. Only four days before, in a proclamation, he had reminded them of Marengo and Friedland, and declaimed, 'The moment has come for all good Frenchmen to conquer or perish.'

Good Frenchmen, it must have appeared, did not necessarily include crafty Corsicans. It was said that on many soldiers faces as they passed him 'surprise was mingled with discontent'. His youngest brother, Jerome, a frivolous worthless creature, was yet able to rise to the challenge of Waterloo. His attempts to capture the farmhouse of Hougomont were pressed with exemplary courage and resolution, and were as heroically repulsed. He recognised what the situation demanded, and asked, 'Can it be possible he will not seek death here?' Spoken like a Bonaparte. But the greatest Bonaparte had stepped aside, abdicated his leadership, helped to pave the way to that awful moment when, for the first time in history, the words *'La Garde recule'* were heard, followed by the very French cry of *'Nous sommes trahis'*.

Even as late as 7 p.m. hopes had been high on the French side. As they advanced up the sloping open fields between Hougomont and La Haye Sainte they could discern no real opposition; indeed they could see little more than a group of mounted officers around an instantly recognisable figure with a low-crowned cocked hat.

A wounded French general, Friant, making his way towards the dressing station in the recently captured farmhouse of La Haye Sainte, shouted exultantly: 'All goes well. The enemy seems to be forming his rearguard to cover his retreat. He will be completely broken as soon as the rest of the Guard debouches. We only need a quarter of an hour.'\*

But Wellington and his staff were not about to turn their horses towards Brussels. Before them, concealed in a sunk road, the patient redcoats awaited the end of their long ordeal, during which some had actually wondered if this was to be the first battle in which *everyone* was killed. As the Imperial Guard came in sight, mounting the slope only forty paces away, with their towering bearskin caps, destined to be among the spoils of war when they were added to the uniform of the British Guards, they looked gigantic against the setting sun. Then, in a strange hush commented upon by many survivors of that day, hundreds heard Wellington's voice — 'Stand up Guards!' For many Frenchmen his voice was to be the last they ever heard. Swept by three mighty volleys of disciplined fire at almost point-blank range they wavered and broke. This was the moment for which the Duke had waited so long. 'Oh Damn it! In for a penny in for a pound' he

\* Translated from an official Netherlands history, which is as vivid an account of the battle as any ever written: *'La Campagne de 1815 aux Pays Bas; d'aprés les rapports officiels néerlandais.'* by F. De Bas & Le Comte J. de T' Serclais de Wommersom. Brussels 1908.

cried, and waved his hat towards the French in an unmistakeable commanding gesture.[8]

In stepping aside into his sheltered spot whilst the men whose lives he had so often demanded of them marched on into the hail of lead which awaited them, proud to die for France and for him, Napoleon stepped down from the pedestal of his military glory and took his first step towards St Helena. As the last of that river of cheering men flowed past, the sound of the *pas de charge* — 'the *rum* dum, the RUM dum, the rummadum rummadum *dum* dum — ' drifted back to the quarry, as the Imperial Guard advanced for the last time. But the man whom they had marched past so proudly was no longer the man for whom they were happy to die — their Little Corporal, France's greatest soldier.

Physically he stood there, but spiritually he was already back where Ney had wished him in 1812. Leaving his soldiers again to fight and die for him he was mentally in the Tuileries, scheming to save what he could from the ruin which he knew to be inevitable. And — yes, of course — he was choosing his scapegoats. Ney for a start. That was easy. Ney was mad. He had spoiled everything. Only a few hours before the Emperor had permitted himself the sadistic pleasure of telling poor Ney — 'You have ruined France!'

But this time, to Napoleon's discredit, he cast the net wider — much wider. He was not at all surprised by his defeat, he told an aide-de-camp, young Charles de Flahaut — it had been the same thing ever since Crécy. That was it. The French had never been really worthy of him — not worthy of the foreigner who bestrode their nation as his war-horse, placing at their disposal his great gifts of leadership, and his genius for war.

But the revelation on the stairway of the Tuileries, an experience approaching Transfiguration, had proved to him that the French would respond to his summons again and again. So it would be well to leave them once again — if leave he must — on a note of pride in what they had done and yet might do, together. This temporary reverse must be explained, minimised. He set to work before long on the composition of an inspiring communiqué for publication as a Special Supplement to the *Moniteur Universel* of June 21st, 1815. Waterloo — or to the French 'The Battle of Mont St Jean — so glorious and yet so disastrous for the French armies', was represented as a splendid victory 'ensuring us a brilliant success for the following day', when Grouchy would have attacked the Prussian rear — all thrown away 'through a moment of panic terror' and quite probably also treachery — 'ill-disposed persons had shouted 'Sauve Qui peut'.

The British, if they read the communiqué must have been quite surprised to learn of 'several squares being broken and six British infantry colours captured'. So much for our national belief that in the long history of our Army a British infantry square was broken only once, and that by Hadendowa tribesmen — 'Fuzzy-Wuzzies' to the British soldier.[9]

The Hundred Days — one hundred and ten, reckoning from Napoleon's landing on March 1st to the Battle of Waterloo June 18th, was followed by The Fifty Days — from June 18th to August 7th, when Napoleon was transferred to H.M.S. *Northumberland* to be taken to St Helena.

During the remaining years of his life, less than six, the master builder of the Napoleonic Legend was to busy himself with the repair of its damaged fabric, in what time he could spare from bickering with and outwitting the insensitive and small-minded man whom the world came to condemn, somewhat unjustly, as a brutal gaoler. A torrent of abuse has been poured upon the country which consigned the hero to his island prison — Perfidious Albion.

We shall have to see, in the following chapters, if there is anything to be said in our defence.

## CHAPTER II

# The Corsican , the French and the English

Your Royal Highness,
Exposed to the factions which distract my country and to the enmity
of the greatest powers in Europe, I have ended my political career, and
I come, like Themistocles, to throw myself on the hospitality of the
British people; I put myself under the protection of their laws, which I
claim from Your Royal Highness as the most powerful, the most
constant, and the most generous of my enemies.

Napoleon, Rochefort, July 13th, 1815.

With this magniloquently theatrical declamation Napoleon
announced a decision arrived at after some weeks of vacillation.
Whilst he was drafting this letter, Baron Richard, an emissary of
Fouché, the President of the provisional Government of France,
was actually on the way to arrest him. Despite all the conflicting
advice offered to Napoleon and the various plans which were
evolved, he had really little choice, for he was no longer in a
position to control his fate. To escape to America, as his brother
Joseph did, would have involved undignified procedures, such as
hiding in an empty brandy cask; and the British Navy would
almost certainly have caught him. France did not want him. Louis
XVIII was anxious to be free of the responsibility, for he was not
a vindictive man, any more than Napoleon himself had been in his
dealings with the king. Surrender to Blücher? 'I am not mad,' said
Napoleon, 'He has promised to hang me.'

The Tsar was an old friend; had indeed been an affectionate,
even an infatuated admirer; and the Emperor of Austria was
Napoleon's father-in-law. But they might have been unable to save
him, if they had wanted to do so, for it was Prussian and British
troops, the victors of Waterloo, who were invading France, and
capture by them was always a horrid possibility. As before, he was
prepared for that. Corvisart had again provided him with poison
and this time, no doubt, if it had had to be done it would have
been done properly.

Finally, whilst Napoleon and General Gourgaud were discussing the situation on July 13th in Rochefort, Fate had spoken to the intensely superstitious Corsican, though not unequivocally to be sure. Gourgaud had caught a sparrow which had flown into the room. 'Give it back its freedom,' said Napoleon, 'Let us read the omens'. Out it flew — 'to the English man-of-war', cried Gourgaud, always an advocate of surrender to the English. But to Napoleon, still undecided, it seemed to be indicating America — and freedom.

Napoleon's letter to the Prince Regent is rightly considered by Claude Manceron to be 'one of the finest documents of his life'. With its unmistakeable Napoleonic style, melodramatic yet noble, linking him, as he so loved to be linked, with a hero of classical history, it was not so much an offer of surrender as an almost condescending notification of an imperial decision. Unbelievable though it may seem, Napoleon had succeeded in infecting his entourage with his own faith in his destiny, which was, he felt sure, to be welcomed in England as an honoured guest, allowed to settle in a country estate, received into the Order of the Garter, and at the end of a life of dignified retirement to be buried in Westminster Abbey. With what in anyone else would be sublime effrontery, he let it be known that in inviting the Prince Regent to show magnanimity to his great enemy, he was offering him the chance to live his finest hour.

Typically he seems to have thought that he had only to express his wishes for them to be carried out, and he was no bad judge, if one may be permitted to disagree on this point with Lord Rosebery, one of the first historians to examine this period of Napoleon's career. Lord Rosebery considered that, although Napoleon had been waging war against Britain for so long, he completely misunderstood the character of the people. Quoting Napoleon's claim 'Had I been allowed to go to London in 1815 I should have been carried in triumph. All the populace would have been on my side', Lord Rosebery commented that in counting on a welcome from the English he was 'betraying the strangest ignorance of their character and habits of mind'. He added:

> Metternich, who had been in England, noticed when Napoleon was on the throne, that as regards England he believed only what he chose to believe, and that these ideas were totally false.

Believing only what he chose to believe was one of Napoleon's worst failings, but about the English his ideas may not have been as false as these two great statesmen believed. Left to himself the impressionable and warm-hearted Prince Regent might well have responded to Napoleon's approach and fallen under the great enemy's magnetic spell. Admiral Lord Keith, the commander-in-chief of the Channel Fleet, certainly thought so. He said to Captain Maitland of *Bellerophon*: 'Damn the fellow, if he had obtained an interview with His Royal Highness in half an hour they would have been the best friends in England.'

In this the Prince Regent might have had the support of a great many of his father's subjects. W.S. Gilbert knew the British character when he put on Ko Ko's little list 'the idiot who praises with enthusiastic tone, All centuries but this and every country but his own.' The British people tend to develop feelings of admiration, not far short of affection, for enemy generals, especially when we have beaten them. Soult was lionised in England once Napoleon was disposed of. Marshal Macdonald received a hero's welcome to South Uist, to which, it has been said, he replied in Gaelic with a strong French accent. Can we doubt that if Rommel had survived his Führer's insane *Götterdämmerung*, he would have attended many an old comrades' reunion in England, as did our German hero of the 1914-1918 War, General Von Lettow Vorbeck?

Hypnotised by the dazzling brilliance of Napoleon's marshals, the British were slow to believe that they had generals of their own who, given the chance, proved themselves equal or superior to the best of them; men such as Sir Ralph Abercromby, Sir John Moore, Sir Rowland Hill — 'Daddy Hill' — and old Tom Graham, the first Lord Lynedoch, a wealthy Perthshire laird who took to soldiering at the late age of 42 to avenge the desecration of his wife's coffin by a revolutionary mob at Toulon. Strange that three of them should be Scotsmen, for the Irish love to claim that Britain gets her best generals from Ireland. Those who make this boast must have recoiled in horror at seeing Wellington described by Sir Arthur Bryant as 'England's Greatest Son'; rather like the shock to a Scottish Nationalist who finds Burns in an anthology of English poets. Wellington, like Napoleon, tended to have the last word, and on the subject of his nationality he said, 'Because a man is born in a stable that does not make him a horse.'

Most of Wellington's fellow-countrymen ultimately came to have in him the confidence which his soldiers always felt. Unlike Napoleon, who was always supremely his own master, Wellington was the servant of an often niggardly Government, watched by a jealous Whig Opposition; and he commanded a small army, of which, as he himself said, he had to take great care as it was England's only one. From his experience in India and in the Peninsula, where a small army got beaten and a large one starved, Wellington made himself 'possibly the soundest of all great generals', in Lord Wavell's opinion. Napoleon, seldom over-generous in his praise of other generals, thought much the same, saying, 'The Duke of Wellington, in the management of an army, is fully equal to myself, with the added advantage of possessing more prudence.'

Wellington had the greatest respect for Napoleon's ability, saying that 'his presence on the field made a difference of 40,000 men'. He had a low opinion of the parvenu emperor's character and honesty, but displayed no rancour or bitterness towards him or his subjects. Before he was 18 he lived for a time in Brussels, and spent a year at the French Royal Academy of Equitation at Angers. He spoke French with confidence, and always treated enemy generals courteously. He understood very well the sources of the vindictiveness and desire for revenge upon the French displayed by Blücher and his Prussians, but he did all he could to restrain his allies.

The British soldiers felt no animosity towards the French, who were very well disposed towards them, particularly towards the Scots, probably more because of their picturesque uniforms than from any lingering memories of 'The Auld Alliance'. In 1814, when the British Army first entered France, Wellington's wise humanity led the French to hail them as liberators, rather than fear them as invaders. The inhabitants were amazed to find that Wellington's troops paid for everything, unlike the retreating French soldiers who plundered their own countrymen as ruthlessly as they had always done in enemy countries. This must not be taken as an indication of inhumanity among French soldiers, nor of saintly forbearance on the part of the British. It was due to the different policies of Napoleon and Wellington. Napoleon, who believed that War must be made to pay for itself, did little or nothing about feeding his soldiers, leaving them to supply their needs for themselves at the expense of the civilian populations.

Wellington in the Peninsula was fighting in the territory of allies, and always knew that his small army needed the friendship of the local inhabitants, which could be lost by looting or ill-conduct. He developed the best commissariat for which his sparse financial resources could pay, and set his face against even moderate plundering. His soldiers often got away with quite a lot of looting, but if things threatened to get out of hand the Provost erected gallows in prominent locations as a grim reminder of the Commander-in-Chief's policy.

In France itself, the once proud French warriors, discharged or on half-pay, naturally had little liking for the soldiers of the armies which occupied their defeated country; but during the campaigning in the Peninsula the British and French soldiers had usually got on very well together. Indeed their tendency to fraternise had often been a disciplinary problem. Friendly intercourse whilst burying the dead; or when, after the long hot July battle of Talavera, parched soldiers from both sides drank from the Portina brook, just had to be tolerated. Officers even turned a blind eye to a good deal of hobnobbing at outposts, where enemies swapped rations, tobacco and brandy. They sometimes even exchanged forage caps, in the friendly spirit in which members of international rugby football teams swap jerseys with their opposite numbers after a hard-fought match.

The unique flavour of these meetings and a pleasing insight into the character of the famous commander of Wellington's Light Division, is beautifully conveyed in the story of an unexpected visit by General 'Black Bob' Craufurd to an outpost just as a French soldier dropped in for a smoke. It is told in the racy memoirs of Rifleman Ned Costello, who was not to be the last author to mis-spell his general's name.

> The French sentry had crossed the plank to light his pipe and was standing carelessly chatting with me, when who should I see approaching, but General Crauford inquiring if Tidy had shod his horse. The Frenchman's red wings soon attracted the General's notice, and he suddenly with his well known stern glance inquired, 'Who the devil's that you're talking with Rifleman?' I informed him the French sentry, who had come over for a light for his pipe. 'Indeed', replied Crauford, 'let him go about his business, he has no right here, nor we either', said he, in a low whisper to his aid-de-camp, and away he walked.

Robert Craufurd, for all his severity, was greatly admired by his men, who were accustomed to meeting him a good deal further forward than it was prudent or quite proper for a general to be. He was killed quite soon after this incident, at the siege of Ciudad Rodrigo.

After a few Wellingtonian victories his soldiers, delighted to find that they could send the dreaded conquerors of the Continent packing, began to feel just like those 'Brave Sons of John Bull', who, the recruiting posters had assured them, could lick any six frog-eating Frenchmen. They felt justly proud to be the first troops to humble the French at a time when to be a Frenchman, and above all a French soldier, must have seemed the greatest thing on earth. Enormous and alarming as the French grenadiers might look in their towering bearskin caps it was a fact that the average height of a Frenchman in the nineteenth century was only five feet five inches, compared to our five feet seven and a half. So perhaps after all they were just a bunch of funny little stage Frenchmen — Frogs — Johnny Crappos. Such an attitude is neatly expressed in W.S. Gilbert's *Ruddigore*, in which the jolly Jack Tar, Ralph Rackstraw, sings patronisingly about the 'poor Mounseers', and the 'hardy British tars who had pity on a poor Parley Voo'. But frontline soldiers knew better than to be patronising towards those wonderful tough fighting men, respected for their soldierly qualities, and likeable for their gaiety and gift for comradeship. Front line troops are not much given to hatred of an enemy who shares their dangers and strains. Prisoners of war not infrequently find that their treatment becomes progressively harsher as they pass into the hands of the inhabitants of the base areas who often bristle with martial ardour.

On their side the French adopted a chivalrous attitude towards men whom they regarded 'as fellow craftsmen worthy of their steel; as pupils who had made good', in Sir Arthur Bryant's words. This mutual regard was somewhat shaken by the sight of atrocities perpetrated by the French, atrocities too appalling even for Goya to portray. Spanish families wiped out, women and children horribly mutilated, peasants nailed alive to the doors of their barns before these were set alight. Possibly the British realised, again to quote Sir Arthur Bryant, that the French 'took brutality, death and destruction as matters of course; they were still the children of the guillotine.'

And then of course violence breeds violence. The French had ghastly Spanish outrages to avenge. Stragglers met horrid deaths; soldiers were found crucified with their amputated genitals stuffed into their mouths; a French general was killed by being sawn between two planks. But what were the French avenging when they left behind them hundreds of hamstrung horses and mules?

The sight of these poor creatures mutely waiting to be put out of their misery affected our tough peasant soldiers especially strongly. But these soldiers of an island which for centuries had not heard the tread of invading armies were not good haters; and it seems that we have not changed very much. The Japanese in the

Second World War outdid those nineteenth century Frenchmen and Spaniards. Well authenticated stories tell of the ritual decapitation of prisoners of war, entitled in our day to the protection of the Geneva Convention; of patients and staff of hospitals massacred;* living men used for bayonet practice, and even of a living soldier's liver being cut out.

Yet a story told by General Sir Frank Messervy shows that his soldiers had nothing to learn from Wellington's men.[1] The general overheard two of them discussing what to do with a Japanese prisoner. 'What shall we do with this little . . . then, mate? What they've done to our chaps?' Unable to bring themselves to cold-blooded murder they took him along, and shortly one of them, having given his friend a cigarette, suddenly turned to the prisoner and said "Ere y'are . . . Tojo, 'ave a fag.' (*Spearhead General*, H. Maule, p. 323.) It would be naive to assume that such brutalities are things of the past. Nazi treatment of those regarded as inferior to the *Herrenvolk*; Chinese genocide in Tibet; Hindu — Mussulman bestialities from time to time; and Roman Catholic-Protestant goings-on nearer home, remind us of what man can do under the stress of war, or differences in religious belief. Man himself is more to be feared than the weapons of mass destruction devised by his ingenuity.

Our soldiers in the Peninsula did not extend their kindly feelings for Napoleon's soldiers to include Boney himself, the monster whose megalomania kept them for long years of campaigning far from their homes, where their wives were using his name to frighten naughty children. But a surprising number of people at home did not hate Boney, and indeed almost worshipped him. According to Chateaubriand, once Napoleon was beaten England conceived for him 'a stupid enthusiasm'; but in fact there had been plenty of stupid enthusiasm about Napoleon in England long before he was beaten. Those who opposed the Government for any reason, those who actively desired revolution in their own country, idealists who applauded the enthronement of *Liberté*, *Egalité* and *Fraternité*, contrived to overlook the manner in which Bonaparte had seized power and, by the *Coup de Brumaire*, had virtually ended the French Republic. They accepted him at his own valuation as The Revolution Made Man, and blindly worshipped him despite his growing megalomania, ambition and ruthless

* Some eyewitness accounts of one shocking example were recently published in the Journal of the Royal Army Medical Corps; October 1972 — '*The Alexandra Outrage. 13th February 1942*' Colonel W.J. Irwin.

conquests; just as they had been able to regard the bloody excesses of The Terror as regrettable, but only temporary, trials along the pilgrim path to the Golden Age and the establishment of the Empire of Reason, which their hero liked to proclaim as his ultimate goal.

That great parliamentarian Charles James Fox said that Napoleon had 'thrown a splendour even over the violence of the Revolution'. No wonder Napoleon said, 'The school of Fox sooner or later must rule the world.' Fox was the presiding genius of the Whig Club with its slogan 'The Sovereignty of the People'. The Duke of Norfolk hailed him as England's George Washington; and the Duke of Bedford enshrined a bust of Fox in a Temple of Liberty (No stately home should be without one: Admission, 5p). But Fox's activities were so nearly treasonable that Pitt had his name removed from the Privy Council and even considered the Tower. That Pitt had cause for concern is clear from a remark made by Fox to Lord Grey, after one of Napoleon's victories: 'I confess I go farther than you in my hatred of the English Government; the triumph gained by France excited in me a joy I can scarcely conceal.'

If there is an excuse for Fox's unpatriotic attitude it may be that it was his frustrating experience to waste a brilliant intellect, wonderful gifts of eloquence and a personality which, in the jargon of today, could be called charismatic, in the dreary wastes of perpetual opposition. He is not the only gifted politician who has come to regard an enemy of a hated government as his friend, even if that friend was an enemy of his country.

Fox was not the only Englishman who applauded the Emperor's triumphs and lamented his reverses. The complex motives of Napoleon's many and varied friends in England, and the astonishing lengths to which they were prepared to go, are explored in great depth in E.T. Lean's study of political disaffection, *The Napoleonists*. Mr Lean tells us that even after the Retreat from Moscow a heroic portrait of the Emperor boldly standing on the imperial throne, 'as if no defeat had occurred', broke all records in drawing crowds to view it in Leicester Square, at a shilling's entrance fee. Napoleon's defeat at Leipzig and his abdication in 1814 were serious setbacks, but gave aristocratic Napoleonists a chance to travel on the Continent, visiting Napoleon's relatives and privately alerting him to the threat of deportation further afield, to St Helena or St Lucia. Among these noble tourists were Lords Holland, Ebrington, and Douglas and the Duke of Bedford, who sent his young son Lord John Russell to visit the shrine of the fallen idol in Elba. The Duke of Bedford himself expressed the opinion that Napoleon's political career was not over for his leadership was needed in Europe — in Italy if not in France.

The curious conduct of Mr David Lloyd George in 1936 provides an illuminating parallel with the attitude of the Whigs to Napoleon. It was perhaps more reprehensible and dangerous, since the man-in-the-street was not likely to suspect our old war leader in the fight against the Kaiser of weak-kneed conciliation of a German enemy. Adolf Hitler's war aims had been made plain enough in his book *Mein Kampf,* and in March 1936 he had shown that he meant business by military occupation of the Rhineland. But in September 1936 readers of *The Daily Express* could leave the worrying to the old 'Welsh Wizard' who had gone to Germany to see for himself, with the promise of an article in due course. So there he was on September 7th, pictured in a friendly posture with Hitler himself, after four and a half hours discussion and a nice cup of tea. Between the 10th and 15th the news was disquieting; massed formations marching past the Führer at the Party Congress in Nüremberg, with '400 fighting air-planes . . . 25,000 blood-red Swastika banners', hysterical denunci-ations of Bolsheviks and Jews by Hitler, Goebbels and Streicher — already named 'the Jew-baiter'. But why worry about the Nazi Monster, when there was some *real* news? — on the 11th, 'Loch Ness Monster seen again'. Hitler was quoted, shouting, 'That you found me among millions is a miracle. That I found you is good fortune'. With this Lloyd George concurred. On September 15th he was shown giving an enthusiastic Nazi salute, and on the 17th the promised full-page article lauded Hitler's achievements and his 'magnetic dynamic personality'. 'He is the George Washington of Germany — the man who won for his country freedom from all her oppressors' cried our elder statesman, dismissing the possibility of Germany intimidating Europe, as he estimated that ten years were needed for Germany to be strong enough to face the armies of Russia or France on any soil but her own.*

It is certainly not for me to criticise the old politician for that error of judgment; but, alas, this was not the last word from Lloyd George for readers of *The Daily Express* that month. On 23rd

---

* In September 1802, during the Peace of Amiens, after dining with Napoleon, Fox declared that he 'did not doubt of his sincerity as to the maintenance of peace'. Napoleon had annexed Piedmont in that month, and within six months the British Ambassador had left Paris.

September they were told that in his memoirs — 'with withering scorn Lloyd George charged Haig with responsibility for the defeats of 1918'; and that he reserved 'his fiercest contempt for Haig'. Is it now fair to ask if the Scottish field marshal, who was dead when his old political chief derided his 'ineptitude', could have stooped like a Welsh mountebank to lick the Austrian corporal's boots, aping his Hitler Salute?

* * *

Napoleon's doings in Elba were closely watched by spies whose reports reached Talleyrand through Mariotti, the French consul in Leghorn. Mariotti found the English obsession with Napoleon mildly amusing; and he wrote to Talleyrand:

> The English have a lively admiration for Napoleon. They have bought up all the alabaster busts of him in Florence. Every ship's captain has a portrait of Napoleon in his cabin.

As for Napoleon himself, Mariotti wrote:

> He makes every effort to be nice to the English, and that fool Campbell is completely taken in.

The lively admiration of the English for Napoleon was enhanced by what they saw of the Bourbons, who had returned to France having forgotten nothing and learned less. Mariotti may have been a bit hard on Sir Neil Campbell, the Allied representative on the island of Elba, responsible for Napoleon's custody. His memoirs show him as having been less than captivated by his illustrious charge. The comment on the ships' captains is very interesting, for there had developed a considerable mutual admiration society between Napoleon and the Royal Navy. The respect felt by British sailors for a great military leader could hardly be a source of embarrassment to the Government, but the activities of the Napoleonists in England were quite another matter.

The British Government, having been asked by the Allied Powers to undertake the custodianship of Napoleon, did not need to worry about the reaction in Europe to the choice of St Helena for his detention. It had been one of the possible places under discussion even before his escape from Elba. But no British government can be entirely regardless of public opinion at home. An embarrassment with which the Government had to contend was the growing feeling, sedulously fostered by Napoleon's friends in England and elsewhere, that by sending him to St Helena

Britain had in some way behaved dishonourably towards a head of state who had appealed to them for sanctuary.

The conviction that this was so helped to sour Napoleon's last years, and in this instance it seems that the wily old actor was not playing a part designed to win the sympathy of his captors, or of anyone who might be induced to intercede on his behalf. The strong Oriental streak in his character, derived it is thought from Arab or Berber strains in the ancestry of the inhabitants of his part of Corsica, convinced him that the most sacred law of hospitality, even to a sworn enemy, had indeed been callously and shamefully violated.

A glance at the first twenty years of Napoleon's life, his Corsican Period, helps to explain the confidence with which the fallen Emperor entrusted his fate to the British people. Like most islanders the inhabitants of the rugged, mountainous, rather poor island of Corsica burned perpetually for freedom and independence, and were said to be 'always in power or in revolt'. We first hear of them in revolt against Carthage, of which the island was a province. The annexation by Rome of Corsica and Sardinia helped to precipitate the Second Punic War in 219 B.C. In the fifth century A.D. the island was part of the Vandal Kingdom under Genseric. The Bonapartes emigrated from Liguria to Corsica in the early sixteenth century, some hundred years after the Ramolinos, the family of Napoleon's mother, had arrived there from Lombardy. The island had been dependent on various Italian states and, when Napoleon's father, Carlo Buonaparte, was a young man, it had been for three centuries under the hated dominion of Genoa.

In 1755 the great Corsican patriot Pasquale Paoli, who had been a soldier in Naples, returned to Corsica and led a successful guerilla campaign which expelled the Genoese from most of Corsica, though they kept a foothold in Ajaccio and some neighbouring smaller ports. As a democratic ruler Paoli governed Corsica wisely, but being still troubled by hostilities with Genoa, he sent Carlo Buonaparte, Napoleon's father, as a member of the Corsican nobility, to Rome to seek the Pope's support for his régime.

Carlo's mission was successful but it all came to naught when in 1768 the Republic of Genoa, helped by some rather underhand dealings between a Corsican called Matteo Buttafuoci and the Duc de Choiseul, ceded Corsica to France for 5,000,000 francs. Paoli did not take this lying down and Carlo Buonaparte, accompanied by his wife, already pregnant with Napoleon, went into the maquis

Napoleon and his fellow exiles, from a contemporary sketch on board *Northumber-land*
*from l. to r.*: Gourgaud, Bertrand, Napoleon, Las Cases, Montholon

Napoleon's 'Malmaison' at St. Helena, The Briars, where he spent the first weeks of his exile. The tent was erected by the sailors of the *Northumberland*

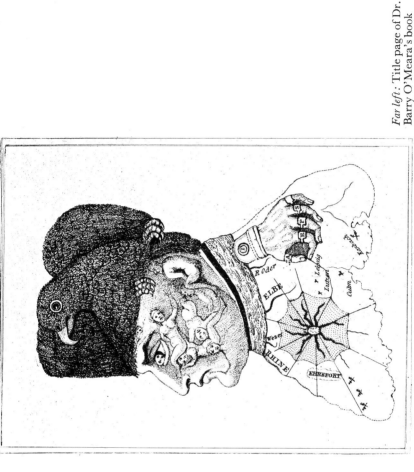

J. Kay 1814.

*Description of the hieroglyphic Portrait of Buonaparte .*

The French Eagle crouching forms the *chapeau en militaire* .
The Red Sea represents his *throat* illustrative of his drowning armies.
The *visage* is formed of carcases of the unhappy victims to his cruel ambition

*Far left* : Title page of Dr.
Barry O'Meara's book
*Napoleon in Exile*

*Left* : Contemporary profile
of Napoleon on Elba

# NAPOLEON IN EXILE ;

OR,

## A Voice from St. Helena.

THE

OPINIONS AND REFLECTIONS OF

## NAPOLEON

ON THE

MOST IMPORTANT EVENTS OF HIS LIFE AND GOVERNMENT,

IN HIS OWN WORDS.

By BARRY E. O'MEARA, Esq.

HIS LATE SURGEON.

Ἐγὼ δὲ ταῦθ᾽ ἅπαντ᾽ ἠπιστά-
'Ἑκὼν ἑκὼν ἥμαρτον, ἐκ ἀρνήσομαι·
Θνητοῖς δ᾽ ἀρήγων, αὐτὸς εὑρόμην πόνους·
Οὐ μήν τι ποιναῖς γ᾽ ᾠόμην τοιαῖσί με
Κατισχνανεῖσθαι πρὸς πέτραις πεδαρσίοις,
Τυχόντ᾽ ἐρήμου τοῦδ᾽ ἀγείτονος πάγου.

ÆSCH. PROM.

IN TWO VOLUMES.

VOL. II.

*FOURTH EDITION.*

## London:

PRINTED FOR W. SIMPKIN AND R. MARSHALL,

STATIONERS'-HALL-COURT, LUDGATE-STREET.

for a campaign which ended in Paoli's defeat by the Comte de Vaux at Ponte Nuovo. Paoli and many of his followers were taken to England in a British warship, but Carlo Buonaparte, unlike the bachelor Paoli, sadly decided that family considerations compelled him to stay in Corsica. Thus Napoleon, who might have been born a Corsican in London, was born in Ajaccio, a French subject but very much a Corsican.

Educated at two French military schools, at Brienne and Paris, at the French king's expense, he was described in school reports as typically Corsican, and he once said to a school friend, 'I will do these French all the mischief I can.' England was already the Mecca of the oppressed and misfits from many countries. The first and only king of Corsica, Theodore Neuhof, had taken refuge there in 1749, and when he died seven years later was buried in the graveyard of St Anne's, Soho. He had spent some time in the King's Bench prison for debt, and bequeathed his kingdom of Corsica to his creditors. His musical comedy reign lasted only a few summer months, and sounds very like W.S. Gilbert's comic kingdom of Barataria, though King Theodore has more in common with the Duke of Plaza Toro than with any of the claimants to the throne of that jolly island.[2]

During Napoleon's youth Paoli was still in exile in London. To the young Buonaparte, dreaming of creating in his island the kind of ideal republic visualised by Rousseau, England seemed to be the home of tolerance and democratic government. The son of his adored nurse Camilla Ileri had joined the British Navy, and Napoleon seriously contemplated following his example. He went to the length of writing to the British Admiralty, but as months went by without a reply he decided to settle for the French navy. But for a time he had also thought of going to serve with the British in India, or even of commanding native troops against them. Such day-dreams provide the plot of an entertaining novel, *The Eagle Flies West*, by Edward Atiyah. Napoleone is taken to England as a child, becomes a soldier and, of course, a general. Before long he is Viscount Buonaparte, Governor General of India. Britain is then shaken when her Governor General proclaims himself Emperor of India; but he ultimately over-reaches himself, when he tries to add much of Europe to his Empire; is beaten at Waterloo by Wellington, this time commanding an Anglo-French army, and is banished to St Helena.

Napoleon's thoughts of joining the British Navy may have been a passing whim, but his intention to join the French Navy was

D

perfectly serious. His mother pointed out that in the navy he would add dangers from the sea to those of enemy shot and shell, and she tried to dissuade him from becoming a sailor. She was almost certainly right, for it eventually became abundantly clear that Napoleon, though born by the sea, was a land animal with absolutely no understanding of naval affairs. To be a soldier was plainly his destiny, but let us imagine for a moment that, with his habitual perversity and determination, he had defied it and insisted on going to sea.

It could well be that his genius for war, his capacity for unremitting hard work and his marked mathematical bent might have combined to make him a master of seamanship and naval strategy. Here is material for another fascinating romance — Admiral Buonaparte pitted against Nelson, and the Invasion Camp at Boulogne under the command of one of the other brilliant generals thrown up by the French Revolution — André Massena perhaps, or Jean Bernadotte. Not the land mass of Europe but the island kingdom might then have been over-run and plundered by the French. What a nightmare. Let us hope that the army of occupation might have been commanded by the stern upright Bernadotte rather than by the wily rapacious Massena. But naturally we must put our money on Nelson, though 'Admiral Buonaparte' would have needed to command the Channel for only a few days, and he might have had a little of the luck which attended General Bonaparte in his early campaigns. His luck even held on three occasions when he ventured into the open sea. First when his invasion fleet on its way to Egypt evaded the Royal Navy, and later when he himself twice escaped capture at sea when he returned to France from Egypt and from Elba.

After the French Revolution Paoli returned to Corsica in 1791 and was hailed by the French National Assembly as a hero and martyr of Liberty. In 1791 Napoleon, hearing that the National Assembly intended to raise four battalions of Corsican infantry, got permission to go to Corsica to help in forming these new units. Before long he was at cross-purposes with his boyhood hero. Lucien Buonaparte, an impetuous republican firebrand, suspected Paoli of being pro-English, and Napoleon, who was now convinced that Corsica's future should be with France, later said that he had been a dupe of Paoli. Paoli, revolted by the excesses of the French Revolutionary régime, did in fact secede from France, declare himself President and offer the suzerainty of Corsica to the King of England. The Buonapartes, unpopular with many factions in

Corsica, escaped to Marseilles in June 1793, a month before the British landed in the island.

It was not much easier for a rather noticeable young Corsican general, who had decided to make a good Frenchman of himself, to keep out of trouble in France than it had been in Corsica; and in 1794 Napoleon spent an uneasy two weeks under arrest, mainly because of his friendship with Augustin Robespierre, who had gone to the guillotine with his famous brother Maximilien. Napoleon now began to think of making a career as a soldier of fortune in Russia or Turkey, and had completed his arrangements to go to Turkey, his passport being ready by September 1795, when a new political upheaval put a stop to these plans. The Convention came to an end and the Directory began. The young artillery general whose 'whiff of grapeshot' had saved the Government on the 12th Vendémiare (4th October 1795) had no need to look abroad for secure employment.

Napoleon's Corsican Period was over, and it was as a rising young French general that he sat down to plan the recapture of his island from the British. In his home town at the time were two British officers who would later cross his path; Lieutenant Hudson Lowe of the 50th Foot, and a Major Lyster, who would one day be proposed by the Governor of St Helena, with incredible but typical obtuseness, to be orderly officer in Napoleon's household. His reminiscences of garrison life in Ajaccio would not have gone with a swing in Longwood House. Lowe himself, speaking good French and Italian, was soon to be appointed to command two hundred Corsican Rangers in British service.

Bonaparte's plans to drive the British out of Corsica were thwarted by the watchful Royal Navy, but pretty soon his successes in Italy made continued British occupation difficult, and they quietly evacuated the island, and the French, as quietly, took it over. Before this Paoli, who did not get on with the British Viceroy, Sir Gilbert Elliott, later Lord Minto, had retired to London, where he died and was buried at St Pancras.

Corsica was French again, but Napoleon, surprisingly, took no further interest in the affairs of his native island. He had failed in his attempt to become the big man in Corsica and to make his clan the most important in the island. Now he had set his sights higher, much higher. He was determined to become a true Frenchman, to shed every trace of his Corsican nature. He taunted his brothers if he detected any lingering traces of Corsican traits in their behaviour; but he knew better than to try such tactics on his mother. At school he had been aggressively Corsican, but now, as he said later, 'I wanted at all costs to be a Frenchman. Being called a Corsican was to me the bitterest of insults.'

During the rest of his life he paid only one visit to his home. This was during his secret voyage from Egypt to France in 1799, on his way to seize power. A word from the First Consul, or later from the all-powerful Emperor, could have brought prosperity to Corsica, but that word was never spoken. Some Corsicans showed their resentment by throwing Napoleon's bust into the sea at Ajaccio, when news was received of his first abdication. But in the long-run Napoleon did a lot for Corsica. He well knew the redoubtable fighting qualities of the fierce islanders, especially the mountaineers amongst whom he liked to count himself, though he was born at sea-level.[3] A great many Corsicans reached high rank in Napoleon's army and navy, the latter including Captain Casabianca, the father of that boy so well-known to generations of British schoolchildren, who 'stood on the burning deck' of L'Orient, before she blew up during the Battle of the Nile. It has been estimated that no less than forty three Corsicans became generals during the Napoleonic wars, and that some ten thousand Corsican soldiers fought for France. This is a most impressive record for what was then a sparsely populated island and the pattern has been maintained, as the long lists of names on the war memorials in small villages prove.

Long before the Bonapartist restoration and Napoleon's apotheosis set him on the path to becoming a major tourist attraction, the greatest of Corsicans had shown by his dazzling career that honour and glory, to say nothing of profit, were the rewards of fighting France's enemies instead of shooting one another in the pursuit of their unending and profitless vendettas. Under Napoleon severe legislation was introduced in an attempt to put an end to the vendetta, but no legislation could tame the fierce and independent islanders. However, more and more of them through the years have risen to high positions in France and in her Empire. Nationalist and separatist movements have been active, but a more sober majority aims rather at more economic independence for Corsica, for which today the Action Régionaliste Corse campaigns actively. Accepting that their destiny should be linked with that of France, they resent being regarded as 'colonials'. Perhaps their attitude is comparable to that of a Scotsman who opposed 'Home Rule for Scotland' on the grounds that it would mean giving up England.

Napoleon's first brush with the Royal Navy was at Toulon, where, after his capture of Fort Mulgrave and neighbouring forts, his professional use of the French artillery drove off the British fleet, which had hitherto had to deal with an ill-led Revolutionary rabble. Bonaparte had been land-based, and it was the last success he was to score against our navy. Throughout his career he displayed a marked lack of understanding of naval affairs. Impatient of opposition, the man who erased the word 'impossible' from his vocabulary, could not understand that in those days of sail man could not impose his will upon the ocean. It was this attitude which precipitated that appalling affair, (referred to in Ch. 1, p. 24) when Admiral Bruix disobeyed Napoleon's orders to embark hundreds of soldiers near Boulogne for a review and invasion practice.

It was the first time in his life that Napoleon, who had been proclaimed Emperor just two months before, had been openly defied. When Bruix bluntly refused to obey because of the danger to men's lives, Napoleon advanced upon him with raised riding whip; Bruix laid his hand on his sword, saying, 'Sire, be careful'; and Constant, who was there, noted that, 'All who stood by were frozen with terror.' Napoleon dismissed Bruix and ordered the embarkation to continue. When the inevitable disaster struck and twenty barges ran aground he was horrified, dashed into a lifeboat, brushing aside restraining hands and did his best to save at least some lives. This horrid sacrifice of over two hundred men to his ignorance, and refusal to admit he could be wrong, taught him nothing. Indeed it hardened his conviction that his naval officers were too timid and unwilling to take risks. He grew to despise his admirals, harassed them, accused them of lack of initiative, even of lack of courage. Here is a sample of what they had to put up with:

> All Naval Expeditions undertaken since I have been at the head of the Government have failed, because the Admirals see double, and have learned — where I do not know — that war can be made without taking risks. If the art of war consisted merely in not taking risks, Glory would be at the mercy of very mediocre talent.

Magnificent — but not much help to poor Admiral Villeneuve, who, it seems to me, may have been much under-rated as a naval commander. One sentence in his instructions to his ships' captains before Trafalgar has a distinct ring of 'The Nelson Touch'. *Tout capitaine qui ne serait pas dans le feu ne serait pas à son poste; et un signal pour l'y rappeler serait une tache deshonorante pour lui.*

However this may be translated the intention is clear. Any captain not under fire would be out of his station and should engage the enemy more closely. He would be disgraced if he had to be told to do this by a signal. Hardly the timid Villeneuve whom Napoleon liked to make a whipping boy. The unhappy man committed suicide by stabbing himself, after his return from captivity in England in 1806, rather than face the formidable Corsican.

Only a professional naval officer could judge if Napoleon's contempt for his admirals was justified to any extent; but I suspect that he did not fully appreciate the depth of experience, the seamanship and, above all, the inspired understanding which existed between Nelson and his captains — his Band of Brothers — which enabled our great admiral to take such calculated risks as those which led to the destruction of Napoleon's fleet in the Battle of the Nile.

In 1799 Napoleon may have loftily asserted that he had decided not to take Acre because of the plague, but privately he always admitted that it was the British admiral, Sir Sidney Smith, who had frustrated his hopes of Eastern conquests. This was the first reverse of his career, and a bitter memory — 'Had Acre fallen I should have changed the face of the world'. His contempt for his own admirals was sharpened by the exploits of Nelson and his Band of Brothers; and he said to Maitland, 'If it had not been for you English I should have been Emperor of the East; but wherever there is water to float a ship, we are sure to find you in our way.'

Whilst the Royal Navy had blocked his path to world dominion it was the British Army which had delivered the *coup de grace*. Napoleon was convinced that he ought to have won the Battle of Waterloo, and indeed in an Army Communiqué on 21st June, 1815, he described the battle as a glorious French victory, thrown away by a moment of needless panic, and, of course, treachery. But his final considered opinion was, 'The French, though fewer in numbers, would have won the victory but for the obstinate and unconquerable bravery of the British troops which alone prevented them.'

For a close look at the magnificent weapon forged by Nelson and other great sailors Napoleon had to wait until he went on board British ships as a prisoner. All that he saw filled him with admiration, which he was not slow to express; indeed he seemed to set himself deliberately to charm the ships' companies. When Napoleon did that only the most insusceptible could resist him. He said of himself, 'If my material power was great, my power over

men's minds was far greater. It almost amounted to magic.' Many
people succumbed to this magic. Men like Caulaincourt and de
Ségur said that when he wanted to charm he was irresistible. What
hope had our simple sailors in the face of this magnetic power,
switched full on expressly to captivate them? When H.M.S.
*Undaunted* landed the prisoner on the island of Elba the
boatswain, on behalf of the ship's company, wished him 'long life
and prosperity on the island of Elba, and better luck another
time'. Better luck another time! It is almost incredible; and he
came within a touch of getting it too.

It was the same on *Bellerophon* after his final surrender, and on
*Northumberland* taking him to St Helena. Captain Maitland of
*Bellerophon* was fascinated and, after the voyage, enquiries among
his ship's company produced the unanimous opinion that 'they
may abuse that man as much as they please; but if the people of
England knew him as well as we do they would not touch a hair of
his head'. To the men of *Northumberland* he was 'a fine fellow
who does not deserve his fate'.

On board *Bellerophon* young Midshipman George Home soon
became a devoted worshipper. Napoleon must surely have been
touched by the delicacy of feeling with which the boy, having
helped him on to the poop deck and told him that the land in
sight was Ushant, then withdrew leaving Napoleon to take his last
long look at France through the pocket glass which he had used at
Austerlitz — a long look which lasted from 5 a.m. until nearly
midday.

Napoleon contrasted the quiet orderly efficiency of our naval
vessels with the relatively chaotic conditions which he had noticed
aboard French ships, where, he said, 'everyone calls and gives
orders and they gabble like so many geese.' Discipline was the
answer and if Napoleon knew how this was enforced among our
sailors, many of them pressed men, he was too tactful to refer to
it, and certainly not as bluntly as Sir Winston Churchill is said to
have done. To an admiral, who had been protesting about some
point and speaking of naval tradition, the 'Former Naval Person'
growled, 'Naval Tradition? I'll give you naval tradition — rum,
sodomy and the lash' (or words to that effect, as the Manual of
Military Law has it).

Napoleon led his troops by inspiration and incentive rather than
by fear; and, in the tradition of the fine rugged Revolutionary
Army which he inherited, flogging a soldier would have been
unthinkable. At this time discipline in our Army was too often

harsh and undiscriminating, and, to our shame, enforced by brutal flogging. It may have been his knowledge of this which caused Napoleon's opinion of our officers to be as low as his admiration for the men they led was great.

Like many French generals of the time he praised the cool sturdy courage of the British soldiers, and is actually on record as saying that they were braver than the French. He once said, 'Had I had an English army I should have conquered the universe'; and he believed that he could himself have led British soldiers better than their own officers did. Here I think we must disagree with him.

Wellington once said to Lord Stanhope, 'There was nothing like him. He suited a French army so exactly! Depend upon it, at the head of a French army there was never anything like him.' Wellington's admiration of Napoleon the soldier was always tempered by somewhat amused contempt for certain aspects of the character of 'Boney' the man; and in thus emphasising the word 'French', he may have been expressing something of the blunt Englishman's attitude to what one of the Duke's biographers refers to as the Emperor's 'melodramatic speeches which set one's teeth a little on edge'.

In Wellington the British soldiers had a commander of outstanding commonsense, who saw to it that they were clothed, fed and cared for; and was extremely sparing of their lives, perhaps the most sparing of all great generals. They could do without bombast, especially bombast in which, with their keen sense of the ridiculous, they would have detected something bogus. Not for nothing perhaps was the bogus poet Ossian Napoleon's favourite poet.

Many of Napoleon's speeches and special orders certainly sound flamboyantly histrionic, but they were, in some small degree, matched on our own side of the Channel in recruiting posters exhorting 'Brave Sons of John Bull' to flock to the colours. The noble words which Shakespeare put into the mouth of Henry V thrill us today, and probably would indeed have steeled his soldiers' hearts; but today our taste is for something simpler. Field Marshal Montgomery's words, few, straightforward and re-emphasised, remain fixed in the minds of those who heard them at a time when victory was our greatest desire. Napoleon's famous proclamation containing those immortal words, 'Victory will advance at the charge; the eagle, with the national colours will fly from spire to spire right up to the towers of Nôtre Dame', is in general much too flowery for British tastes, and far far too long — over six hundred words. Wellington or Montgomery would have boiled it down to half, and allowed the residue to crystallise in a few telling phrases.

Whether or not the real Napoleon would have been as great a success in command of British troops as the hero of Edward Atiyah's novel, he would certainly have liked to have a try. It was not only after his defeat, or from any idea of ingratiating himself with his captors, that he praised our sailors, our soldiers and our great general Wellington. Whilst he was still in power, still commanding French armies, he gave it as his opinion that our soldiers were braver than the French, who in turn were braver than the Russians, the Germans, and the Italians, who came last of all.

His bitter comment to Flahaut when he saw his soldiers running at Waterloo (Ch. 1, p. 36) was but an echo of what he said to General Foy, who had been sent home from Spain to explain to the Emperor in person the problems of the war in Spain. Napoleon asked him bluntly if the French were afraid of the English soldiers; and said, 'Well you see the English have always beaten them — Creçy, Agincourt, Marlborough.' Foy could only counter with a reference to Fontenoy, which Napoleon brushed aside. But did Foy notice his Emperor's use of the word 'them'? — a curiously detached attitude to the people whom he had chosen as his war-horse.

In Elba he told Colonel Sir Neil Campbell how greatly he admired the English, and, choking with emotion, said that he had hoped to raise the French nation equally high. He admitted his failure in this, when he told General Gourgaud, 'The British Navy would be much less able to carry on the struggle with us if we had but half the English National Spirit.' On another occasion he said, 'The English character is superior to ours.'

He always liked to turn a blind eye to the difficulties facing his brother Joseph in the Peninsula, but he knew only too well that Wellington's superb generalship had made of that campaign 'the Spanish ulcer' — a creeping ulcer which eroded the reputation of one marshal after another, draining away resources which he could ill afford. True the British Army was ridiculously small by Continental standards, but there was that formidable national spirit — and, as he added thoughtfully, 'They have Wellington.' Then Britain's enormous wealth — ah! the good old days — was as great as her army was small; and her subsidies maintained in the field the armies of any of the Continental powers who were willing to fight on. England provided a refuge for all who were opposed to

his regime. It had been in England, during the Consulate, before he
had seated himself firmly on the imperial throne, that the plots of
Georges Cadoudal and General Pichegru had been hatched.
Desperate men prepared to lose their lives in attempts to
assassinate the usurper were trained in a camp at Romsey.

Little wonder that he sometimes cursed the British, as he gazed
across the Channel at their impregnable island. Once, seeing some
English children playing in the gardens of the Tuileries, he
exclaimed, 'English! I wish the earth would open and swallow
them up.' But such violent feelings stemmed from respect, not
from the contempt which he often expressed for other nations,
even for the French who had done so much for him. He said once,
'There are only two great nations, France and England; the rest are
nothing.' Perhaps he really did sincerely want to make peace with
us; almost to divide the world with us.

Romantic people presumably believe, as did Midshipman
George Home, that Napoleon, brooding during those long hours on
the poop deck of *Bellerophon*, was indeed paying his last farewell
to a land he truly loved. Was he not to direct in his will that he
was to be laid to rest 'on the banks of the Seine, in the midst of
the French people whom I have loved so greatly'. But, as I have
said, it was not only in the bitterness of defeat that he expressed a
certain contempt for the French. Even when his Corsican period
was over and he was striving to be thought French, he wrote and
spoke of France in a way which French critics have asserted no
true Frenchman could have done. France was his mistress; never
his mother. It has been French writers much more than English
ones who have depicted him in harsh colours as a Corsican
brigand, who exploited and robbed his adopted country to
aggrandise and enrich himself and his rapacious Bonaparte clan.

Just fourteen months before that sentimentalised farewell to
the receding coastline of France he had been cowering in his coach
in fear of an ugly death at the hands of a French mob; listening to
stones cast by Frenchmen rattling on the coach. When he then
cried out: 'I was right to despise mankind' it was not his enemies
who were uppermost in his mind.

The three weeks between Napoleon's second abdication and the
signing of his fine letter to the Prince Regent were occupied in
endless debates about his personal future. He himself seemed to
veer from one plan to another. He would escape to America; the
necessary ships were secretly made ready by wildly enthusiastic

young sailors. He would yet again place himself at the head of French armies; he briefly donned his old uniform, and his supporters gaily grasped their swords. But he had almost certainly privately made up his mind. He had told Colonel Campbell in Elba of his desire to end his days in England; and as recently as June 21st he had told his stepdaughter Hortense that he would never surrender to any ruler, adding, 'I prefer to turn to a people, to England.' To General Gourgaud he said that although the Tsar Alexander was his friend, he could never feel safe in Russia, where 'the rope that throttles Alexander will strangle me the same day.' As for the Emperor of Austria, the brash and tactless Gourgaud saw that he had 'dropped a brick' in mentioning the possibility. How could Napoleon go to Austria, where his wife Marie Louise was openly living in sin with Count Neipperg, whom her father had appointed to be her 'knight of honour'?

Queen Hortense had not thought much of the idea of turning to the English people, but this course was vigorously advocated by such people as Las Cases, who hoped that his knowledge of English might strengthen his position with the Emperor; by Fanny Bertrand, wife of the grand marshal of the Palace, who was the daughter of General Arthur Dillon, an Irish exile in the French service; and, of course by Gourgaud and his sparrow — how could a French sparrow point the way to America? — it could *see* the British ships. Perhaps Gourgaud's reading of the omens was right. In any case all these well-intentioned people were merely commending the course to which his heart had prompted him from the start — an appeal to the English. 'They are a great nation, noble and generous; they will treat me as I ought to be treated.'

So in the end we see Napoleon approaching the shores of England, basking in the respectful admiration of British sailors; warmed by the grave courtesy of a Scottish aristocrat (he had been careful to find out that Maitland was related to Lord Lauderdale) and the puppy-like adoration of young Midshipman George Home, also well-connected, which helped because Napoleon was a snob. He confidently expected that the attitude of the ship's company of *Bellerophon* would prove to be a foretaste of the friendly reception in England on which he was counting.

He was magnanimously prepared to let byegones be byegones; to embrace the Prince Regent, whom he would have addressed as 'cousin' with the sublime effrontery which had permitted him to refer to the murdered King Louis XVI as 'my poor uncle'. Next no doubt he would have inspected the fine country estates from which he would be invited to make his choice. In a letter to the British Government, entrusted to General Gourgaud, he had specified his requirements; a house large enough for all his household, some thirty to forty miles from London. He added, 'If the Government wishes to keep an English commissioner near me, it will see to it that this has no appearance of servitude.' 'Will' — the word reserved in military usage for those entitled to give orders.

So superb is this man even in defeat, so powerful is the magic of the Napoleonic Legend, that, even if one considers that he deserved all that lay in store for him because of the suffering which his megalomaniac ambition had brought upon the world, it is easy to wish that things might have fallen out differently. Almost anything seems preferable to the sordid existence and boredom of St Helena. If only the wind had changed during the five days he was aboard the frigate *Saale* and he had not been mesmerised by thoughts of Trafalgar, but had attempted to slip past the British ships, as he had done in escaping from Egypt and Elba. How brightly would his Legend have glowed if he had found that 'glorious grave' at Waterloo, spoken of by Jerome, or even the martyrdom which would probably have been his fate if Major de Colomb, with the 8th Regiment of Prussian Hussars, had pressed on more quickly to Malmaison, where the quarry was deeply, if belatedly, mourning the discarded Josephine, who had died whilst he was in Elba.

It is even pleasant to think of Prinny making that magnanimous gesture so confidently expected of him by Napoleon. Pleasant indeed, but that is not to admit that Napoleon had any right to expect such generosity, or that the British Government, even if a little ungenerous, deserved unqualified condemnation.

# CHAPTER III

# Britain's Task

Various factors contributed to the bland assurance with which Napoleon contemplated the shores of England from the hospitable haven of *Bellerophon*. Accustomed as he was to getting his own way, especially with the rulers of Europe, it is unlikely that anything he may have heard of the Prince Regent made him expect a collision with a will as strong as his own. Lord Keith's opinion about the result of a personal encounter between these two was never put to the test, because the Prince Regent acted correctly, accepting the advice of his ministers. Indeed before Napoleon sailed for St Helena the Prince Regent personally ordered that a strict guard should be kept upon his person, whilst expressing the hope that the prisoner's freedom would not be unnecessarily restricted.

This insistence on a strict guard is hardly surprising. It was the too easy-going surveillance of the British Commissioner, Sir Neil Campbell, which had permitted Napoleon's escape from Elba, with all its terrible consequences. Now the unenviable task of safe-guarding the disturber of the world's peace had again been inflicted upon Britain by the Allied Powers, who, Sir Arthur Bryant says, 'had almost bled dry the one constant opponent of the tyrant, and given as little as possible in return; each of whom, at one time or another, had given up the struggle and joined the enemy, only to be brought back into the fold with fresh gold from the Island Treasury.'* Napoleon was right to call Britain 'the most powerful, the most constant' of his enemies.

Although it was to the Prince Regent that Napoleon had addressed his appeal, it was, as we have seen, really in the English people that he placed his trust. Las Cases, rashly assuming that nearly ten years living in England as an emigré had made him   an

* Prologue to *The Capel Letters*, ed. Marquess of Anglesey. Jonathan Cape, 1955.

authority on our laws, confidently pronounced that on *Bellerophon* they would all be on British soil, bound by the sacred laws of hospitality and governed by the civil laws of England. This misplaced confidence was echoed by Napoleon, in his own striking words, 'They are a great nation, noble and generous; they will treat me as I ought to be treated.' *Ought* to be treated — in his own opinion of course. Did he really expect them to expunge in a moment the memories of twenty years of bitter struggle? Remembering that he had really no choice; that he had been lucky to escape with his life and knew it, was he bluffing, as he had so often been in the past?

In a brief and brilliant foreword to M. Jean Duhamel's book *The Fifty Days*, Dr Felix Markham, the Oxford historian and authority on Napoleon, says that Napoleon's letter was 'probably a bluff, a gamble, a forlorn hope'. It was most certainly the last two; but, although he may have been bluffing, it is hard to believe that even that consummate actor could have entirely feigned the profound shock with which he seemed to receive the news of his fate. As a realist he might have expected nothing better, but he was to retain for the rest of his life that almost Oriental conviction that the sacred laws of hospitality had been outraged, not by the 'noble and generous' people to whom he had appealed, but by the hated oligarchy which ruled them, and had frustrated his ambitions throughout his career. His sense of outrage and injustice intensified his bitter hatred of the British Government, which he bequeathed as a legacy to the French people, many of whom to this day cannot forgive our country's treatment of their hero.

The catastrophic fall of one who aspired to be the greatest man on earth has naturally attracted the attention of historians from the nineteenth century to the present day. During the ten years from 1961 to 1971 The Fifty Days, between Waterloo and Napoleon's embarkation for St Helena, have been exhaustively analysed in no less than five books, four by Frenchmen, those of Claude Manceron, Jean Duhamel, Gilbert Martineau and Henri Lachouque; and one by an American, Michael Thornton.

These authors make use of contemporary sources of information which were not available in 1900, when the fifth Earl of Rosebery wrote his classic *Napoleon, The Last Phase*.

To Commandant Lachouque, a robustly Bonapartist soldier and author of fine books about Napoleon's battles and his Imperial Guard, England is naturally enough the enemy. However, although he heads one chapter 'Hypocrisy and Breach of Faith', he is far from blind to the humane motives of many of our countrymen at that time. He generously acknowledges Napoleon's high opinion of us, quoting his noble tribute, 'The English are really of a calibre superior to ours. If I had had an English army I would have conquered the world.' Manceron, Martineau and Duhamel are historians who know our country and our language, share Napoleon's feelings for our nation and, like him, find it hard to condone the actions of a Government unworthy of the people to whom the Emperor had entrusted his future.

An exception in this last respect must be made in the case of M. Duhamel, a lawyer trained and qualified both in France and in England, and thus able to express an informed opinion on the legal and constitutional problems with which His Majesty's Government had to wrestle. He endorses the view expressed by Lord Campbell, a great lawyer, a judge and Lord Chancellor in the middle of the nineteenth century. Lord Campbell supported the decision of the Lord Chancellor of the day, Lord Eldon, that Napoleon's case was unique, but the law of self-preservation justified keeping him 'under restraint in some distant region, where he should be treated with all the indulgence compatible with a due regard for the peace of mankind'. This seems very fair, and Britain would have deserved no blame and possibly avoided the increasingly severe judgment of successive generations, had certain petty irritations, which must be mentioned later, been avoided.

In all the books dealing with this brief phase of Napoleon's career the familiar dramatis personae play their parts in the three act drama. On stage throughout are Napoleon and his small band of followers, the faithful few (though some of them scarcely deserve the adjective) who were to accompany him to St Helena, and those who would not be allowed to do so. Two of these latter were among the most devoted — Generals Lallemand and Savary, Duke of Rovigo. Savary, Napoleon's 'hatchet man', deeply implicated in the assassination of the Duke of Enghien and other murders, including probably that of the English sea-captain Wright; and in the tricking of the Spanish Bourbons out of their throne, was high on the 'wanted list' in France.

Act I of this historical drama of The Fifty Days is concerned with France's attitude to the re-established Bourbons and the fallen Bonaparte. One character, careful to avoid the limelight, is the one of whose villainy there is no doubt. The intriguer Joseph Fouché, determined that whatsoever king might reign he'd be the Chief of Police, stealthily edged Napoleon towards the British ships waiting to capture him; sending him to Rochefort where *Bellerophon* was already stationed. Napoleon was later to say that his greatest mistake during the Hundred Days had been that he did not hang Fouché, and few could have blamed him if he had done so, for Fouché was one of the most evil creatures bred in the Revolutionary jungle.

Minor officials could not be blamed for waiting to see which way the cat would jump. Unlike Fouché they could not manipulate events and had had to make two right-about turns in loyalty in the recent past. Such a one was Casimir de Bonnefoux, the maritime prefect of Rochefort, a ship's captain who would not go to sea. He feigned illness to avoid going to meet Napoleon at Tours; but in the end the old loyalty prevailed. When the provisional Government had finally decided to arrest Napoleon and sent Baron Richard, a regicide and friend of Fouché, to do this, Bonnefoux confused the land-lubber with seaman's talk of tides, and warned Napoleon, who gave himself up to the British Navy, thus sparing not only Bonnefoux but France herself the shame of handing him over to his enemies.

This was a relief also to General Beker, the Alsatian soldier appointed by Fouché to guard Napoleon, who was a valuable pawn in his negotiations with the Allies. Embarrassed by the assignment, Beker offered to withdraw, but Napoleon put him at his ease; and the polite convention was adopted whereby Beker appeared more as the commander of a guard of honour than the custodian of a state prisoner. At the end he did nothing to prevent Napoleon's voluntary surrender, but Napoleon forbade Beker to accompany him to *Bellerophon*, so as to avoid any impression that he had handed him over to the British.

Beker, Bonnefoux and several other officers were subsequently punished in various ways for taking an 'active part in the escape plans of the usurper' — an official French attitude and wording which many French writers prefer to overlook. General Beker had been a sympathetic, more or less neutral, observer of the action of the play from Malmaison to the Isle of Aix, refraining from interfering in the various plans, ranging from a bold bid to regain power, to exploration of possible methods of escaping to America.

The resolute brother, Lucien Bonaparte, urged the first course, whilst the placid older brother, Joseph, still absurdly calling himself King Joseph, advocated the latter, even offering to impersonate Napoleon to enable him to sail on the ship which eventually took Joseph to America. Several ships, French and

neutral, were ready to make the attempt, but Napoleon, quite
unlike the man who had braved the Royal Navy in escaping from
Egypt in 1799 and from Elba in 1815, was half-hearted. So was
Captain Philibert, commanding the frigate *Saale*, which with a bit
of luck could have outsailed *Bellerophon*.

A very different stamp of sailor was Captain Ponée of *Méduse*,
who pleaded to be allowed to hurl his ship at *Bellerophon*,
sacrificing himself and his ship's company in engaging the old
ship-of-the-line, whilst Napoleon slipped out into the open sea in
*Saale*.

Then there was a splendid band of six young naval officers who,
with reckless lack of secrecy, prepared the *Zélie*, a *chassemarée* or
decked whaleboat, for a dash past the watchful British vessels.
Although Napoleon had given them some encouragement he
would not go through with the bold attempt. His indecision and
unadventurous spirit at the end of his active career were mainly
due to a praiseworthy desire to avoid further bloodshed and not to
abandon his small band of remaining adherents to fend for
themselves; as well as a determination to leave the European stage
with dignity.

Act II, nearly all sunshine and smiles, opens with Napoleon
boarding *Bellerophon*. Captain Maitland and Midshipman George
Home have left charming accounts of the events of the voyage to
England with the wonderful passenger. With the arrival of the
battered old man-of-war off the English coast the curtain falls on
the high hopes of Napoleon and his followers and the action
becomes increasingly tragic; for in Act III, still on *Bellerophon*,
they are fighting to avert his deportation to St Helena, which in
the end they have to accept with varying degrees of indignation or
resignation, as they embark in *Northumberland* for Napoleon's last
voyage.

Napoleon's last conquest, that of the ship's company of
*Bellerophon*, is well illustrated by the transformation of young
George Home from one of a cheerful bunch of skylarking
midshipmen into a hero-worshipping slave of the Emperor — his
man for life, as his *Memoirs of an Aristocrat* proclaim.

But for us the most important character must be another
Scotsman, the attractive, sensitive Captain Frederick Lewis
Maitland of *Bellerophon* (later Admiral Sir Frederick). To many
Bonapartists he is almost as black a villain as Fouché, an opinion
which can be sustained only by blind prejudice and ignorance. The
charge against him is that he tricked Napoleon into giving himself

E

up to England by false promises of generous treatment.

Of course Maitland was intensely eager to capture Napoleon, to gain for his ship the prestige of having on board the great enemy who for twenty years had kept officers and men of the Royal Navy almost constantly at sea, far from their homes. His country was still at war with France. He had been ordered to prevent Napoleon's escape and he knew that it had been decided that no peace could be concluded whilst Napoleon was still at large. If Maitland did play a cat-and-mouse game with the French he was himself a cat on very hot bricks. The naval force under his command was barely adequate to guard all of the three channels from Rochefort by which the fast-sailing frigates *Saale* and *Méduse* could reach the open sea. Spies reported to him that plots were being discussed to secrete his quarry on neutral vessels. Naturally the thirty-seven year old captain was consumed with anxiety about the outcome of the important task entrusted to him by his admiral.

When at last Napoleon's mind was made up and, in the early hours of July 15th, he was approaching *Bellerophon* all too slowly in the brig *Epervier*, unable to make headway against a contrary wind, whilst Admiral Hotham's flagship *Superb* was rapidly bearing down upon the scene, Maitland, determined not to be robbed of his prize, sent his First Lieutenant, Andrew Mott, in a longboat to take Napoleon off *Epervier*. Commandant Lachouque, reporting that the rowers saluted Napoleon, suggests that they may have been French prisoners. Whether he is ignorant of the peculiar fascination which Napoleon exerted over our sailors, or is unwilling to credit them with kindly feelings for a captured enemy, the idea that Maitland could have chosen Frenchmen for this delicate duty is laughable.[1]

Maitland was later to tell Sir Walter Scott that he had trembled with anxiety during the negotiations with the envoys sent by Napoleon to discuss his surrender. But he kept his head and repeatedly stressed that he could not give any undertakings on behalf of his admiral or of His Majesty's Government, nor guarantee anything whatsoever about his country's intentions towards so illustrious a prisoner. He made it abundantly plain that, although he was prepared to receive Napoleon on board his ship on his own responsibility, he could not be sure that this 'would meet with the approbation of the British Government'.

He firmly told the French that he did 'not approve of frequent communications with an enemy by means of flags of truce'. It was the French who desired these communications, yet French historians have held that it was deceitful of Maitland not to tell them what his orders were. These orders were secret. It would have been most improper of him to discuss them with representatives of a country with which his own was at war. He bluntly warned them that he 'must use every possible means to capture Buonaparte'; and at the last meeting he once again reminded Las Cases that he 'was in no way authorised to agree to any conditions whatsoever, and that he could only transport him [Napoleon] and his suite to England', where he would be 'entirely at the disposal of His Royal Highness the Prince Regent'. Las Cases replied that he had already explained this to Napoleon.

During the three weeks of Napoleon's stay on board *Bellerophon* Maitland only twice betrayed the strain and anxiety he was experiencing. He nearly lost his temper on being accused, first by Mme Bertrand and later by Las Cases of having deliberately tricked the Emperor. His personal honour was so important to him that he took the unusual and risky step of writing direct to the Admiralty when he heard that Generals Savary and Lallemand were to be returned to France, where they would certainly have been shot.

Admiral Keith supported him in this, and the generals were sent to Malta. Maitland felt that they had come to England under his personal protection; and even some French historians have conceded that, had he really given any sort of guarantee to Napoleon, he would have risked as much for him. M. Martineau suggests that Maitland, by thus venturing to raise the case of the two generals, may have hoped to convey a hint about similar concessions for Napoleon. Whatever historians may have subsequently thought, Napoleon himself knew very well that Maitland had not betrayed him. Count Montholon reassured Maitland on this point, earnestly clasping his hand whilst telling him:

> Las Cases negotiated this business. It has turned out very differently from what he and all of us expected. He attributes the Emperor's situation to himself, and is therefore desirous of giving it the best countenance he can. But I can assure you the Emperor is convinced your conduct has been most honourable — and that is my opinion also.

Napoleon himself twice told Maitland that he had no complaint about his conduct, which, he said, had throughout 'been that of a gentleman and man of honour'. He tried to get Maitland to accept costly gifts, and wanted to petition the Prince Regent to make him an admiral. On leaving *Bellerophon* he thanked Maitland for the way he had been treated, first formally through Montholon, and finally in person, when he took off his hat — a rare concession — and publicly thanked him most warmly, asking him to convey his thanks to the officers and men. Before stepping on to the gangway he turned, again removed his hat and bowed three times to the ship's company. When the admiral's barge was some thirty yards from *Bellerophon* Napoleon stood up, pulled off his hat and bowed one last time to his devoted custodians.

Alas, for all this courteous charm and dignity, there was always an unpleasant side to Napoleon. In his final protest Napoleon did not hesitate to claim that he had come to England as a free agent trusting in English hospitality promised by Maitland. The Frenchman Jean Duhamel and the American Michael Thornton are among those who bluntly state that Napoleon was lying — 'blatantly lying' says Thornton. M. Duhamel says, 'In his misfortune the Emperor deceived himself and deceived posterity.' M. Duhamel admits that Napoleon was ready to sacrifice the reputation of a man he trusted and liked in order to show himself in a favourable light. Nobody seems to have asked if Napoleon would ever have considered himself bound by an undertaking given by one of his own naval officers. Far from being a free agent, as he claimed, Napoleon knew that he had escaped at the eleventh hour. Although he had the superb effrontery to refer to his 'magnanimity' in surrendering, it should not be forgotten that he had said more than once, to General Beker and others, that above all he must save France the shame of handing him over to the Allies. After writing his 'Themistocles letter' he said to Bertrand, (or according to some accounts to Marchand, perhaps to both), that although there were dangers in surrendering to the enemy it was 'better to trust in their honour than to fall into their hands as a prisoner'. Free agent indeed!

We certainly should not be too censorious about the devious conduct of the desperate man and his advisers, fighting for their lives. This was true of Napoleon himself to an extent which he could not as yet have realised. But it is hard to forgive the self-seeking, scheming Las Cases, who was not on any 'wanted list'. His motives for insisting on accompanying Napoleon into exile are obscure. He was always careful to ensure that his rather hysterical protestations of lifelong devotion were made in the Emperor's hearing. His zeal to live and die for his hero had developed perhaps a little late. He had been a naval lieutenant before the Revolution, but when he returned from exile in England after the *Coup de Brumaire*, when there was fighting to be done, he settled for a chamberlain's post.

After Napoleon's first abdication, although Louis XVIII had made him a captain in the French Navy, he returned to England, where he stayed until the events of The Hundred Days drew him back to Paris. Before embarking on *Bellerophon* he rigged himself up in a shining new naval uniform, to everyone's surprise. When Napoleon chaffed him a little unkindly he explained: 'a uniform carries much more consideration in a foreign country'. He was determined to make himself indispensable to Napoleon, and he succeeded, though not as an authority on English laws and customs, nor as a naval expert. He pushed his claims in both these fields. It was during a discussion with Las Cases about the chances of sailing to America that Napoleon said, 'Had the mission been confided to Admiral Verhuell, as was promised on our departure from Paris, it is possible that he would have sailed.' Claude Manceron's comment on this is, 'Napoleon I was therefore bemoaning the absence of the father of Napoleon III.' Verhuell had been a Vice Admiral of France at the same time as a Marshal of Holland; and Queen Hortense found in this subject's arms a passing solace for the impossible conduct of her unbalanced husband, Louis, the absentee King of Holland, and once Napoleon's favourite brother.

It was as a secretary, amanuensis and fellow-polisher of the Napoleonic Legend that Las Cases was to render useful services to his master; but even here self-interest cannot be excluded. It is generally accepted that he was a diligent Boswell in attendance on a particularly garrulous Dr Johnson; almost a journalist fastening on to a promising source of 'copy'. Lord Rosebery, after a mocking portrait of Las Cases, including the splendid sentence, 'He even had the complaisance to be much shorter than the Emperor', concludes 'We confess to a sneaking kindness for the devoted rhetorical little man.' I think his Lordship was too kind; Maitland could, with justification, have applied the word 'sneaking' to Las Cases himself.

Napoleon and his small court were not alone in denouncing the St Helena decision as shameful. Midshipman George Home probably spoke for the majority of his comrades on the old 'Billy Ruffian' when he said, 'It will be a vile stain on our name for centuries to come.' He prophesied accurately. A century and a half later Commandant Lachouque proclaimed the view that

Napoleon's protest 'had branded England with eternal dishonour'. Even the less excitable M. Martineau concludes that the decision exposed our country 'to the judgement of History, which is the conscience of nations'. However the legal expert M. Duhamel calls Napoleon's protest 'a masterpiece of propaganda', which it most clearly was, so perhaps our own conscience need not prick too fiercely.

M. Martineau is the latest and surely the last historian to put The Fifty Days under the microscope, and his examination covers the whole field fairly evenly. M. Manceron and Commandant Lachouque concentrate upon Act I, and M. Duhamel and Mr Thornton upon Act III. *England and the St Helena Decision* is the secondary title of Mr Thornton's book, and his extracts from contemporary newspapers reflect the irreconcileable views of the two sides in the furious controversy.

On the one side, those who were pro-Government or simply anti-Bonaparte howled for vengeance on the monster responsible for so much suffering. Let us beware of being duped by the Corsican Trickster who had lured the weak-witted Ferdinand of Spain to Bayonne, there to be told that the Bourbon dynasty was ended and his life was in Napoleon's hands. Many murders, such as those of Enghien, Pichegru and Captain Wright, were cited in protest against lenient treatment of the perpetrator of so many dark deeds. The escape from Elba had cost sixty thousand Allied soldiers their lives at Waterloo, and added £30 million to the vast expense of the Napoleonic wars. Why should the Treasury be further burdened with the cost of this criminal's custody; with the expense of saving his life? Let him be handed over to the French for summary justice.

Predictably, in a country with a traditional aversion to hitting a man when he is down, those who cried for vengeance were rebuked by humanitarians, including the type who can readily forget a victim's sufferings in their agony over his killer's punishment. To this chorus were added the voices of those who were already Napoleonists or who had joined their ranks once the arch-enemy was beaten; and also those who were ready to use any stick to beat the Government.

We had some experience in Hitler's day of appeasers and peace-at-any-price politicians. Winston Churchill sometimes had to fight not only Hitler but parliamentary critics. Such back-biting is customary in a democracy when reverses shake confidence in the leadership, but in the Hitler war it was mild in comparison with the activities of the Whig Opposition in Napoleon's day. During the Hundred Days prominent Whigs were all for peace and trusting Bonaparte; and long before that they had strongly opposed continuance of the war. Many had felt sure that no country could hope to oppose Napoleon, and that our small army would soon be driven from the Continental battleground on which it should never have been allowed to set foot. To some of them that army's leader was obnoxious; a haughty aristocrat who never deigned to explain his plans, or to excuse his strategic withdrawals, which they saw as defeats, confirming their belief that he was an unskilled amateur, unfitted for the professional ring dominated by Napoleon and his marshals. The Tory Government deserves great credit for defending Wellington and supporting him, even if at times half-heartedly. After all they could not know, as we know now, that he was one of the greatest generals in history.

Opponents of military adventures knew that we had been pushed off the Continent in 1794, when 'The Grand Old Duke of York' (he was 34 at the time) had 'marched his men to the top of the hill and marched them down again'. Then, in 1809 we had scuttled home leaving behind the body of our great Scottish general, Sir John Moore; and some six months later Napoleon, after winning the Battle of Wagram, had been the unchallenged master of Europe. Far safer to skulk in our island fortress protected by our invincible Navy. Should we today feel inclined to boast of how much braver we all were in 1940 let us reflect that we had then become habituated to victory, even if cynics told us that we always lost every battle but the last. Like Queen Victoria, who had said, 'We are not interested in the possibilities of defeat; they do not exist', we felt in our bones that the British Empire *must* win in the end, that it could not fall to a common brute with a Charlie Chaplin moustache. Luckily we did not then know how soon it was to disintegrate with a little help from 'disinterested friends'.[2]

In 1815 our Allies gladly availed themselves of Britain's unique facilities for guarding the common enemy. St Helena had long been the favoured place for his exile, and the Honourable East India Company was prepared to lend the island to the mother country. Our army was commanded by Europe's greatest general, now that Bonaparte was disposed of. Our immense wealth had been depleted by the cost of the wars against Napoleon — according to one estimate, a thousand million pounds sterling — but we were still rich. Above all our powerful Navy could guarantee that there would be no repetition of the regrettable slip of letting Napoleon escape from Elba.

The British Foreign Secretary, Lord Castlereagh, accepting the burden, said that, by undertaking to guard Napoleon, Great Britain 'will ensure the gratitude of Europe'. That included France. Ralph Waldo Emerson wrote that 'the universal cry of France and of Europe in 1814 was "enough of him"; *assez de Bonaparte*'. In 1815 the French Government, eager for peace on any terms, echoed Talleyrand's heart-felt cry, 'Anything rather than the Emperor, even the Bourbons.'

But however convinced the Government might be that the decision about his disposal was right and proper, putting it into effect was not to be all plain sailing. The term 'political asylum' may not then have been in the common man's vocabulary, but the powerful feelings which it stirs in his mind today were deeply rooted in the British conscience. Not only Capell Lofft, a passionate Whig firebrand, who wrote letters six times as long as any newspaper editor would tolerate today, but reasonable middle-of-the-road citizens, invoked the magic words *Habeas Corpus* — apparently unaware that this peculiarly English protection was not legally available to Napoleon. Was he a prisoner of war? Then he must be released as soon as possible after a peace treaty was concluded. Apart from those unfortunate enough to be deemed insane, there was, it seemed, no class of person for whom permanent incarceration could legally be ordered. (There were of course no Great Trains to rob.)

The complex ethical dilemma was hotly debated, publicly in the newspapers, and privately in the Cabinet, where the final arbiter was the Lord Chamberlain, Lord Eldon. The French lawyer Jean Duhamel, quotes extensively from Lord Eldon's legal opinions and from his letters to his brother Sir William Scott, also a lawyer. Eldon professed himself not unduly worried by Party or Posterity, which he was sure would be as ill-informed on this as on most other issues, 'but to do the thing that is right is really a matter of most anxious concern with me'. The trouble was that Napoleon was a very special case, unique as he had been in so much else. To some his uniqueness seemed to demand leniency rather than harshness.

Among the schemes for delaying Napoleon's deportation none was stranger than the attempt by an eccentric West Indian lawyer, Anthony Mackenrot, to serve on Lord Keith, as Napoleon's guardian, a subpoena requiring him to produce his prisoner as witness in a lawsuit.[3] If successful this would have kept Napoleon in or near England for at least three months. The Commander in Chief of the Channel Fleet was subjected to much anxiety and some indignity in keeping just ahead of the half-crazy litigant, brandishing his writ. Bonaparte's presence on *Bellerophon* was already a source of some embarrassment. Thousands of sight-seers in small boats jostled around the ship. Some had been drowned as a result of the efforts of the guard-boats to keep the crowds away.

M. Jean Duhamel, having expertly reviewed the legal position, sums it up by saying that the Government's decision was 'based on the necessity of self-preservation and legitimate self-defence'. He asks:

> How could one expect them not to adopt an implacable attitude? The war, with its great loss of life, had lasted twenty years; the dead of Waterloo had just been buried.

Frenchmen, less forgiving than M. Duhamel, who still feel that the Government disgraced our country by rejecting Napoleon's noble offer to settle peacefully in an English estate with the alias of Colonel Muiron, must surely also denounce France herself and her allies for hanging the Nazi leaders in the more enlightened twentieth century. Do they feel that a château in France should have been placed at the disposal of a peace-loving Hitler? Which dead comrade might have provided his alias? Not Captain Roehm or Field Marshal Rommel.

Napoleon's English admirers must have sincerely believed in his protestations of his peaceful intentions. His English admirers, such as Mr Vincent Cronin, do so to this day. French writers seem less convinced. Count Vandal saw him as an aspirant to absolute power all his life; and Marshal Foch said that 'he forgot that war is not the highest aim, for peace is above war'.

Unlike Hitler, Napoleon did not outline his true aims in a book; and his outbursts, such as, 'I hear nothing but the word Peace, when everything should resound to shouts of War', were inaudible on our side of the Channel. But his firm resolution never to accept France's pre-Revolutionary frontiers was well-known. He could have had peace in 1813, but would not give up territory which he had sworn at his coronation to defend. So he turned his back on his losses of half a million men in Russia, and scraped the manpower barrel again and again for new armies.

When French deputies blamed him for rejecting offers of peace, and denounced the endless wars which drained away young men who should have been at universities or working for the prosperity of the country, Napoleon furiously abused them, and turned to what he was supremely capable of doing. With wonderful words he inspired his boy-recruits to die for their country and for him. They could not know that during the prolonged negotiations with Metternich, the Austrian Foreign Minister, he had said that he was a soldier to whom the lives of a million men meant nothing. Like his threat that, if he were brought down, he would bury the world beneath the ruins of his throne, this must have been among the terrible words and deeds which he deeply regretted once he had regained control of his explosive temper.[4]

Well, said the Whigs at the beginning of The Hundred Days, that is all in the past. He is a new man now, having learned his lesson in 1814. Liberal-minded Britain should learn to live in peace with him instead of following the line of the European Powers, who in any case, as Samuel Whitbread, one of the most loquacious of them, pointed out, had given Napoleon legitimate cause for complaint by withholding his pension. If the Whigs were right the leopard had indeed changed his spots. Changed his spots? He was incapable of doing so. He may have said that a man was too old for war at forty. The occasional lethargy which overtook him after he had become very fat did seem to make him sigh for peace. But he said that his self-made dynasty could endure only by conquest; unlike hereditary monarchies which could survive defeats. When he returned from Elba and went to his old work-room in the Tuileries, he scornfully threw out the books and missals left by Louis XVIII, saying, 'The cabinet of a French monarch should not resemble an oratory, but a general's tent.'

Only the day after Waterloo he had been still full of fight. Urging his brother Joseph to see to it that the deputies gave him their support, as the only general who could save France, he wrote in his own hand 'Courage and Firmness'. He was most contemptuous of the poor spirit shown by the French, saying, 'How can one count on a people who are ready to surrender after losing a single battle.'

On March 13th, 1815, the Duke of Wellington, Britain's representative at the Congress of Vienna, had signed the declaration whereby the Allies proclaimed Napoleon an outlaw, an enemy and disturber of the world's peace, who, by his actions in breaking his word, had delivered himself to public vengeance. Some thought that we should not have signed. Napoleon had not been the first to break the Treaty of Fontainebleau. The miserable Bourbons did so

first, and even gloried in depriving the Usurper of the money
needed for his existence in Elba. Lord Rosebery thought that they
had hoped that 'Britain might be jockeyed into providing the
funds'. This is a French concern. So far as our country was
concerned Napoleon at large was unquestionably a danger to
peace. We had fallen into line with our Allies, and had signed with
them that declaration. We had no choice but to stand by them
through all the bloody consequences of the outlaw's breach of
faith, and in the end to accept the heavy burden of his custody.

If there had been any duplicity in Maitland's dealings with
Napoleon, or in any of the subsequent actions of the Government,
which I certainly do not admit, they were dealing with the World
Champion of Duplicity. Benjamin Constant wrote in June 19th,
1815, 'No nation can depend on his word'. It was a Whig Member
of Parliament, the Hon William Lyttelton, who, in a long interview
with Napoleon on board *Northumberland*, told him, 'From the
moment that you invaded Spain there was hardly an individual in
England who trusted your word.'

Napoleon in England or in America would have been a
quiescent volcano. Fears of its eruption would have kept Europe
in constant anxiety and readiness for war. In Colonel Muiron we
would have entertained a de-hydrated Napoleon, ready for instant
reconstitution in favourable circumstances. One day in St Helena,
learning of unrest in France, he exclaimed, 'Oh! If only we were in
England.'

Fleury de Chaboulon, who had brought to Napoleon in Elba the
messages which encouraged him to return to France, had a most
revealing interview with him after his final abdication. He had told
Napoleon that he felt sure that England would not allow him to
settle in America. 'Then I shall go to Mexico. I shall find patriots
and put myself at their head.' When Fleury de Chaboulon
observed that they already had their leaders, Napoleon said that he
would go on to Caracas, Buenos Aires, California — anywhere,
until he found 'asylum from the ill-doing and persecution of
men' — and of course someone, anyone, to lead.

In building these castles in the air Napoleon's feet were well
clear of the ground, but he regained contact with a bump when he
asked rather sharply if he was expected to stay in France like a
fool to be captured by Wellington and led in triumph through the
streets of London. This was certainly more realistic than his
day-dreams of a hero's welcome in London, such as had been given
in 1802 to his aide-de-camp General Lauriston, whom he had sent

to announce the Peace of Amiens. The crowd had un-harnessed the horses from his carriage and drawn it through the streets to loud cries of 'Long Live Bonaparte'. The excited crowds which had surrounded *Bellerophon* made a similar welcome for himself seem quite a possibility.

Napoleon's brother Joseph was eager to help him to get to America, and whilst Napoleon lived there was a good deal of desultory plotting to that end.[5]

America might have found that in Napoleon she harboured a viper in her liberal bosom. Proscribed Bonapartist officers had established a so-called *Champ d'Asile* in Texas, where the French had originally settled for a time in 1687. The leading spirit in this venture was the rumbustious Baron Charles François Antoine Lallemand, one of the two generals for whom Captain Maitland spoke up so courageously in 1815. Lallemand, who had been condemned to death in France in his absence, was soon allowed to escape from Malta and, after journeying to Turkey, Greece, Persia and Egypt, he joined his younger brother, also a general, and many other Bonapartist refugees in the United States. After a great deal of plotting to rescue Napoleon and restore the Bonaparte regime, the *Champ d'Asile* was founded with a view to creating a new province of France, ready to provide a nucleus for a new army for Napoleon, if he should ever reach America. Some time after Napoleon's death Lallemand was allowed to return to France and, towards the end of his life, Louis Philippe appointed him to be governor of a department of Corsica, a post which he held with considerable distinction for two years.

Like the various plots which were cooked up in America to rescue Napoleon, the *Champ d'Asile* eventually failed because of poor organisation and lack of funds. Had Napoleon's powers of organisation, and the considerable fortune which he had managed to salvage, been available the chequered progress of that great State towards membership of the United States of America might have suffered quite a set-back. But Napoleon's presence in America would have been more likely to have embarassed Britain, against whose interests in that Continent the French had long been active. In 1791 a strong French fleet commanded by the Comte de Grasse, and more than five thousand soldiers, had helped Washington to defeat Cornwallis; and it was to a French general, the Comte de Rochambeau, as well as to General George Washington that the unlucky British commander had surrendered at York-town. Also present at the surrender was the Marquis de Lafayette, who had been particularly active in urging the French Government to help the American colonists, and had commanded French volunteers fighting against the British troops.

Napoleon had kept his nose out of American affairs. Six years before his birth France had ceded to Great Britain a large part of New France. Napoleon himself sold to the United States the vast territory of Louisiana in 1803, for the paltry sum of 60,000,000 francs. When weighing up the possibilities of a new career, in that interview with Fleury de Chaboulon, he had said that America was not yet strong enough to oppose England. He himself might have brought closer the time when they could do so. Lazare Carnot had actually pressed him to escape to America, saying, 'From there you will again make your enemies tremble.'

This was precisely what Britain had to fear. In Napoleon America would have had a general capable of taking Canada for her, which she had only recently failed to do for herself. Britain in the past had had to fight not only France, but America for possession of Canada. Our preoccupation with the Napoleonic Wars had given America new hope of adding Canada to the United States, and her attempt to do so by armed invasion had been ended only on December 24th, 1814, by the Treaty of Ghent.

To some extent that war had ended in stalemate. James Madison, the fourth President of the United States of America, had been a singularly inept war leader, and had had to flee with his family to the woods of Virginia when his capital, Washington, was captured. However, some victories during the closing months allowed 'Mr Madison's War' to be blown up into a school-book triumph for America.

One can imagine the impact on the situation if General Bonaparte had been able to put his sword at the disposal of the United States, which already possessed a fine and enterprising Navy under spirited leaders.[6]

What if it had been Napoleon the Great, and not that would-be Napoleon of our own day, 'Charles the Great', who had trumpeted that ill-mannered and historically out-dated cry — 'Vive Québec Libre'.

No — let us not listen to Bonapartists who would have us believe in the kindly Colonel Muiron, anxious only to live as a peacable country squire.

Great Britain was right to chain the Eagle to his rock.

# CHAPTER IV

# Medical Board

Up to this point I hope that unbiased readers may be willing to agree that the British Government, mindful of the Lord Chancellor's 'most anxious concern . . . to do the thing that is right', were justified in their decisions. But here loyal support for one's country, right or wrong, wavers a little. If His Majesty's Government did the right thing they did some of it the wrong way.

Who were these 'oligarchs' who incurred Napoleon's lifelong hatred, and the reproaches of generations of historians, by failing to show that noble magnanimity which Napoleon had so confidently expected from our country. These ministers of a supposedly mad king and a madly unpopular Regent were all lords — Liverpool, Castlereagh, Bathurst, Sidmouth and Eldon, a law lord. The Home Secretary, Viscount Sidmouth, as Henry Addington had been First Minister at the time of the short-lived Peace of Amiens, and four years after Waterloo was to be linked with the less glorious field of Peterloo. In 1822 the suicide of the Foreign Secretary, Lord Castlereagh, removed from the political scene a man whose name will always be remembered for the rôle he played in those days of Britain's greatness.

The names of the other ministers cannot be said to shine like beacons in our history. But it is a little surprising to find some of Queen Victoria's best-known ministers already on the political scene. Lord John Russell, who had visited Napoleon in Elba, was a Member of Parliament, aged twenty-three; Peel, at twenty-seven, was Chief Secretary for Ireland; and Palmerston — *ce terrible Palmerston* of the gun-boats — who had chosen in 1809 at the age of twenty-five to be Secretary at War rather than Chancellor of the Exchequer, was in Paris with Wellington, enjoying the fruits of victory when Napoleon's fate was being debated in August 1815.

If His Majesty's Ministers failed to respond to a unique challenge in a spirit of high-minded generosity they had certainly served their country and her allies very well. Despite the dwindling national wealth, the plaints of the City as business interests withered in the protracted blight of war, and the relentless sniping of the Opposition, they never thought of giving up the struggle. In the end they had earned for the Prince Regent Napoleon's tribute to the most powerful and most constant of his enemies – but the most generous? Perhaps not, but those who remember the nation-wide hostility to 'Kaiser Bill', Hitler and Mussolini may forgive the implacable oligarchy for regarding a much greater enemy as an enemy still.

The first reaction of Lord Liverpool, the Prime Minister, to the relief of the final defeat of Napoleon was expressed in a letter to Lord Castlereagh: 'We wish that the King of France would hang or shoot Buonaparte as the best termination of the business.' Doubts whether Louis XVIII was as yet strong enough to punish Buonaparte as he deserved were, it seems, the chief obstacle to handing him over to the French to be shot, like Marshal Ney. The views and the personality of the greatest living subject of George III helped to cool tempers heated by a dearly-bought victory.

Wellington unobtrusively curbed Blücher's bloodthirsty zeal, opposed the suggestion of handing over Napoleon to Louis XVIII, and let it be clearly understood that the British Commander-in-Chief could never consent to be an executioner. The Opposition had deplored the vindictiveness of the Congress of Vienna in declaring Napoleon an outlaw and enemy of the human race. They had denounced Wellington for signing that declaration, but once Napoleon was beaten Wellington was too great to be vindictive. 'If the Sovereigns wish to put him to death', he said, 'they should appoint an executioner, which should not be me.'

In the end, influenced perhaps by Wellington's sensible attitude and the Prince Regent's wish that Napoleon should not be treated with unnecessary severity, the Government framed regulations for his custody which were neither vindictive nor ungenerous. One decision was that large sums of money, or valuables liable to be converted into funds to assist an escape, were to be temporarily confiscated, but returned in due course or used to supplement the expenses of Napoleon's household. The French themselves admitted that this distasteful procedure was carried out with extreme delicacy. French writers describe the cunning with which almost all the money and diamonds were concealed in body belts, leaving only a paltry 80,000 francs to be found. This would have been impossible with a proper search or a strict regime of custody, neither of which the Government enforced.

The Government, in fact, having accepted the guardianship of the common enemy, now complacently regarded themselves as the benefactors of Europe, and even the saviours of Napoleon's life. In France Napoleon's supporters were suffering under the so-called 'White Terror'. Lord Keith, in one of the interviews demanded by Napoleon, tried in a kindly way to get him to see this point of view. Surely to be Britain's prisoner was better than to be handed over to France or Russia. To this Napoleon's reply was the exclamation *'Russie! Dieu m'en garde'*. In St Helena, Keith pointed out, much greater freedom would be possible than if Napoleon were incarcerated in the United Kingdom — The Tower of London, Dumbarton Castle on the Clyde, and Fort George on the Moray Firth had all been suggested.

Napoleon however made a strong formal protest against St Helena, saying that he preferred death, and averring:

> In St Helena I should not live three months; with my habits and constitution it would be immediate death. I am used to ride twenty leagues a day. What am I to do on this little rock at the end of the world? The climate is too hot for me. . . . If your Government wishes to put me to death they may kill me here.

There was of course nothing to prevent Napoleon riding his twenty leagues a day in St Helena, except his own obstinate refusal to allow a British orderly officer to accompany him.

The First Lord of the Admiralty had particularly directed that Napoleon's doctor should accompany him to St Helena. One of the regulations for his custody in St Helena was this:

> If the General should be attacked by any serious indisposition the Governor and the Admiral will each direct a Medical Person in whom they may have confidence, to be in attendance on the General, in addition to his own Medical Assistance, and direct them severally to report daily on the state of his health.

This clause, as we shall see, could never be implemented because of the attitude of 'the General'; but at least it showed a proper concern for the prisoner's well-being. It was not the fault of the British Government that no French doctor was willing to share the Emperor's exile.

The Government was later to prove extremely sensitive to allegations that Napoleon's health was suffering, even that he was dying, as a direct result of being kept in St Helena. It would have been a wise precaution if, before sending him there, they had had his own opinion of his unfitness to withstand a tropical climate put to the test of medical opinion.

Let us suppose that they did decide to convene a board of medical men to examine him and give an opinion, as would certainly be done today, in anything like comparable circumstances. What might such a medical board have found?

If given time and the opportunity to interview those who had recently seen a lot of Napoleon, and his own doctor, this hypothetical medical board might well have decided that Napoleon was in perfect health, despite the rumours which they might have heard that at Waterloo he had been lethargic, below par, even ill. Maitland and Keith had both thought that he was in excellent health. Napoleon himself said that he was well. He had often said so in the recent past, was to say the same in St Helena, and, if the board had questioned him, he would probably have claimed, as he had often done, that he had never been ill in his life. He was always contemptuous of those who were often ill — 'What a rabbit the fellow is,' he would say; '*Quelle mazette que cet homme-la*'.

In fact, although he had a share of the family tendency to hypochondria, he was not the man to confess to any kind of human frailty. Just over a month before arriving in England he had assured Jacques Lafitte, the banker, 'I am still in good health and I have fifteen years more ahead of me. I sleep and wake up when I want to; and I can ride four hours on end and work ten hours a day.'

He had always been proud of his ability to sleep and wake at will, and regarded this as a sign of a good constitution. Sleep however had eluded him in the anxious days of his advance on Paris after leaving Elba, where life had become too easy for a man like him. The admiring and observant young doctor, Foureau de Beauregard, who had accompanied him from Elba, had to give him soporific broths.

It is usually stated that Napoleon was a good sleeper throughout his life, and Vincent Cronin takes this as evidence of a calm and peaceful mind. Not surprisingly he had many sleepless nights in St Helena, and, in fact, several of his contemporaries said that he was a bad sleeper. Although I do not agree with Mr Cronin that Napoleon had a calm and peaceful personality, I think that those who believe that he was unable to sleep peacefully may have been misled by his habit of deliberately waking himself to work through the small hours.

Dr Foureau could have told the board that his patient had often

F

boasted of his robust health and freedom from the need to consult doctors, whose remedies he affected to despise. He had attributed his perfect health and digestion partly to not overeating, and used a curious expression. He said that he knew his 'draught' — *son tirant d'eau* — and if he passed it his stomach rejected the surplus. Could this have indicated incomplete emptying of the stomach? The point may be kept in mind, for he was to die in less than six years of some illness associated with vomiting, and the post-mortem finding of some obstructive growth at the outlet of the stomach (the pylorus).

Unfortunately Dr Foureau de Beauregard would not have been available for questioning. He had loyally volunteered to stay with Napoleon, but Napoleon unselfishly refused to allow this, because the doctor had just been offered a good appointment in France.

Before Napoleon left France his family physician, the great Baron Corvisart, was asked to select a doctor to accompany him, and chose one of his pupils, the thirty-two year old Dr Maingault. Maingault told Napoleon's valet, Marchand, that, apart from the honour of being with Napoleon, he had agreed because he wanted to go to America and later to bring his family to join him there.

When he learned that Napoleon's destination was not America but St Helena, he said that he had been deceived and refused to go. Everyone, including Lord Keith, tried to persuade him, but although he had given his word he had signed no agreement, and he insisted on backing out. Dr Maingault had been incapacitated by seasickness on board *Bellerophon* and the ship's surgeon, Dr Barry O'Meara, had deputised for him.

Dr Maingault might have had little to tell the board, apart from anything he may have learned from Corvisart. From Dr Paul Ganière's biography of Corvisart we learn that the famous physician was almost obsessional about professional secrecy, but he would surely have told his pupil what he needed to know about the medical history and the personality of his new and somewhat alarming patient. He may have had little to tell. Dr Ganière concludes that Napoleon suffered from no serious illness throughout his reign. As we have seen, he prided himself on his physical fitness. He despised doctors for what he regarded as their unscientific approach to their profession. He scoffed at all drugs, saying, '*Je ne suis pas un homme à potions*'.

He used to say that he had no confidence in medicine but every confidence in Corvisart. What he liked about Corvisart was that he prescribed, not drugs, but a régime — diet and so on — and gave his patient moral support. When Corvisart advised Napoleon against his second marriage it would seem that he did so, not on account of any specific condition, but on general grounds, deeming it inadvisable that the Emperor should change his way of life at the age of over forty. Corvisart may also have been motivated by loyalty to Josephine whom he adored, as he knew Napoleon did himself.

Corvisart is known to have suspected that epilepsy was the cause of the strange convulsive seizures from which Napoleon suffered; but he also recognised the neurotic disposition — *une nervosité exacerbée* — which aggravated any symptoms which he may have had.

It was apparently not Corvisart who suggested that Napoleon's transient losses of consciousness might have been due to Stokes-Adams seizures. These are fainting attacks, unconsciousness lasting from a few seconds to a minute or more, associated with a persistently slow pulse rate of around forty to the minute. Dr Ganière tells us that Mme de Rémusat said that Napoleon's slow pulse, said to have been about forty beats to the minute, was 'a congenital malady known as Stock-Adam'. (Mme de Rémusat got both names wrong. The syndrome is named after two Irish physicians, Robert Adams (1791-1875) and William Stokes (1804-78). Although first described in the early nineteenth century, American and other textbooks refer to it as Morgagni-Adams-Stokes syndrome, giving priority to Giovanni. B. Morgagni (1682-1771).)

Whoever may have given Mme De Rémusat her information, we can be sure, says Dr Ganière, that it was not Corvisart.

Leon Daudet, gratuitously and without proof I am sure, deduced that Napoleon's slow pulse and possible heart-block resulted from congenital syphilis. Some hostile critic always has to drag in this unpleasant insinuation.

A military surgeon, Revillé Parise, even denied that Napoleon had a slow pulse at all, saying that his heart beat was very hard to detect, even before he had begun to get fat.

No doubt the medical board would have accepted Napoleon's assurance that he had a good digestion, but, since the point has importance in discussion of the cause of his death, we must probe a little more deeply.

Dr Paul Hillemand, the author of the most recent medical biography of Napoleon, accepts the official theory that Napoleon died of cancer of the stomach, but believes that there was a long-standing gastric ulcer which ultimately became cancerous. He points out that the Bonapartes had a strong family history of gastric ulcer, which was very prevalent in Corsica. Blandly dismissing the fact that Napoleon himself, both before going to St Helena and whilst he was there, strenuously denied that he had ever suffered from stomach trouble, Dr Hillemand postulates a callous healed perforated ulcer of the lesser curvature of the stomach, dating from about 1802. He believes that Napoleon suffered for a long time from pain relieved by taking food, that he kept food by his bedside to relieve such pains during the night and constantly ate cachous and other titbits.

Now it is a fact that Napoleon often woke himself by an effort of will in the early hours of the morning in order to put in some hours of hard work at his desk before the Palace was astir. Perhaps that food by the bedside helped to keep him going at such times, whilst the nibbling of cachous, like his compulsive snuff-taking, might have been a manifestation of his life-long nervous irritability. Fat people do tend to indulge in frequent snacks, but Napoleon's obesity was not due to overeating but to pituitary dysplasia.

Dr Hillemand includes occasional vomiting among the signs pointing to a gastric ulcer, though Napoleon himself, as we have seen, regarded this as a safety valve, a sort of Plimsoll Line, rather than an indication of digestive disorder.

Dr Hillemand mentions Napoleon's habit of bolting his food and his irregular mealtimes, and also touches on probable psychosomatic factors. In support of his theory of gastric ulceration he quotes Dr Yvan, who was Napoleon's personal doctor on all his campaigns from 1796, but he weakens his case by selecting only one sentence from Yvan's report written for General de Ségur in 1812. Hillemand only quotes 'Le spasme chez lui se partageait entre la vessie et l'estomac', whereas that whole section of the report points quite clearly to emotional stomach upsets and not to gastric ulcer. Here is what Yvan wrote:

> The constitution of the Emperor was highly nervous. He was very susceptible to emotional influences and the spasm was ordinarily divided between the stomach and the bladder. When the irritation affected the stomach he had a nervous cough which exhausted his nervous and physical forces to such an extent that his mind was not the same.

Dr Yvan is, in fact, our best authority for the marked psychosomatic or, as it was then called 'nervous', element in Napoleon's illnesses during his active life. Many people who knew Napoleon well knew that he was liable to stomach upsets when things were not going well. Corsicans are said to have for long been very subject to psychosomatic ailments, and much addicted to seeking treatment from a variety of individuals who in some countries would be called witch doctors. Dr Hillemand admits that there is one point which tends to disprove his theory of long-standing peptic ulceration. This is the fact that Napoleon was completely free from stomach trouble from 1813 to 1817. It is hard to believe that Napoleon, a man much given to discussing his own health, could really have allowed this period of four years to have erased from his mind the memory of eleven years of constant pain and stomach trouble so completely that he would ever thereafter vow that he had never had stomach trouble at all. For that is the way he talked before going to St Helena and during his early years there. When Dr Antommarchi pressed him to take medicine and warned him that the liver disease 'might provoke an illness of the stomach', Napoleon replied vehemently, 'Never in any place, or in any circumstances have I suffered the slightest pain from it' (the stomach). This was on 15th November, 1820. Well, with Napoleon anything is possible, and his repeated denials of any previous history of stomach trouble could, I imagine, have stemmed from his determination to maintain that he was ill only because he was in St Helena and could only be restored to health by being removed from there.

Dr Paul Ganière, in his three volume work on Napoleon's captivity, written ten years before Dr Hillemand's book, also reviews the evidence for a gastric ulcer, particularly a callous ulcer, and points out that Napoleon fitted to perfection the modern idea of an 'ulcer personality' — intelligent with a hyperactive brain, independent, self-reliant, ambitious, choleric and tending to eat too fast and unwisely. To this one might add the restlessness and inability to sit still, of his early years; and his tendency to overwork and to drive himself and others to the point of exhaustion.

It has been pointed out that Napoleon's doctors could not have diagnosed gastric ulcer, since that condition was not recognised until ten years after Napoleon's death, when it was described by the surgeon Cruveilhier.

Dr Hillemand is not the first writer to suggest that Napoleon's hand, typically thrust into his waistcoat, was pressing upon a painful stomach. Incidentally Hillemand says it was the left hand, though in the majority of portraits it is the right hand, which is the most likely one in view of the way in which masculine clothing is normally buttoned. The point is worth mentioning only as an indication of how difficult it is to find agreement about the smallest details concerning the Emperor.

It has been also suggested that the Emperor's hand could have been pressing upon a painful liver, but as he never complained of liver trouble before he was in St Helena that possibility will be discussed later. Personally I cannot see why any medical explanation for Napoleon's best-known stance need be sought. Those who have to inspect soldiers, if they are not carrying a stick, must find something to do with their hands, and so must others in the public eye.

Even if Napoleon made no mention of liver trouble the board ought to have investigated the possibility if they knew that he had been suffering severely during the Waterloo campaign from prolapsed piles. Piles were a cross which the Bonaparte family had to bear. Napoleon had written to Jerome recommending the application of leeches, which he said he had found very effective. This is an indication that his piles were no mere transient minor trouble. The first occasion on which Napoleon had had to resort to leeches was during his Italian campaign. His piles were probably associated with his tendency to chronic constipation; but the condition is sometimes due to trouble in the liver.

Napoleon might not have volunteered any information about his piles, for, as Dr Hillemand points out, such conditions were apt to be the subject of ridicule in those days. But he was seldom reticent about any of his symptoms, and in particular he was never in the least diffident about discussing his urinary troubles.

Of course it is pure guess-work, and some may think impertinent guess-work, for any doctor to speculate about Napoleon's reactions to being confronted by a panel of inquisitive doctors. Surmise, however, can be based upon information supplied by Napoleon himself. Although he affected to despise almost all doctors, calling them charlatans and quacks, his overpowering interest in the human body and its ailments, especially his own, drew him into discussions with them. With his logical and analytical mind and his interest in science, he readily detected the prevailing dearth of accurate knowledge based on scientific observation, and he complained that medical treatment founded on conjecture was usually useless and often fatal. 'Well doctor, how many patients have you killed today,' was a favourite greeting from which even the trusted Corvisart was not spared. He told Dr Barry O'Meara in St Helena: 'My opinion is that physicians kill as many as us generals'; and he went on to assert that they did so with the same cool lack of concern.

Surgeons were different, and he 'acknowledged the great utility of that science'. He called the great surgeon, Baron Dominique Larrey, the most virtuous man he had ever known. It was so easy to watch Larrey being virtuous, heroically lopping off limbs on the battlefield; the mobile surgical units which he had organised, his famous *ambulances volantes*, bringing succour to wounded men well forward in the combat zone. These services were available only to the Imperial Guard. The rest of the French army suffered horribly. Heroic activity of this sort appealed to the practical soldier. With his low opinion of men, of human nature, Napoleon could not appreciate the human side of doctoring, the art of psychiatry, which really good doctors must have been practising long before the word was used. Corvisart employed it in his dealings with Napoleon, and he alone was occasionally permitted to answer back.

Realising that the medical board might be persuaded to advise the Government against sending him to St Helena, Napoleon might well have proved co-operative, even talkative. His remarks, based upon things which he is known to have said, might have been on the following lines. 'I always said that I expected to become very fat at forty, and you can see, gentlemen, that I was right. I live only by the skin; and that is why I must spend many hours in very hot baths.'

Making his usual claim to have enjoyed robust health, he might have pointed to his remarkable capacity for hard work, his ability to sleep and wake at will, and the fact that he possessed what he used to call 'two o'clock in the morning courage'. He would certainly not have felt called upon to mention that when his iron self-control failed him he often gave way to the most violent outbursts of rage, sometimes culminating in loss of consciousness. He would have needed little questioning about his 'waterworks' to say, as he had often said before, 'My bladder is my weak point. I shall perish from that.'

Napoleon's urinary trouble, or dysuria, consisted mainly in difficulty in starting to pass water. He was often seen leaning against a tree, or with his forehead against a wall or the breech of a gun, trying to pass water, sometimes for several minutes. He did not often complain of pain, but it has been suggested that he had a stone in the bladder. There is really no evidence to support this. Dr Hillemand thinks that the trouble was of nervous origin. I agree with him, and in my own book *Napoleon: Bisexual Emperor* explained why I believe that the dysuria may have been a manifestation of what the psychologist Alfred Adler called Organ Inferiority.

I also referred to an extremely interesting theory, which in fact offers a more convincing explanation of Napoleon's dysuria than any other. Professor Wardner. T. Ayer of the State University of New York, has developed at considerable length the theory that Napoleon's urinary troubles and many other symptoms, can be attributed to schistosomiasis acquired during the Egyptian campaign of 1799.

Schistosomiasis, familiarly known to British soldiers as 'Bill Harris' from its alternative name of Bilharziasis, is one of the interesting diseases the causal organism of which spends part of its life cycle in man and part in some other creature. *Schistosoma haematobium* and *schistosoma mansoni*, the types found in Egypt, spend part of their life cycle in freshwater snails — *S. haematobium* in *Bulinus* and *S. mansoni* in *Planorbis*. Free-swimming larvae, called *cercariae*, leaving the snails would soon die if they cannot enter a human being, whose skin they penetrate. Entering the blood stream they reach the portal vein, in the liver, whence they reach the bladder or rectum. In due course embryos (miracidia) escape from the bladder or rectum, and infect the appropriate snail, if one is handy, and the cycle begins again.

The disease is extremely prevalent in Egypt, where people are infected whilst bathing or washing in canals or rivers. In Napoleon's day his soldiers were severely affected, and many of them suffered from what was then called Egyptian haematuria. The incubation period before serious symptoms occur ranges from two months to two years, and thus an infection of this sort could account for Napoleon's urinary troubles, which first became serious at Marengo in 1800. A more severe attack partially incapacitated him at Borodino in 1812. Other conditions which Professor Ayer believes could have resulted from such an infection were Napoleon's skin irritation and rashes (due to the *cercariae*) dry cough, tender enlarged liver and haemorrhoids, which are caused by the activity in the rectum of *S. mansoni*.

Professor Ayer's theory seems much more convincing, and is also more acceptable to those who try to believe the best about people, than the insinuations of those who believe that Napoleon's dysuria was caused by some form of venereal infection. The so-called evidence for this is flimsy and rests entirely on the deductions of Count Truchsess von Waldburg, the Prussian Commissioner who accompanied Napoleon on his journey to the port of embarkation for Elba. Von Waldburg, a very hostile witness, wrote that Napoleon openly applied remedies for an 'amatory complaint' in the presence of the Commissioners. Whatever von Waldburg thought he saw, it is probable that all he saw was Napoleon having his customary difficulty in starting to pass water. Though Napoleon liked to say that he expected to perish from the trouble with his bladder, his weak point, he had, like many a patient before him and since, a deep-seated fear of cancer; a fear which, in his case, was sharpened by his belief that cancer of the stomach, from which his father had died, was hereditary.

Napoleon's previous doctors and many of his close associates could have enlarged upon his story of having become very fat at forty. He had in fact suffered a most remarkable change in his physique and personality, beginning about 1805 to 1808, when he was thirty-six to thirty-nine, with increasing obesity and periods of lethargy, sleepiness and indecision, which astonished those who had known and worked with him in earlier days.

Dr Hillemand, describing this as *Le syndrome neuro-endocrinien des dix dernières années*, dates the change from about 1811, though he says that the increase in weight had begun around 1804. The tendency to sleepiness, which he calls *Le Syndrome de Pickwick* (or as we might call it 'The Fat Boy Syndrome') led to some remarkable scenes, when Napoleon would even fall asleep on the battlefield. One of the earliest examples occurred at the Battle of Jena in 1806, where De Ségur observed a company of grenadiers forming a square around the slumbering Emperor.

After the Battle of Leipzig even the tremendous roar when the Elster bridge blew up failed to awaken the Emperor. Dr Hillemand asks, 'Is it not remarkable to see the Emperor sleeping thus, instead of controlling the retreat of the army after a defeat?' Yes indeed — but perhaps Macdonald's disillusionment and subsequent hatred of the emperor (see pp. 25, 26) might have been tempered if he had but known that Napoleon could not help it.

The usually accepted cause of all this is that it was due to pituitary dysplasia. Napoleon's pituitary gland, overactive in the early stages of his career, became exhausted, 'burned out', with subsequent failure of its all-important secretion.

Turning now to the physical examination of Napoleon, the board would have found themselves confronted by a very different kind of man to the Emperor described by visitors to France during the short-lived Peace of Amiens. Napoleon was now extremely fat with a pudgy unlined face of a curious olive colour. Although not very short, five feet six inches in fact, his corpulence and fat round thighs made him look shorter than he really was. His legs were quite shapely and he was proud of his delicate little hands and small feet. Maitland thought that it was to show his legs and feet to good advantage that he always wore silk stockings on board *Bellerophon.*

If our doctors had been allowed to examine the obese body they could have confirmed the impressions of many of Napoleon's intimate friends, who for some years had observed his increasingly feminine appearance and had written of 'a roundness not belonging to our sex . . . breasts plump and rounded' — gynecomastia is the medical term.

It must remain a matter of conjecture if Napoleon would have concealed the nature of his curious body or displayed it openly, even defiantly, for the board's inspection. We shall see, in due course, that he refused to allow a doctor, whom he quite liked, to examine him except in darkness. On the other hand he exhibited himself naked to the Corsican doctor, Francesco Antommarchi, whom he disliked and despised, lightly drawing attention to his curious shape, and boasting ' . . . any beauty would be proud of a bosom like mine.' And this was by no means the first occasion on which he had 'joked about the fatness of his breasts', as his secretary de Méneval said he loved to do. He compared himself to a young female beauty; but that was not quite how he struck others. As he sat in his state coach beside his new young empress he was taken by a bystander for her elderly governess.

This feminine shape — gynandromorphy — a cruel disability to such a man as Napoleon, resulted from the pituitary dysplasia. The secretions of the pituitary gland influence the activities of other internally secreting, or endocrine glands, including the parts of the sex glands which are responsible for producing the secondary sexual characteristics, which distinguish male from female bodily development. In 1913 Dr Leonard Guthrie in the light of the knowledge of endocrinology in his day, diagnosed Napoleon as a case of Fröhlich's Syndrome, but today we might substitute a diagnosis of Pituitary Eunuchoidism, as I suggested in my first book, the theme of which was the effect which such a condition might have had on Napoleon's personality.

Now it was nearly a hundred years too early in the story of medical knowledge for the mid-nineteenth century doctors to know all about this. They might however have felt, on general grounds, that a man of Napoleon's physical type should not be sent to live on a tropical island. Understanding of the scientific justification for that decision also lay far in the future.

Very stout people do not thrive in the tropics, especially if there are factors which could impair the functioning of the heat-regulating mechanism of the body, which depends on the evaporation of sweat from the skin surface, thus extracting the latent heat of evaporation from the blood in the tiny blood vessels in the skin. What used to be called sunstroke, thought to be due to the dangerous actinic rays of the sun, is now called heatstroke, or Heat Hyperpyrexia. In the early nineteen thirties many Europeans in India still wore, buttoned to the back of their shirts, thick quilted 'spine-pads' to protect the spinal cord from the dreaded rays. Soon turned into sweat-soaked poultices they merely impeded the necessary evaporation of sweat from that area of skin. Delicate brains (pickled in alcohol and curry, if we can believe detractors of the British Raj) were shielded from the sun by solar topis; not only lightweight comfortable pith hats but the heavy cork Wolseley topi, smart but uncomfortable, which in the British Army crowned the white man's burden.

Old beliefs die hard in most armies, and even in the 'forties' a certain general, unable to spend his energy in chasing Rommel, made his soldiers' lives burdensome by compelling them to wear this archaic headgear, though in the Western Desert we, like the Afrika Korps, had for long been happily bare-headed or wearing an assortment of caps and berets.

To the protective paraphernalia some rather old-fashioned people in India would add a flannel belly-band, called a cholera belt. The imaginary protection conferred by this quaint item was supposed by some to be conferred upon the Scottish soldier, by the broad thick waist part of the military kilt. Healthy he certainly was, but it was not on account of his often over-heated middle, for that part of the kilt, like the futile spine-pad, could be unpleasantly warm in hot weather, but because the free-hanging lower part of the kilt allowed the free circulation of air and evaporation of sweat from all extensive skin area. It is no exaggeration to say that this could have been literally life-saving in 1857 and 1858, when the British soldiers, trudging across the burning plains of India in pursuit of mutinous sepoys, died in hundreds from 'apoplexy', which was clearly due to heatstroke more often than to cerebral malaria or any other cause. By no means all regiments had at that time been provided with khaki light-weight uniforms, and too often ignorant martinets refused to allow their soldiers to remove their thick scarlet serge tunics, or even to unfasten the high stocks at the neck.

Because of the importance of the skin in heat loss, and for other good reasons, army medical authorities do not like to send to the tropics men who have suffered from intractable skin disorders. Napoleon would certainly have qualified for a reprieve from St Helena on this score. His lengthy battle with a tiresome skin complaint, usually called scabies or the itch — *la gale*— has been exhaustively studied and written about by doctors. James Kemble thinks it was neuro-dermatitis. After the Battle of Wagram, an anxious period in Napoleon's life, his doctors were so worried about his skin trouble that, fearing that he was seriously ill, they sent for Corvisart to come from Paris. Dr Jean Pierre Franck, a former physician of the Austrian Emperor, had thought that it was a scorbutic condition, but Corvisart decided that it was a neglected skin rash, probably started by the rubbing of a coat collar. Napoleon himself made light of it, as he usually did of his 'itch', which he erroneously believed had all been started by handling an infected ramrod during the Siege of Toulon.

Mr Kemble's diagnosis of neurodermatitis is supported by the fact that Napoleon's skin troubles tended to be made worse by anxiety. During some nerve-wracking moments during the *Coup de Brumaire* he scratched the pimples on his face so fiercely that he drew blood. Early August 1815 was a very anxious time for Napoleon, and if the doctors could have examined his skin it is likely that they would have seen places at which he had scratched or torn to the extent of drawing blood. A favourite place was a sinus on his left thigh, which resulted from a wound at Toulon. He used to tear this open with what Dr Antommarchi called 'a kind of eager delight'. When he had opened it up and the blood flowed he felt mental and physical relief, which he attributed to Nature relieving herself. He said that it did him more good than anything in the doctor's pharmacy.

According to Kemble there were various places on his body 'where he chose to "open a vent" for the bad humours as he imagined'. One might imagine that his curious ideas about the beneficial nature of such practices could be explained by the medical belief, in his day, in the efficacy of blood-letting. But this sort of thing hardly suggests a calm untroubled mind.

More important than Napoleon's dermatitis was the likelihood that he suffered from anhidrosis, or impaired functioning of the sweating apparatus, which could be as crippling for a man in a hot climate as is the disabling 'non-sweating disease' to a horse. This is probably why Napoleon spent so much time in very hot baths; and why he said, 'I live by the skin.' Dr Yvan knew all about his patient's dependence on his skin, and wrote in his report:

> As soon as his pores were contracted from either an emotional or an atmospheric cause the appearance of irritation was manifested, with a result more or less serious, and the cough or ischuria became pronounced. All these manifestations ceased with the re-establishment of the function of the skin.

We must be careful not to judge by the standards and knowledge of today those who made the decision to send Napoleon to St Helena; but it can be said that there were adequate reasons for doctors to advise against sending a man of his constitution to live for the rest of his life in a tropical climate. There were in fact to be no special complaints by the French about the heat of St Helena. They were more troubled by the damp of the plateau on which Longwood House stood, and by the constant winds which blew there. But, even if Napoleon did not suffer from the effects of heat, it is I think almost certain that his life was shortened by being sent to St. Helena. He was after all only forty six years old when he went there. He was four months younger than Wellington who had many years of service ahead of him.

The purpose of my first four chapters has been to show the nature of the problem with which the British Government saddled itself in accepting responsibility for the custody of the disturber of the world's peace. Some aspects of that problem were to drive them into defensive actions, including one which doctors must find hard to condone — the trial by court martial of a doctor who had tried to do his best for a patient.

The Bourbons were glad to see the last of Bonaparte, and many of their subjects cordially agreed with them. The gross and bloated old king, his distorted gouty feet encased in small carpet bags, rather than slippers, could offer none of the glamour and glory, the feeling of superiority over the whole world, which had fed the national spirit for twenty years — but at what a cost. The mothers of young sons and the war-weary of all sorts were glad to be rid of him; and so were the Germans, Austrians and Russians whose lands he had ravaged and pillaged. But Britain had never suffered the threatened invasion and there, perhaps more than anywhere else save among ardent French Bonapartists, that almost inexplicable and ultimately well-nigh universal fascination which Napoleon and his Legend were to exercise over men's minds was growing strongly.

Napoleon's decision to place his fate in the hands of the British people was only partly the result of a cool appraisal of the situation. Predominantly it came from the heart. Even in Elba he told Sir Neil Campbell of his desire to end his days in England. When he realised that, swayed by emotional considerations and by his usual determination to see things as he wished them to be, he had seriously misinterpreted the position, he was deeply wounded. But his confidence in the kindly feelings which many of the British people had for him was not really misplaced. In that summer of 1815 he might have encountered less hostility in England than in France. The London crowds would not have drawn his carriage in triumph through the streets, but they would not have stoned him and tried to kill him as the people of Provence had done in 1814.

In France Saint Napoleon's Day quietly dropped out of the calendar; but Napoleon was determined to ensure that the graven image was still worshipped, and he was to spend his remaining years assiduously polishing it and smoothing away its rough edges. In this he received, and has received ever since, as much help from English admirers as from the French. In recent years Napoleon and his Legend have been subjected to very hostile treatment by at least three French writers — Jean Savant, Maximilien Vox and Henri Guillemin. Guillemin indeed has savagely mauled the nation's hero, seeing him as a brigand chief who pillaged Europe and France herself to enrich himself and his clan, without a single redeeming feature.

In sharp contrast to this is the Napoleon of Vincent Cronin, the last major biography in English, which is comparable to the last great French one, that of the academician Jacques Bainville. Both are splendid and noble portraits worthy of the great Court painters, examples of whose art beautify their covers — the Emperor in his coronation robes, by Baron Gérard (Bainville) and the First Consul in a beautiful red velvet court dress, by Antoine de la Gros (Cronin). But, whilst Jacques Bainville gives us

Napoleon 'warts and all', Vincent Cronin's portrait would have given its subject unalloyed pleasure, for he has averted his eyes from the less attractive side of the Emperor and presents him exactly as he himself wished to be seen by posterity. Our national tendency to see the best in our enemies, or at least to refrain for as long as possible from seeing the worst in them, rises above political party, so far as our statesmen are concerned. It was the Whigs who were all for appeasing the French dictator. More recently Conservative statesmen, though they may not have stooped to Lloyd George's adulation of the German dictator, certainly went dangerously far in their efforts to appease him and his mentor and subsequent lackey, Mussolini.

Feelings about Napoleon, whether for or against, tended to run high, and it was only to be expected that there were many in Britain who execrated him and called for severe punishment, even for his death, so long as we ourselves did not have to execute him.[1]

His Majesty's Government wisely did not attempt to justify their treatment of Napoleon by indulging in vilification. It would have done them no good, for their chief problem was the great sympathetic heart of the British public, full of the traditional spirit of shaking hands with the beaten enemy and never hitting him when he is down. Many who had feared Napoleon, even hated him, using his name to scare naughty children, were now impelled by sympathy for the fallen colossus, who no longer threatened them, to join the ranks of the Napoleonists. These ranks were swollen by the kind of woolly-headed do-gooders who are always on the look-out for evil in high places, and by those who merely welcomed any stick with which to beat the Government. A considerable army of Napoleonists was thus on the watch for any rumours of harsh treatment which might be brought home by visitors to the prison isle, which was a port of call for all those who were returning from Africa, India and the Far East. There was really very little for these watch dogs to growl about, and the Government could feel fairly complacent, trusting as they did in the man on the spot. They were not to realise for some years what a deplorable choice they had made in Sir Hudson Lowe.

Ultimately the prisoner's health, and particularly his liver, became the one serious issue upon which the critics could fasten. The French in St Helena, Bonapartists in France, Napoleon's family in Rome and elsewhere, and Napoleonists in Britain insisted that the British Government, defying the sacred laws of hospitality, had sent Napoleon to an unhealthy tropical island, where he was dying of liver trouble acquired there — his doctors said so. Nonsense, replied the Government, Napoleon is perfectly well, the Governor says so, and anyone who disagrees is little better than a traitor. The doctors were simply playing Napoleon's game, helping him to use his bogus illness to force the Government's hand and secure his release. Moreover the climate of St Helena, far from being dangerous, is positively delightful, the Duke of Wellington says so. And so he did; but then he had only had to stay there for ten days. Five and a half years of it were to prove too much for Napoleon.

CHAPTER V

# St. Helena and Sir Hudson

Many writers have dwelt upon the irony of an entry in one of young Lieutenant Buonaparte's notebooks, describing British overseas possessions. He had written: 'St Helena – small island . . .' and here his pen had stopped for lack of more to say. In 1804, as First Consul he planned an expedition to capture the island. In 1815 he inaugurated the convention, followed by all who have written about his exile, of calling it a rock.

M. Gilbert Martineau, an acknowledged authority on Napoleon's life in St Helena, who as French consul now lives in Longwood House, obediently follows this convention in his book *Napoleon Surrenders*, calling St Helena a rock and Longwood House a 'henhouse'. However his first book, *Napoleon's St Helena* includes descriptions of the richly varied scenery of this rock, with pictures of the mountains and plateaus of an interesting looking island, and of Longwood House – a not altogether unimposing residence, as it was in Napoleon's day. The Longwood hens, it appears, had the use of several rooms, including a 'long, light spacious billiard room' and a 'drawing-room, only moderately large but with a handsome black stone chimney-piece'.

But I must not mock at M. Martineau's hyperbole. Living where he does he could not fail to be a dedicated Bonapartist. His books are enchanting, authoritative and essential to an understanding of the last phase of his hero's life. If he criticises our country he does so more in sorrow than in anger, and his castigation falls upon the ruling oligarchy and the inadequate men whom they chose to carry out their policy, all of them unworthy of the 'great nation, noble and generous' in which Napoleon had placed his trust.

M. Martineau is very fair to Wellington, acknowledging the part he played in saving Napoleon from summary justice, which for a time was a hideous possibility – ' "Put to death". This was the issue under consideration at Malmaison, in Fouché's gilded study, Wellington's tent and Blûcher's camp'. I cannot entirely agree with

G

M. Martineau's opinion that the regulations drawn up by His Majesty's Government, designed 'to convert St Helena into the safest prison in the world, and the Emperor into the best guarded prisoner in history', were simply the product of minds 'better fitted to govern a penitentiary than a ministerial department'. Ministers had not forgotten their responsibility for the escape from Elba and the outpouring of blood and treasure which resulted from it. They cannot be blamed if, this time, they were determined to be 'covered' — always an essential requirement to the bureaucratic mind.

The practice of consulting The Duke — and for many years those words meant Wellington and no other duke — about every conceivable subject had not yet become a national obsession. Much trouble might have been avoided if the Government had taken his advice. Some years later he told Lord Stanhope what his opinions had been at the time. The Allies were unanimous about St Helena and Wellington did not oppose the choice. He had spent some time there ten years before and had found the climate excellent. He said that he would have guarded only the very few landing places, and required Napoleon to report his presence night and morning; 'but for the rest of the time I would have let him do or go wherever he pleased. This would have avoided most matters of dispute and then he might have received or sent as many letters as he chose'. It might have worked — without Sir Hudson Lowe.

It is hard to forgive the unbelievable obtuseness of the Government in choosing a soldier for the delicate and formidable task of Governor of St Helena without consulting Wellington. It is certain that no worse choice could have been made from among all the subjects of King George III. Wellington thought that it was a great mistake to replace the East India Company's Governor, Colonel Wilks, of whom he said, 'He was a very intelligent, well-read man, and knew everything that had been passing in Europe, and Napoleon had become really attached to him.' Napoleon himself was to say, *'Pourquoi n'ont ils pas laissé ce vieux gouverneur? Avec lui je me serais arrangé, nous n'aurions pas eu de querelles'.*

Of Lowe, Wellington said, 'I always thought that Lowe was the most unfit person to be charged with the care of Bonaparte's person'. Wellington knew his man and said that Lowe was a damned old fool. 'He was a stupid man. He was not an ill-natured man. But he knew nothing of the world and, like all men who know nothing of the world, he was suspicious and jealous.'

In the hands of this narrow-minded unimaginative man there was to be placed a goad with which he would madden his victim and wreck any hopes of a reasonable relationship between them. This was the decision that Napoleon was to be referred to by no other title than General Buonaparte. It is even possible that the restoration of the 'u' which Napoleon had dropped from his surname, when trying to make himself seem more French, was maliciously intended, though there is in fact no consistency in the spelling of the name in various official documents. Lord Rosebery thought that the use of the old spelling was intentional, pointing out that when the Act of Indemnity was brought before Parliament to sanction the detention of Napoleon, he was referred to as General Buonaparté, 'as if to deny that he had ever been French at all'. If the Government had realised how much the question of title meant to Napoleon and the faithful few, and had been broad-minded enough to give way on it, even a little, they might have forestalled half the troubles of the captivity. For the French would accept no communications in which the title General Bonaparte was used, and the Governor refused anything, even a medical report, in which it was not.

The Government seem to have been led into this ridiculous nonsense by pride in the fact that, alone among the Great Powers, Britain had never recognised Napoleon as Emperor. First Consul — Yes; Emperor of the French — Never. This was partly an expression of sympathetic support for the Bourbons, living in England as emigrés.

The First Lord of the Admiralty heard with pain that, through the innate courtesy of the Royal Navy, Napoleon had been received on board Admiral Hotham's flagship with almost royal honours. This would never do. Henceforward he must be treated as a general on the retired list. Napoleon poured scorn on this nonsense. Why general? Why not archbishop? He had been head of the Church as well as of the Army. No one played out this dreary farce more childishly than the admiral who took Napoleon to St Helena, Sir George Cockburn. He took a slightly malicious pleasure in putting Napoleon in his place during the voyage.

Napoleon seems to have found the bluff sailor too childish to quarrel with. Eventually in St Helena Sir George felt compelled to make his position quite clear to the French. He wrote to Bertrand:

> You oblige me officially to explain to you that I have no cognisance of any Emperor being actually upon this island, or of any person possessing such dignity having (as stated by you) come hither.

The composition of this piece of puerile pomposity surely earns Rear Admiral Sir George Cockburn a place in the Valhalla of the 'Humourless Scotsmen' of English traditional belief. On such a man Napoleon's gentle irony was wasted. The admiral having graciously invited the general to a ball, Napoleon directed Montholon: 'Send this card to General Bonaparte. The last I heard of him was at the Pyramids and Mount Tabor'. But it was never really a joke to Napoleon. He had been twice crowned, once as Emperor and once as king; had been annointed by the Pope, accepted, even grovelled to, by most of the crowned heads of Europe. The titles which he had invented and conferred upon his relatives and supporters were recognised in France, as many are still recognised today. To refuse him his title was an insult to France, to the memory of thousands who had died for him. In a sense it seemed like an attempt to erase from the history of France some of its most shining pages. Poor stupid Sir Hudson Lowe took over Cockburn's part in this fatuous farce, and played it to the end.

Napoleon, three weeks before his death, had presented to the officers of the 20th Regiment his copy of Coxe's *Life of Marlborough*. The vigilant Sir Hudson, seeing on the title page the words *L'Empereur Napoléon*, ordered that it must be torn out. Happily the officers refused and the book was sent home for a decision by the Commander in Chief, the Duke of York. He wrote that, 'such a gift from Napoleon to a British regiment was most gratifying to him'. His ruling came too late for Napoleon to learn that the hated oligarchy and its shoddy servants did not necessarily speak for England.

But Hudson Lowe had the last word. He rejected a French request that Napoleon's coffin should bear the one name which never could be — never has been — obliterated. The French refused all alternative wording, so a nameless coffin was consigned to a nameless grave, to await apotheosis and translation to the *Invalides* nearly twenty years later. In this 'silly subject of dispute', as Sir Walter Scott called it, the British Government were not so much malicious as insensitive. They seemed to be unable to comprehend the depth of Napoleon's feelings about it and, like many people, felt that he simply used the argument as one more cause for complaint with which to embarrass them. For Napoleon was determined that they should never succeed in their pathetic attempt to pretend that no person who had possessed the dignity of an emperor was actually present in St Helena, as their representative, the admiral had put it.

When Lord Liverpool, disappointed in his hope that the French might summarily dispose of Bonaparte, had written to the Foreign Secretary about the advantages of St Helena as a place of exile, he added that 'being withdrawn so far from the European world, he would very soon be forgotten'.

Perhaps in the case of the frivolous pleasure-loving Prince Regent it may have been a case of 'out of sight, out of mind'. He had been King George IV for little more than a year when he was told of Napoleon's death — 'It is my duty to inform your Majesty that your greatest enemy is dead'. 'Is she by God' said the delighted king. — In less than three months his real enemy did die — the impossible, flamboyant Queen Caroline, Germany's most damaging export to our country, not excluding the Volkswagen. But Europe and its kings had too many reasons for remembering Napoleon to be able to forget him then or ever since.

The story of his last years has fascinated historians to this day. Lord Rosebery said:

> There seems to have been something in the air of St Helena that blighted exact truth, and he who collates the various narratives on any given point will find strange and hopeless contradictions.

Despite the emergence since Lord Rosebery's day of many valuable contemporary sources of information the contradictions persist, mainly because we are so dependent on gossip.

Napoleon and his captors between them created conditions in which the universal thirst for any detail of his life in exile could be satisfied chiefly by gossip; Napoleon, by progressively withdrawing himself from all outside contacts, hoping that his gaoler's life would be made wretched by rumours of escape plots; and the Government, by grossly overcrowding the island with largely idle soldiers, 2,280 of them, multiplying mouths to devour its scanty produce, mouths to spread the gossip to eager ears of thousands with nothing better to do than collect it and pass it on.

Napoleon and his friends had very little difficulty in so manipulating the gossip that the captivity soon became martyrdom in the eyes of the world.

It cannot fairly be claimed that the martyr was subjected to any really harsh treatment, but petty meannesses and irksome restrictions, in the case of such a man, are as unpardonable as cruelty, and were felt by him even more acutely. But it is only fair to point out that the very first Bonapartists of all, those who were actually there with Napoleon, have left us plenty of evidence that most of their complaints were a deliberate propaganda campaign, in order to have the conditions of their captivity ameliorated, and particularly to have them all removed from the island which they hated.

On one occasion, after Hudson Lowe had quite reasonably drawn attention to the mounting costs of the establishment at Longwood, Napoleon ordered some of his silver plate to be broken up and sold in the market. This was done with the maximum publicity, within sight of army officers who were about to sail for England. It was explained to them that the silver was being sold to obtain enough food to sustain life. Sure enough, by such means, rumours of Hudson Lowe's meanness and severity spread to Europe. But in fact the French were provided for with exceptional generosity, and Napoleon admitted this to his doctor, O'Meara; whilst Bertrand expressly confirmed the fact in a letter to Hudson Lowe.

Staggering quantities of food and wine were supplied to Longwood House, in an island where the inhabitants lived meagrely and in bad times near to starvation. The servants received a bottle of wine a day and the officers even more. Sir Walter Scott wrote that the claret provided

> was that of Carbonel at £6 per dozen without duty. Each domestic of superior rank was allowed a bottle of this wine, which is as choice, as dear certainly, as could be brought to the table of sovereigns. The labourers and soldiers had each, daily a bottle of Tenerife wine of excellent quality.

For all that, Sir Walter regretted that the extravagant and wasteful habits of the internees should have been the subject of official enquiry, since however costly might be the maintenance of the family at Longwood it was less costly than maintaining an army of three hundred thousand men, had Napoleon been still at large. Napoleon, always a critical auditor of his Palace household accounts, and inclined to meanness, even to his own servants, did not care what extravagances went on behind the green baize door at Longwood, so long as his gaolers were paying. Why should he care if the generous Government allowance of £8,000 was exceeded in one year by as much as £10,000? The effect on Sir Hudson Lowe, a somewhat parsimonious man who had to explain things to the Government, can be imagined. He just did not have the kind of noble mentality which could encompass Sir Walter Scott's opinion that:

It would have been better to have winked at and given way to the prodigality of a family, which had no motives of economy on their own part, than be called upon to discuss such petty domestic details in the great council of the nation, sitting as judges betwixt England and her prisoner.

However justified the judges in the great councils of Britain and her Allies may have felt in their treatment of Napoleon, the juries of the common people tended to side with the prisoner. Waves of sentiment, such as those which washed away thoughts of a victim when his killer lay under sentence of death, surged throughout Europe and crashed on the luckless British Government.

It was particularly easy for anti-Government circles to whip up such feelings in Britain itself, where the only French soldiers to set foot had been prisoners. Eventually the unlucky Governor of St Helena became one of the most hated men in England. Since he has come down to posterity as the villain of the piece it is only fair to remember that many people who were in St Helena at the time did not condemn him. Among the French they included two of those best qualified to judge, Bertrand and Montholon. But, as we shall see, they waited until they had left the island, by which time it was too late for Hudson Lowe's reputation. No one should blame them for this. From books and films about prisoners of war we all know that the teasing and tormenting of one's captors is the chief occupation and solace of those in that frustrating situation. Indeed it is a military duty to keep one's guards on their toes, perpetually worrying about the possibility of escape. The French in St Helena all regarded General Gaspard Gourgaud as a traitor to their cause when it became known that, after leaving Longwood and St Helena, (following a curious quarrel with Napoleon which is examined in detail in my first book) he had spread it about in Europe that Napoleon was in good health, even planning to escape; and that conditions at Longwood were satisfactory. The rest of them reserved such honest admissions until they were all safely back in Europe. Whilst in St Helena they waged the skilful war of propaganda designed to excite the sympathy of any who might help to end their exile.

They had been profoundly prejudiced against St Helena even before they left the shores of England. They would have been unimpressed by Wellington's opinion that it was almost a health resort; 'a pleasant place for gentlemen with little left to do', as Rudyard Kipling was to call it in his poem, 'St Helena'. As *Northumberland* approached the island Napoleon commented: 'It is not an attractive place. I should have done better to remain in Egypt.' According to M. Martineau 'one of the ladies of Napoleon's suite is supposed to have remarked "the devil must have s---t the island as he flew from one world to the other";' which sounds like Albine de Montholon, who was certainly 'no lady'.

At first however things began to go not at all badly. Napoleon had adapted himself to much worse conditions during a life of campaigning. Having decided that escape was, at any rate for the present, out of the question, he set himself to be pleasant to Admiral Cockburn, hoping for some betterment of his treatment. He hoped that he had only to await a change of Government, perhaps the succession to the throne of Princess Charlotte, for a change of heart towards him.

After a night in Jamestown in an unsuitable bug-infested inn or boarding-house called Porteous House, Napoleon was taken to view the place chosen for his residence, Longwood House, a fairly large converted farmhouse on a high plateau some miles from the port of Jamestown. On the way there they passed a most attractive property, 'The Briars', belonging to William Balcombe of the East India Company. Here, in a chalet or Chinese Pavilion in the grounds, Napoleon was to live most happily from 18th October to 10th December 1815, whilst Longwood was being made ready for his occupation.

In many ways this was one of the happiest times, certainly the last completely happy time, of his life. He enjoyed his proximity to a pleasant family, and the unaffected friendship of their little daughters, especially the fifteen year old Betsy. The vivacious little girl soon overcame her initial awe of Boney, and an almost flirtatious comradeship developed. It all sounds idyllic as told by Betsy, when she had grown up and become Mrs Abell. For Napoleon it was a period of pleasant relaxation, in preparation, though he could not know this, for his last battle — *La Lutte Contre Hudson Lowe*, as Dr Ganière calls the third volume of his work on Napoleon's exile.

Napoleon, it must be said, had entirely concurred with Admiral Cockburn's choice of Longwood House as his place of residence and, stupid though Cockburn may have been, he cannot be blamed for the fact that the choice proved to be a bad one. When the choice was made neither Napoleon nor Cockburn had any experience of the climate of the island. Sir George may not have bothered overmuch about his prisoner's comfort, but, in selecting

Longwood, he clearly felt that any normal person would prefer to live on this upland plateau, 1,600 feet above sea-level, rather than in the steamy tropical heat of Jamestown, overcrowded and plagued by flies.

Up there, of course, Napoleon could be more easily guarded, and it is likely that it hardly occurred to the Scottish sailor that his Mediterranean-born prisoner might have endured the sultry heat with more equanimity than the perpetual winds and damp rainy climate which were to prove the drawback to life on the upland estate. If anyone was to blame for failure to foresee this it was Colonel Wilks, the Governor, and the Lieutenant Governor, Colonel Skelton. Skelton and his wife were occupying Longwood when Napoleon first inspected it, and could have told him that they came there from their house in Jamestown only during the months of October to February. The plateau was deserted by sensible people for the rest of the year. M. Martineau has made a detailed analysis of the much debated subject of the climate of St Helena and we can unhesitatingly accept his opinion that Longwood was a bad choice; and that 'with its winds, damp, fogs and sharp changes of temperature' it was, and is, a place in which most people do not feel well.

To Napoleon this converted wooden farmhouse on an exposed, damp and windswept plateau, with only a few eucalyptus trees, was to become a hateful contrast to the Elysée Palace. As Wellington said, 'The truth is that when a man is dissatisfied with being confined and thinks you have no right to confine him, if even you were to build him a palace of gold he would say this won't do'. Longwood was no palace of gold. In Napoleon's day many aids to comfortable living in the Tropics, which no doubt make the place bearable today, did not exist. The French were undeniably cramped for space, especially in the staff quarters; and this was the main reason for the Bertrands deciding to live about a mile away at Hutt's Gate. Finally we cannot overlook the fact that what accommodation there was had to be shared with a large and active population of rats.

In due course the inevitable request was made that Napoleon and his suite should occupy Plantation House, the spacious official residence of the Governor. I am afraid that most of those who have served overseas and had to do battle for the best available quarters for their wives and families, would endorse, perhaps a little selfishly, Hudson Lowe's reaction to this request. He told the Russian Commissioner: 'I do not want to hand over Plantation

House to the French. They would do too much damage there, and besides Lady Lowe would not be so well at Longwood, and I will never sacrifice my wife's health to Bonaparte's comfort.'

But Lowe did not just selfishly leave things there. He decided to build a new house for Napoleon on a less exposed site, and collected materials for the purpose. But when he invited Napoleon to choose a site for the house Napoleon was in a completely unreasonable frame of mind, and had decided to force a quarrel on the Governor. There is no doubt that the appointment of Sir Hudson Lowe as Governor of St Helena was unhappy for the exiles and disastrous for the good name of our country and for Lowe himself, who otherwise could have ended his days in retirement, unknown outside a circle of friends. But the disaster, the complete breakdown in normal relations between Lowe and Napoleon, resulted from defects in the characters of both, and if anyone's conduct was most to blame it was undoubtedly Napoleon's. When Wellington supposed that things would have gone more smoothly with Colonel Wilks as Governor he was underestimating Napoleon's capacity for picking a quarrel with someone whom it suited him to antagonise.

Lowe was not a cruel man, only one of the stupidest generals it is possible to imagine, and worst of all a chronic worrier, and the possessor of an unconquerably suspicious mind. The true flavour of that obsessional mind can be appreciated only by studying his voluminous correspondence; but for those with no patience for its arid wastes the famous 'haricot beans case' is a good representative sample. He suspected everyone of being in league with Napoleon and of plotting, or being bribed, to help him to escape. Even the Allied Commissioners, who were in St Helena to assure their Governments of the prisoner's continued presence on the island, did not escape suspicion. Count Montholon once offered the French Commissioner, the Marquis de Montchenu, a few beans to plant. They were both white and green. Most suspicious, thought the Governor, and he wrote to Lord Bathurst:

> Whether the haricots blancs and haricots verts bear any reference to the drapeau blanc of the Bourbons, and the habit vert of General Bonaparte himself, and the livery of his servants at Longwood, I am unable to say; but the Marquis de Montchenu, it appears to me, would have acted with more propriety if he had declined receiving either, or limited himself to a demand for the white alone.

Lowe was undoubtedly in a class by himself, but it may be admitted that, as a general who had failed to distinguish himself in action against his country's enemies and sought, by diligent observance of his orders in every pettifogging detail, to gain a reputation at least for administrative efficiency, he was a type not unknown in any army. Hell hath no fury like a promotion-hungry senior officer, striving to 'keep his nose clean'.

Lowe was naturally intensely keen to succeed in his onerous appointment, the most important task with which he had ever been entrusted. From the start he could see that it would not be easy. When he accompanied Admiral Cockburn to Longwood for his first interview with Napoleon, the footman banged the door in the Admiral's face as he was attempting to follow Lowe into the room. This was Napoleon's little plan to snub Cockburn, and the malicious pleasure which its success afforded him might have warned Lowe of what to expect. But at least it may have been due to a desire to make a completely clean start with the new Governor. Lowe on his side was determined to establish good relations, and at first there were genuine efforts on both sides.

Lowe, as it happened, had been present at the battles of Bautzen, (where he had actually seen Napoleon) Montmirail and Champaubert; and this in Napoleon's opinion augured well for the future — 'We probably fired guns at each other. With me that always makes for a happy relationship.' After their first meeting both felt that good progress had been made, though Napoleon had not liked the look of Sir Hudson. He told Bertrand that he looked like a Sicilian policeman; and to Montholon he said, 'His eye is that of a hyena caught in a trap.' At least one portrait of Lowe makes this impression quite comprehensible (see facing p. 112.)

However, both of them were trying, and Napoleon when he chose to try could be charming. Lowe unfortunately could not; but in his rigid way he did try to be accommodating. But Napoleon's initial impression, together with his indignation about his treatment by the Government which Lowe represented, and a deep inner conviction that he could never be legally deprived of the rights of an annointed sovereign, were at work. Finally some dark inexplicable Corsican superstitiousness welled up in him and he actually thought that Lowe's evil eye might have poisoned a cup of coffee, which he promptly threw out of the window. How could an inelastic, insensitive Englishman comprehend the devious imaginings of such a Corsican mind?

Lowe seems to have dimly realised that something was amiss, for on the 16th May after an interview he complained to Bertrand, with more perception than he is usually credited with, 'I went to see him determined to be conciliatory. He wants everything to be as he wishes and precisely as he understands it. He has created an imaginary Spain, an imaginary England. He wants to make an imaginary St Helena.' But, as Mr Cronin comments, what poor Lowe did not realise 'was that Napoleon had already created an imaginary Hudson Lowe.'

Lowe was in fact, presumably quoting a comment by the Abbé De Pradt, who, as French ambassador to Poland had met Napoleon when he arrived in Warsaw after leaving his beaten army in Russia. De Pradt wrote:

> Whoever followed his career saw him create for himself an imaginary Spain, an imaginary Catholicism, an imaginary England, nay even an imaginary France.

Now Lowe knew his man at least, and he kept repeating that Napoleon was impossible to deal with in anything, that he had a most extraordinary way of going on. Bertrand could sympathise with Lowe, and he told Napoleon that it seemed to him that Lowe had gone to the interview with the best intentions. At their next meeting the final row flared up which made any further meeting impossible.

The row was entirely sparked off by Napoleon, but to some extent it arose from one more important reason why Hudson Lowe should never have been sent to St Helena. This reason was one for which he could hardly be blamed; but the Government deserved severe censure for not realising what a serious disability it was. During a not entirely undistinguished career Lowe had raised and commanded the Royal Corsican Rangers, who to Napoleon, naturally enough, were simply traitors and renegades. Lowe took with him to St Helena to be Inspector of Hospitals, Dr Baxter who had been with him and his Corsican Rangers during the Siege of Capri, which ended in Lowe's somewhat ignominious surrender.

Even worse, he also took Lieutenant Colonel Thomas Lyster, who as a major had served in the British garrison of Ajaccio, Napoleon's birthplace. This, as the Russian Commissioner rightly commented, showed 'an inexcusable lack of tact'. Napoleon seldom bothered to exercise tact himself but he was not a man to overlook lack of it in others. During the terrible quarrel which ended all hopes of peaceable dealings with the Governor, Napoleon taunted Lowe in a manner quite unworthy of a great general. 'You never commanded any men, but Corsican deserters . . . You do not know how to conduct yourself towards men of honour, your soul is too low.'

After this he often asserted that he was sure that Lowe meant to assassinate him, and he habitually referred to him as a *sbirro* — or brigand, in allusion to his unforgivable Corsican command. All the foul temper at that last interview had been on Napoleon's side, and he freely admitted his responsibility for the breakdown in relations, saying to General Gourgaud, 'That is the second time in my life I have made a mess of things with the English. Their complacency is more than I can stand and I say more than I should.'

He went still further in taking the blame for the quarrel when he said to Las Cases, 'I behaved very ill to him, no doubt, and nothing but my present situation could excuse me; but I was out of humour and could not help it; I should blush for it in any other situation.'

He went on in this vein for some time, and ended with the significant remark that he wished that Hudson Lowe had also lost his temper and showed some spirit. I know of no other instance in which Napoleon made quite such a handsome admission of faults on his side. It should certainly increase our sympathy for Hudson Lowe, who had been bewildered by Napoleon's verbal assaults. But it is at the same time so human and understandable that I think it must also increase our sympathy for Napoleon himself.

Sir Hudson's incurably suspicious mind was tortured by fears that Admiral Sir Pulteney Malcolm was undermining his position and authority during the long friendly meetings which he had with Napoleon, with whom he was always on excellent terms. Such jealous apprehension was unfounded and unjust. The Admiral was doing his best to heal the breach and to persuade Napoleon to adopt a more reasonable attitude, as we know from notes of the conversations published by his wife and also from the record of Captain Henry Meynell, who took part in many of the conversations. On one occasion Napoleon, claiming that he was a man who could live tranquilly if he was treated with the regard to which he felt he was entitled, admitted that the Governor had never had a chance to understand his true character, since, in Captain Meynell's words, 'The G has never seen me except when I was irritated and spoke *Bêtises*.'

Lowe was unlucky in his own staff at St Helena, especially in his secretary, a thoroughly nasty little toady, Major Gideon Gorrequer. Lowe was blindly convinced of his loyalty, but Gorrequer was spying on him and deriding him behind his back. His tedious diary may be a useful source of information about

Lowe and Plantation House, but among the assortment of nasty tastes which it leaves in the mouth none is more nauseous than the revelation of its author's character. The diary was recently published and Gorrequer's use of nicknames deciphered and explained by the English surgeon and author, James Kemble. Lowe was equally unlucky in his biographer and official apologist. In the three massive and dreary volumes of William Forsyth the points in favour of his subject are lost in great wadges of tasteless and indigestible matter, like the currants in a wartime cake. Another apologist for Lowe, who somehow failed to make much impact, was T. Dundas Pillans, whose book *The Real Martyr of St Helena* was published in 1913.

Some British officers who had been in the garrison of St Helena spoke up for Sir Hudson, in addition to members of his immediate staff, who had their own reputations to consider. Lieutenant Basil Jackson, an observant and intelligent young officer, considered that Lowe had been unfairly condemned. He quoted Sir John Moore's very high opinion of him in his earlier service. Basil Jackson visited Montholon in France and obtained from him a generous admission that in fact the Governor, in an impossible situation, had done his best for the French. Dr Walter Henry mentioned Lowe's many acts of generosity to the exiles, especially after Napoleon's death, and concluded that 'Sir Hudson Lowe was a very different man from what he was represented by his enemies at the time, and what the world still believes him to be.'

When Lowe's unhappy assignment ended with the death of Napoleon, he was shabbily treated by the Government which he had tried to serve to the best of his ability. The fair-minded Wellington said to Lord Stanhope: 'Without being any great admirer of Sir Hudson Lowe, I must say that I think he has been shamefully used about this business — shamefully'.

Lowe has certainly had a long long wait for any sort of understanding, let alone justice; but I think that he has at last received the best he can expect, perhaps the best he deserves. Napoleon's most recent English biographer, Vincent Cronin, in one of the best chapters in a fascinating book, *The Last Battle*, analyses the progress of the famous quarrel with a deeper perception of the feelings on both sides, and with more sympathetic understanding of the dilemma of Sir Hudson, than has hitherto been displayed even by his defenders.

From the French side one expects, and understands, implacable condemnation of the gaoler, but several French writers have defended him and thought him ill-used. One example of such generous treatment of the enemy is an article by Count L. de Viel Castel, written in 1855 (see bibliography).

More important however is the fact that the two senior members of Napoleon's household spoke up for Lowe, once they had left St Helena and had no axe to grind.

General Bertrand, who knew better than most how impossible Napoleon was to deal with, told Lord Bathurst, the Secretary for the colonies, that the French had nothing to complain of in Sir Hudson's conduct. Count Montholon went even further and was honest enough to admit to Basil Jackson that 'an angel sent from Heaven would not have satisfied us as Governor'. Montholon had shared Napoleon's captivity for six years and he was later to spend exactly the same number of years in the fortress of Ham as a fellow-prisoner of Louis Napoleon, later Napoleon III. He said that the Emperor had been much better treated by the English than his nephew was by the French.

One of the by-products of the break-down in relations between Napoleon and the Governor was Napoleon's steadfast refusal to see any doctor whom he could regard as a nominee of Lowe. Consequently we depend for professional reports about his health on the writings of only a few doctors.

During the first two years of his stay in the island Napoleon's health was very good. This time he had no small kingdom of his own to inspect and to organise, as he had had in Elba. He settled down fairly philosophically in his small estate, surrounded by his last little Court whom he required to conduct themselves as if they were still servants of an Emperor. They needed no encouragement for he was now, even more than before, the centre of their lives, the justification for their own existence in this detestable place. So they wore out their delapidating court dresses, whilst the domestic staff — 'The Service' as they liked to be called — all wore livery; and all behaved with the old formality.

Napoleon went for drives around the island, meeting a few of the inhabitants. He did a little gardening and transplanted some trees which quite soon furnished both shade and fruit, so the soil cannot have been too bad. But his main preoccupation was with endless talking, reminiscing, dictating. He had set himself the task of writing the history of his reign, or really re-writing it. Ralph Waldo Emerson, the American essayist, spoke for one strong school of thought when he wrote that Napoleon spent his time in his lonely island in 'coldly falsifying facts and dates and characters, and giving to history a theatrical *éclat*'.

Well, Napoleon with his theatrical tendency, had always had a remarkable facility for believing only what he chose to believe, and it may be overstating the case simply to accuse him of lying, as so many writers have done. How many of us have never been guilty of embroidering some of the tales of our past adventures, perhaps to make them more entertaining, a better story, even more creditable to ourselves; and after a few tellings have come to believe in the improved version?

In 1814, during his emotional and theatrical farewell to his Old Guard, Napoleon had promised them to consecrate the rest of his life to writing about the great things they had done together. Since then the story had had a sequel, which had not ended too heroically. The French, although enjoying the story of General Cambronne's reply when called upon to surrender at Waterloo (which consisted of the familiar expletive *'Merde'*, thenceforward known as *le mot de Cambronne* in polite society) naturally preferred the glamourised version: *La Garde meurt mais elle ne se rend pas'*. The Guard had not died — by no means all of it anyway; and it had most certainly surrendered. Cambronne had humbly and unsuccessfully sought an interview with Wellington, still grieving over his own terrible losses. Wellington sent him and General Mouton packing because he thought 'they had behaved so very ill to the King of France.' Every army has some blots on its copybook which it prefers to overlook, and the erasure of this one can have presented no problem to the man whose communiqué of June 21st 1815 had presented Waterloo as a brilliant French victory. Nor can it have been difficult to dictate the heroic saga of the march of the Napoleonic armies — the greatest successful 'run' in any theatre of war. Easy enough to remind his old *grognards*, his *vieux moustaches*, of the great deeds which they had done together, the Glory which they had won. But since it had all ended in disaster, how to point the moral, how to convince the limbless veterans now on the scrap-heap, the widows and fatherless children, that it had all been worthwhile; that the sacrifices had been made in a noble cause? That was a challenge which could be met only by the first world champion of propaganda. No man has ever been his equal in presenting himself in a favourable light, in finding scapegoats to account for any apparent failures.

The easier dictation, the straightforward story of campaigns, was taken by de Montholon sometimes, but usually by the strange

Two views of Sir Hudson Lowe. *Left:* Sir Hudson Lowe – as his friends saw him. *Below:* Sir Hudson Lowe – Napoleon's 'Sicilian Policeman'

Frederick Lewis Maitland, Captain of H.M.S.
*Bellerophon.* 15 July, 1815

Louis Marchand

young bachelor general Baron Gaspard Gourgaud, who had himself taken part in all the campaigns of the Empire with some distinction. Promotion had come to him after Austerlitz, Friedland and in the Peninsula; and in 1811 he had become one of Napoleon's aides-de-camp. In 1812 he had been appointed to the specially created post of First Orderly Officer. We have already met him in Chapter 2 as an interpreter of omens and an advocate of surrender to the British. His name was not on the first list of those who were to accompany Napoleon to St Helena, but he made such a fuss that he was allowed to go.

Having, like the others, re-transferred his allegiance from the Bourbons to Napoleon, St Helena was safer for him than France where the 'White Terror' was raging. But with Gourgaud it went much deeper than that. He had conceived a deep personal love for the Emperor, which, for a time at least, was reciprocated. 'He was my First Orderly Officer. He is my work. He is my son', said Napoleon.

Before the eyes of the Emperor, like so many young men of his age, which was thirty-two, Gourgaud had performed the dashing deeds designed to impress their God of War; deeds which epitomised the glory and pride of his manhood; which were a valued part of his chosen career as a soldier, now miserably ended. His adoration of Napoleon was both obsessional and obsessive, and he fiercely and jealously resented anyone or anything which came between him and his idol, or deflected Napoleon's attention from the absorbing game of fighting over again the old battles. He once challenged Montholon to a duel. Montholon's flighty wife was doing her best to lead Napoleon's thoughts to idle dalliance. Everyone knew that Albine de Montholon was a 'tart'. Gourgaud was the one who did not hesitate to say so.

Montholon had been an aide-de-camp to the Emperor for a time and had some slender claim to military standing. But that the absurd, mincing little sneak Las Cases should seek to establish such a claim was too much. The naval uniform had been bad enough, but what infuriated Gourgaud was that, in order to set off his fine new uniform, Las Cases had actually solicited for the Legion of Honour, and had been allowed to put up the sacred ribbon. Gourgaud could not bear to see Napoleon closeted with this detestable creature. After Las Cases' departure Napoleon soothed the angry young general with this explanation: 'You possess the rough virtues, whereas Las Cases has the disposition of a woman. You were jealous of him.' Strange words indeed; but Gourgaud's

H

ill-repressed homosexual passion for his former Emperor is outside the scope of this book.

For Napoleon, Las Cases had something which Gourgaud lacked — brains. He was cultured, well-educated and a good linguist. He had already proved his usefulness as a translator, and even as the author of some of the most noble phrases in Napoleon's dignified letters of protest.[1]

He was clearly the man to record Napoleon's political testament; the attempted justification of his acts of cruelty, tyranny and aggression. He could match the Emperor's interest in History, and could help in the construction of the desired image of Napoleon as a benevolently noble modern Charlemagne. Las Cases was a good listener, and Napoleon, a compulsive talker, was God's gift to an interviewer. It was to exploit this gold-mine that this effete member of the old aristocracy had insinuated himself into the household, proclaiming his lifelong devotion, but somehow contriving to escape from the island once he had accumulated enough nuggets for his massive *Mémorial de Sainte Hélène* — a bit stodgy, except where we hear the authentic voice of Napoleon.

When the day's work was over, and a well-cooked and ceremonially served dinner had been disposed of rather too quickly, coffee was brought into the drawing-room. There would be more conversation, more monologues by the Emperor, or perhaps the reading of a play — Corneille, Racine, Molière. As First Consul and as Emperor Napoleon had been a generous patron of the theatre. When the Emperor had retired the candles were lit in various rooms and the scratching of pens began, for everyone was keeping a diary. Napoleon knew all about this. He had forbidden one of his valets, Etienne Saint-Denis, to keep a diary. Saint-Denis, nicknamed Ali when he became one of the Emperor's Mamelukes, had a good memory and the book which he eventually wrote is one of the best. Napoleon, an exception to most rules, *was* a hero to his valets, but not, it seemed, to his *huissier* or usher, Santini. However the book attributed to him proved to be a forgery.[2]

Through all these memoirs we can share Napoleon's life in St Helena and listen to his conversation. The relentless voice sounds on day after day, usually about himself and his opinions. If it were anyone else we would say the man was a crashing bore, and reading between the lines it seems that Napoleon did degenerate into that unhappy state. He could not resist the desire to boast about his conquests and seductions; the ladies of high society who had competed for his favours. His close friend Caulaincourt said that Napoleon only engaged in affairs in order to talk about them, and towards the end of his life he began to talk about certain charming girls in the coarse unprintable language of some leering public-house Don Juan.

The most charitable view which one can take of this, and I am convinced that it is a fully supportable view, is that it was a symptom of the condition, whatever it was, which was killing him, rendering him feverish, sometimes delirious, toxaemic, poisoned in body and mind. What that condition may have been will be discussed after hearing about the findings and opinions of the four doctors who attended Napoleon during his last illness — O'Meara, Stokoe, Antommarchi and Arnott.

# CHAPTER VI

# Two Stiff Surgeons

And the stiff surgeon, who maintained his cause,
Hath lost his place, and gained the world's applause.

Byron *The Age of Bronze, III*

The stiff surgeon of whom Lord Byron wrote was Napoleon's first doctor in St Helena, Barry O'Meara. The second of those for whom this chapter is named was O'Meara's friend and colleague, Dr John Stokoe. He also lost his post but has received little of the world's applause. In fact it cannot be said that the world's applause for O'Meara proved to be either loud or sustained, despite the approval of Lord Byron, who, it must be remembered was an ardent Napoleonist. 'The Age of Bronze' is a paean of praise for the fallen emperor, in which we are invited to

Sigh to behold the eagle's lofty rage,
Reduced to nibble at his narrow cage.

There was no doubt in Byron's mind as to who was the real martyr of St Helena, and he does not spare 'the paltry gaoler' arguing about 'curtailed dishes . . . and o'er disputed wines.'

O'Meara was one of the busiest of the memoir writers in Longwood House, and is the main source of information about Napoleon's health up to 1818, when he was expelled from the island. His book is a tedious and badly written one, but it is not on account of his defects as a writer that he has been universally condemned. English and French historians, without exception so far as I know, have represented him as a devious Irishman, interested mainly in money; a kind of double agent, spying for both sides. To be sure in two recent studies Doctors Jean Baelen and Jules Bertaut paint much kindlier portraits, but both accept the allegation that O'Meara was a spy. I believe that this may well be unfair.

In this chapter consideration is given to the political implications of Napoleon's last illness as well as its clinical course, about which fairly detailed descriptions can be read in such books as those of Brice, Cabanes, Chaplin, Hillemand and Kemble (listed in the bibliography). About this aspect of the sad story of Napoleon's last years there are fewer of the 'hopeless contradictions' complained of by Lord Rosebery, because information can be gleaned from the writings of only a few doctors.

Napoleon was unwilling to see any British doctor, suspecting them all of being agents of the Governor. Understandably he regarded his health as entirely his own affair and would have liked to be the only person to be given reports about it. But, as a realist, he knew that Hudson Lowe had to be told about it, since he was responsible for keeping the Government informed, and if possible reassured. Here was a source of conflict between the doctors' duty to their patient and their duty, as serving officers, to the Governor.

Barry Edward O'Meara was born in Ireland in 1786, his parents being of the professional class. It is not known where he received his medical education and it has been suggested that he had no formal training, but remedied by experience his deficiency in theoretical education. In 1804 he joined the Army as assistant surgeon to the 62nd Regiment, with which he served in Sicily, Calabria and Egypt; but after getting involved in a duel as a second, he was ordered to leave the Service. He later joined the Royal Navy as assistant surgeon on board H.M.S. *Victorious*.

In the last two ships in which he served as a surgeon his captain was Frederick Lewis Maitland, who warmly commended him to Napoleon. When Maitland left *Goliath* he had written a glowing testimonial for O'Meara, in which he said, 'I know of no man in the service I should wish to have as surgeon so much as Mr O'Meara'. This testimonial, given in full in Note 1, praised O'Meara for a quality to which I attach the highest value. It is one which did not, it seems, characterise every service doctor in those days — tenderness. Such a tribute from a man like Maitland, earned at a time when relationships between surgeons and their executive commanders were not always very warm, is a strong point in O'Meara's favour. During the voyage of *Bellerophon* from France to England O'Meara had attracted Napoleon's favourable attention by his fluency in French and Italian and, learning from Maitland that he was a reliable doctor, Napoleon asked that he should be appointed in place of Dr Maingault, who had refused to go to St Helena. The Admiralty agreed and O'Meara's fate was settled. He did not really very much want to go, and insisted that he should not be removed from the Navy. Admiral Cockburn supported him in this and, when Napoleon offered O'Meara a stipend of 12,000 francs, he ruled that O'Meara should remain an officer of the Navy on full pay.

O'Meara was a cheerful, talkative young man and also an excellent listener. Dr Jules Bertaut writes that Napoleon, wearied by the bickering of Montholon, Bertrand and Gourgaud, found O'Meara a most acceptable person to talk to, *le plus charmant des causeurs*. Napoleon himself was one of the most formidable of conversationalists and, when he set himself out to enslave someone who could be useful to him, the most charming and seductive. O'Meara who had foreseen that his position might become delicate and difficult, soon succumbed to the personal magnetism which had seduced more hard-headed men than he.

He soon found that his new appointment could be an interesting and rewarding one. Quite possibly he also began to realise the market value of the fascinating conversations. Indeed Napoleon himself encouraged O'Meara in that direction. Advising him to think of writing a book, he told him that he had seen far more of him than any French doctor had done. This need imply no slight on Corvisart or Yvan, for in France Napoleon was always busy; usually too busy for long conversations with doctors whom he tended to tease, calling them quacks. Whatever he may have thought of O'Meara as a doctor, and there is more than one view on that, he certainly valued him as a sympathetic listener and one, moreover, who might be induced to serve his patient's interests in a wider sphere than that of his health. If the impressionable young Irishman slowly became 'Napoleon's man' it is hard to blame him.

At first Hudson Lowe liked O'Meara. He had wanted to appoint his old friend Dr Baxter, whom he had brought with him to St Helena, to be Napoleon's doctor, but finding O'Meara entrenched in Longwood House he accepted the situation gracefully, and even raised his pay. But inevitably his suspicious mind began to get to work. Not only was the doctor spending hours in conversation with Napoleon, but he was writing letters to a friend in the Admiralty called Finlaison.

Many writers have accepted these letters as evidence of spying, though why one should unhesitatingly share Hudson Lowe's suspicions is beyond me. O'Meara was finding life in Longwood unexpectedly exciting, and may well have wanted to share his impressions with a friend in England. Hudson Lowe ordered O'Meara to send his reports only through the Governor's office;

and, after he had threatened to replace him by Baxter, O'Meara capitulated. But he dug in his heels about another command, that he must confine his conversations with Napoleon to medical matters. There is evidence that O'Meara was quite a good doctor and a sympathetic, understanding one. A good doctor knows the value of a sympathetic ear to a patient who feels the need to talk, especially if he has cause to be depressed.

Lowe, who suspected hidden meanings in the most innocent remarks, could not believe that these long talks were innocent. He had to know about everything which went on in 'his island'. He felt sure that secrets were being kept from him. Ridiculous — for, as Dr Baelen points out, Napoleon now had more to reveal than to conceal, and had no need to confide secrets to his doctor, apart from purely personal ones. When O'Meara produced his book it was full of the usual Napoleonic self-justification, often expressed in identical terms to those which we can read in other memoirs. But there is also a lot of airy persiflage about subjects unrelated to Napoleon's career, which suggests that he did find O'Meara a stimulating conversationalist.

As time went on O'Meara realised more and more that Napoleon was not just a difficult patient. He was a political prisoner whose conception of the correct doctor-patient relationship was diametrically opposed to that of his custodian. O'Meara had to make up his mind which should be his own conception. He sided with his patient against his commanding officer. It was a courageous course, especially with a man like Hudson Lowe. If duplicity were at work I would suspect the crafty Corsican, expert at bending men to his will, rather than the gay, companionable, chatty though aggressive young Irish doctor.

The American authors Dr Chester Bradley and M.D. Bradley, assert that Napoleon craftily chose O'Meara because he was Irish, and France and Ireland had long been intriguing against Great Britain. This is probably going too far. After the defection of Dr Maingault at the last minute, the choice of doctor open to Napoleon was a limited one. As relations between Longwood and Plantation House deteriorated and Napoleon's last battle began its sickening course, the Governor soon opened a second front — against the medical spy.

It would be tedious to relate in detail the progress of the quarrel between Lowe and O'Meara. As with all Sir Hudson's dealings it was complex, and marked by absurd conduct and futile correspondence. O'Meara, loyal to Napoleon's wishes, refused to refer to him as General Bonaparte. Hudson Lowe refused to accept reports in which any other appellation was used. He even refused to allow O'Meara to refer to Napoleon as 'the patient'. So the childish practice was adopted of O'Meara reporting verbally to Dr Baxter, who then prepared a written report for the Governor. Even this did not always satisfy Lowe and Baxter was often ordered to make many corrections before the medical reports were acceptable.

It was a situation in which an explosion was inevitable, especially when Dr Baxter, knowing the kind of report which Lowe wanted, disagreed with O'Meara's diagnosis, without of course examining the patient. At first there was no medical reason for quarrels. Napoleon's health for most of the first two years of his stay in the island gave no cause for alarm. O'Meara advised him to get out and about, especially on horseback. This Napoleon refused to do so long as the Governor insisted on orderly officers and sentries dogging his footsteps. Reasonably enough, on O'Meara's recommendation, Lowe relaxed the régime sufficiently for Napoleon to go for rides on horseback and in his carriage; and to get out in his garden whilst the sentries made themselves inconspicuous.

O'Meara had little to report about his patient. An occasional cold, a bout of toothache, and, more significant, the gums were 'spongy, pale and bled at the slightest touch'. Clearly suspecting scurvy O'Meara gave good advice about eating more vegetables. Towards the end of 1816 there was one curious attack, to which little attention was paid, at the time or subsequently by historians. O'Meara's entry for December 14th 1816 reads:

Napoleon very unwell. Had passed a very bad night. Found him in bed at eleven p.m. 'Doctor', said he, 'I had a nervous attack last night, which kept me continually uneasy and restless, with a severe headache, and involuntary agitations. I was without sense for a few moments. I verily thought and hoped, that a more violent attack would have taken place, which would have carried me off before morning. It seemed as if a fit of apoplexy was coming on. I felt a heaviness and giddiness of my head (as if it were overloaded with blood) with a desire to put myself in an upright posture. I felt a heat in my head, and called to those about me to pour some cold water over it, which they did not comprehend for some time. Afterwards the water felt hot, and I thought it smelt of sulphur, though in reality it was cold.' At this time he was in a free perspiration, which I recommended him to encourage, and his headache was much diminished. After I had recommended everything I thought necessary or advisable, he replied, '*si viverebbe troppo lungamente*' (One would live too long). He afterwards spoke about funeral rites, and added that when he died he would wish that his body might be burned. 'It is the best mode', said he, 'as then the corpse does not produce any inconvenience; and as to the resurrection, that must be accomplished by a miracle, and it is easy to the being who has it in his power to perform such a miracle as bringing the remains of the bodies together, to also form again the ashes of the dead'.

If this was one of those curious emotional upsets culminating in unconsciousness to which Napoleon had been subject, no precipitating cause was mentioned. In the index to O'Meara's book it is referred to as an 'Attack of nervous fever'.

We shall see in due course that only the Army surgeon, Arnott, was sufficiently ahead of the clinical practice of the time to take and record Napoleon's temperature. But of course, to the clinician, the term 'fever' implies a great deal more than the raising of the body temperature. On this occasion, when Napoleon was feeling so wretchedly unwell that his thoughts turned morbidly to impending death, it is quite possible that he was affected by some sort of infection. In March 1817 an attack of diarrhoea lasted only for a day; in May headaches were troublesome and about the same time Napoleon's legs were often swollen. It was in October 1817 that the condition which was to kill Napoleon came out into the open; and it might be helpful at this point to name the two main contenders.

First, of course, is the almost universally accepted diagnosis of cancer of the stomach, with or without the complication of some form of tropical fever. Secondly, and here I declare my own partiality, is an amoebic abscess of the liver. Of course Napoleon could have suffered from hepatis with liver abscess, and cancer of the stomach as well.

The organism which causes amoebiasis, the *entamoeba histolytica*, was unknown in Napoleon's day, and so were the specific drugs which are now used in its treatment. The organism causes intestinal amoebiasis, which may or may not be sufficiently serious to lead to symptoms of dysentery — amoebic dysentery, as opposed to bacillary dysentery, the disease of camps, of campaigning soldiery and of holiday-makers abroad. Actual dysentery is, in fact, the exception rather than the rule in amoebiasis. In association with a history of intestinal amoebiasis we may encounter hepatic amoebiasis, in which the liver is invaded.

Hepatic amoebiasis, like intestinal amoebiasis, may be acute or chronic, a long-standing condition in which the defences of the body almost, but not quite, keep the attackers at bay. If the invaders win they destroy more and more of the liver tissue, liquifying it and turning it into a reddish chocolate coloured substance. Unless it is secondarily infected an amoebic abscess of the liver does not contain pus, but this broken-down detritus of the liver tissue, which has been compared to anchovy sauce. (It is one of the less attractive practices of pathologists to compare diseased tissues to items of diet.) Amoebiasis may be said to have a world-wide distribution, though it is more prevalent in tropical and sub-tropical countries.[2]

In Napoleon's day, although the offending amoeba was unknown, the results of its attack were well-recognised. Corvisart the world-famous physician to Napoleon's family, studied liver abscess in 1808; and the possibility of such an abscess perforating into the lungs, the peritoneum or the stomach was realised. Dominique Larrey, the leading surgeon in Napoleon's army, operated on many cases in Egypt, and in 1812 wrote about them in his *Mémoires de Chirurgerie Militaire et Campagnes*. (Tom. II, p. 94). Larrey did not mention the connection between abscess of the liver and dysentery; but O'Meara clearly knew all about this. He declared that both conditions were prevalent in St Helena where many soldiers had fallen victim to them.

The terms hepatitis and liver abscess used in this and subsequent chapters refer to hepatic amoebiasis passing on to abscess formation, as distinct from the type of hepatitis due to virus infections, and the type of abscess in the liver following suppurative conditions in the abdomen. Both of these would have been more rapidly fatal than the amoebic infection.

O'Meara was possibly not taken by surprise when Napoleon began to have pain over the liver and in the right shoulder. This shoulder pain is an important sign. It is called 'referred pain' and is very characteristic of disorders in the liver and gall-bladder. Napoleon had not been completely well since about the middle of 1817, with occasional diarrhoea, headache and swelling of the legs, but O'Meara now felt that there was cause for worry. In September Hudson Lowe had wanted to send Dr Baxter to see

Napoleon, but he refused to see the principal medical officer, and indeed became rather reserved towards O'Meara, suspecting him of siding with the Governor. When refusing Baxter's services he told O'Meara, 'Calling in Baxter to me would be like sending a physician to a man who was starving with hunger'. He refused to take exercise although he said that he knew as well as any physician that it was what he needed; but he vowed that 'as long as the present system is in force I will never stir out'. This attitude simply confirmed Lowe in his opinion that Napoleon was using his alleged illness in order to obtain some alleviation of his captivity.

On October 1st, for the first time, Napoleon told O'Meara of a curious pain in his right side, making him want to 'lean or press his side against something — *vorrei appoggiarmi incontro a qualche cosa*'. The 'sensation in the right shoulder, which he described to be more of a numbness than of pain', helped to warn O'Meara of what might be amiss. On October 3rd he found that he could feel the liver, which was firm and tender. Napoleon himself said that he had been able to feel this swelling for two months, but had attributed it to obesity. Now, however, 'from its being attended with pain, he imagined that it might be connected with enlargement of the liver.' O'Meara was sure that Napoleon was right about this, and he diagnosed hepatitis. Lowe was unwilling to listen to any such suggestion.

Unfortunately 1817 had been marked not only by this gradual deterioration in Napoleon's health, but by a much more rapid deterioration in relations between O'Meara and Hudson Lowe. The Governor, naturally, felt that he had to be kept informed about Napoleon's health, but it was too much for the impetuous Irishman to be dictated to about his dealings with his patient, and by the middle of May tempers were frayed on both sides. On 23rd May there was a row because O'Meara had lent newspapers to Napoleon, which Lowe pompously said was 'a violation of the act of parliament', but by the winter Lowe had added to the list of offences against Government policy, of which he thought O'Meara was guilty, a much more serious crime than lending newspapers.

On October 4th 1817 O'Meara had presented his report, in which he said that Napoleon had hepatitis, to Hudson Lowe in person. The Governor, unable this time to hide behind his principal medical officer Dr Baxter, said the report was too long, and must be shortened so that it could be made public. He also hinted that O'Meara had written it in collusion with the French. Indeed the French, like O'Meara, were now openly speaking of

Napoleon's hepatitis, and Lowe, realising the significance of such a disease, acquired in St Helena, forbade the use of the word.

Inevitably quarrels now became more frequent. Napoleon's health was giving cause for alarm and the Governor was not yet ready to dismiss O'Meara, or to allow him to resign from his impossible situation as he tried to do at least twice.

A flaming row erupted on 25th November, when O'Meara refused to repeat to the Governor the subject of his conversations with Napoleon.

Lowe fulminated: 'You are no judge, Sir, of the importance of the conversations you may have with General Bonaparte. I might consider several subjects of great importance, which you consider trifling or of no consequence'. (Such as green and white beans, one may suppose.) He insisted that it was the doctor's duty to report everything that passed.

O'Meara hotly refused to become a spy, or *mouton*, which he defined for Sir Hudson as 'a person who insinuates himself into the confidence of another for the purpose of betraying it'. Furious now, striding about and bawling, the Governor ordered O'Meara out of the room. After this things went from bad to worse; and eventually O'Meara was ordered not to leave Longwood, as if he too were a state prisoner. His desk was forced and his trunks rifled; money and valuables disappeared.

In venting his spite on the doctor Hudson Lowe influenced others to shun him. O'Meara had been an honorary member of the Officers' Mess of the 53rd Regiment, and when the 66th relieved them they also invited him to share their mess. The Governor now requested the commanding officer to deny O'Meara this privilege; but, when the officers refused to be dictated to and continued to welcome O'Meara, Hudson Lowe made it an official order transmitted through General Bingham. When the commanding officer, Colonel Lascelles, submitted, great indignation was felt towards him by his own officers, as we learn from their medical officer, Dr Walter Henry.

The Colonel had made it plain in writing to O'Meara that the action had been forced upon him; and the officers also wrote to O'Meara to assure him that they had always found his conduct consistent with that of a gentleman. Officers of the Royal Navy, in their own way, also showed that they sided with their brother officer against the military tyrant whom they had come to detest.

Finally on July 15th, 1818, on orders received from Lord Bathurst, O'Meara was told to quit Longwood House. The

Governor was told to replace him by any doctor who might prove acceptable to the awkward prisoner. At first O'Meara was determined not to leave his patient, but had to submit in the end and, after giving Napoleon all the advice about his health which time permitted, he sadly departed with the last words of the man whom he had come to admire printed on his mind: '*Adieu O'Meara. Nous ne nous verrons plus. Soyez heureux*'. In paying his touching farewell Napoleon had given O'Meara messages for his mother and his sister Caroline; for Lady Holland, the wife of one of his Whig admirers, and for his wife Marie Louise, in whose faithfulness he still pretended to believe. The letter to the ex-Empress was smuggled out of the island in one of O'Meara's shoes.

Hudson Lowe, somewhat late in the day, had finally passed on to Lord Bathurst on the 18th May, 1818, O'Meara's opinion that Napoleon was suffering from 'hepatitis in a chronic and insidious form'. However the Government felt no compunction about recalling O'Meara, for they felt reassured by General Gourgaud's statement, when he came to England, that Napoleon was not really ill at all. Like Hudson Lowe they were always more ready to listen to anyone who could give them the reassurances they craved, rather than to the doctors who had the responsibility of looking after the patient.

Lowe cannot have felt quite so complacent. O'Meara had really worried him by warning him that Napoleon might die without medical aid if a suitable replacement was long in arriving. Napoleon's own reaction did little to ease Lowe's anxiety. He commented that although he had made a prisoner of the Pope he would sooner have cut off his right hand than remove his surgeon. Furthermore it seems almost certain that by now the principal medical officer, Dr Baxter, was beginning to repent of his extraordinary, unethical, indeed professionally almost criminal, conduct in fabricating out of O'Meara's reports the sort of news about Napoleon which the Governor wanted to hear. Baxter's own violent quarrels with his old friend lay less than a year ahead, but he knew he had been used for Lowe's own ends. I hope that his conscience as an Edinburgh graduate was pricking him unmercifully.

It is possible that doubts about his conduct and worries about Napoleon's health were by now troubling even Hudson Lowe, and he must surely have begun to wonder if O'Meara could have been right after all. Whether O'Meara's diagnosis was right or wrong, few doctors, and certainly none who have served in the armed forces, could fail to commend him for sticking to his opinion, based on personal observation, against the ignorant criticism of the Governor and his subservient principal medical officer, who knew nothing whatever about the case. It is possible that, at this point, if O'Meara had quietly reported to the Admiralty all that he knew about Napoleon's case some sort of impartial investigation might have saved Hudson Lowe from pursuing the course along which his obstinacy was to drive him.

Unfortunately anything so tame was alien to the nature of our impetuous doctor, whose conduct from his arrival in England in October 1818 was to make him world-famous. In letters and articles he published abroad his views about the conditions of Napoleon's captivity, his illness and his treatment by Sir Hudson Lowe. If we can commend him for thus, at great risk to his own career, trying to better the lot of his former patient, we can only deplore a major indiscretion which he immediately blundered into. He wrote officially on 28th October to the Secretary to the Admiralty, John Wilson Croker, stating that Napoleon's life was not safe in Hudson Lowe's hands. He stated that Lowe had tried to have Napoleon poisoned. The response of the Admiralty to this was justifiably prompt. O'Meara was removed from the list of naval surgeons, the main charge against him being 'traitorous correspondence with the people at Longwood'.

In O'Meara's position personal dealings with the people at Longwood had been unavoidable, and without to some extent identifying himself with their interests he could hardly perform the function with which he had been entrusted. But it does seem that his hatred of Lowe and his partiality for Napoleon combined to make him lose his head. Napoleon had for some time been paranoically obsessed with his self-made image of the evil Governor seeking to encompass his death.

O'Meara's devotion to Napoleon may have led him to accept his view that attempts to poison him were really in Lowe's mind, though a moment's reflection could have convinced him, as his friend Dr Henry was convinced, that this must have been the last thing which Hudson Lowe could want. The death of Napoleon would terminate his own lucrative and important appointment; and, if the circumstances were in any way suspicious, could only lead to serious trouble for himself.

In sharing Napoleon's obsession about Lowe O'Meara went against his own sound clinical judgment. He thought he knew what was killing Napoleon and had told the Governor officially. His conduct now was no help to Napoleon; but, if it was inspired by a malicious desire to get his own back for his dismissal and the humiliating treatment to which he had been subjected, it was supremely successful. He became the chief architect of the image of the evil Governor, and by the time Sir Hudson got home the damage was done. He was even too late for legal action against O'Meara for some undoubtedly libellous writings.

Deprived of pay and pension, O'Meara began a pamphlet war to attack Lowe, to do what he could to help Napoleon, and presumably to make money. The glittering prizes open to him could be glimpsed from the success of Dr William Warden's *Letters written on board His Majesty's Ship 'Northumberland' and at St Helena*, published in 1816, which went into five editions in as many months. Warden the senior surgeon on board *Northumberland*, spoke no French and had to rely on Las Cases and Mme Bertrand as interpreters. Napoleon always denied that Warden's versions of his views and conversation were accurate. Warden was attacked by Government supporters for his favourable attitude to Napoleon, and by Sir Hudson Lowe, who complained that some comments in his letters amounted to a breach of discipline. Warden was struck off the list of naval surgeons, but reinstated after intervention by Sir George Cockburn.

In 1817 O'Meara had himself commented on Warden's book in an anonymous pamphlet, *Letters from the Cape of Good Hope*, which was severely criticised in a long article in the pro-Government *Quarterly Review* (Vol 17, pp 506-30). *The Quarterly Review* was always hostile to Napoleon, and its criticism of O'Meara's pamphlet was that it was no reply to Warden since it was equally favourable to Bonaparte.

The amazing success of Warden's worthless book was a clear indication that Europe was eagerly awaiting news of the man who so recently had absorbed its interest and troubled its peace for twenty exciting years. No doubt O'Meara had duly noted the indications of profit to be had from an association with Napoleon very much closer than Warden's. His first major work was published in 1819, in reply to an anonymous pamphlet praising Hudson Lowe. This proved to be the work of one Theodore Hook, who had spent only two days in St Helena.[3]

O'Meara's reply — *An Exposition of some of the Transactions that have taken place at St Helena since the Appointment of Sir Hudson Lowe as Governor of that Island*, was well received. A review of both pamphlets in *The Edinburgh Review* of July 1819 strongly supported O'Meara, and warned the country of the blow to England's reputation if Napoleon, deprived of the services of the only doctors in whom he had confidence, should die before the mysteries surrounding his illness had been resolved. The reviewer demonstrated his impartiality by trouncing both the 'Napoleonists' who unduly exalted Napoleon, and those who sought to minimise his greatness. His captivity should be alleviated, if not ended, at once, before it was too late.

This was the sort of talk which O'Meara wanted; and he set to work to expand his *Exposition*, and in 1822 published his famous *Voice from St Helena*.

Its full title, shown in the illustration facing page 49, amounted to an advertisement of precisely what the world was awaiting, and was enough to ensure fantastic success, and translation into five or six languages, for what is, in fact, a maddening book.

The gold is there all right but the 'panning' required to extract it is inordinately difficult and tedious. O'Meara's turgid style would earn him an honoured place today among speech-writers for the hierarchy of the Trades Unions. Here is an example, recording a minor tiff with the Governor, who had objected to General Bertrand writing to the French Commissioner:

> I observed that Count Bertrand had said, that at the time the letter was written, there had existed no prohibition against epistolary correspondence with persons domiciliated in the island as the marquis was.

One looks in vain for a coherent medical history of O'Meara's famous patient. In a footnote near the end of the second volume O'Meara declares that it is not his intention 'to tire the reader with the detail of a medical journal'. This is a pity for he was the only man who could give us the facts.

The book is written as a Journal with meticulous insistence on the date of every conversation or statement by Napoleon, often on trivial subjects. Having nothing much to do, Napoleon kept recurring to certain subjects, often in the same words, and, even if it is the genuine voice of the Emperor, honesty compels me to say that much of it is pure waffle. For example he harped on the question of whether our ambassador to China should have refused to *kotow* or prostrate himself before the Emperor. For the record the ex-Emperor's opinion was that Lord Amherst should not have refused to conform to the custom of the country.

Dr. Barry O'Meara

Dr. Archibald Arnott

Dr. John Stokoe

Dr. Francesco Antommarchi

The book is permeated by hatred of Hudson Lowe and, human nature being what it is, the criticisms of the Governor and of His Majesty's Government made the book especially popular. Sir Hudson never had a chance.

Opposition became O'Meara's profession. He espoused the cause of Queen Caroline, collecting witnesses for her trial. Although not a Catholic he took a prominent part in the agitation for Catholic Emancipation, and campaigned for the First Reform Bill, becoming an ardent follower of O'Connell, 'The Liberator'.[4]

O'Meara's diagnosis of Napoleon's illness has been supported by many medical experts, whose opinions will be mentioned later. His bad reputation among historians, who regard much of his testimony as unreliable, has grown chiefly from the belief that he spied for both sides and took money for doing so.

From Sir Hudson Lowe's character and his subsequent dealings with O'Meara, it seems likely that, in securing a rise of pay for O'Meara he intended to buy him; but I cannot see why the young doctor should have suspected this at the outset. His responsibility was a heavy one for a junior officer and a little 'extra-duty pay' was well-earned. At first, perhaps because of Lowe's threats to replace him by Baxter, he tried to keep in with both sides, but in November 1817 he had given up hope of placating the Governor, who, he now realised, genuinely regarded it as the doctor's duty as a British officer to spy on his patient.

Showing himself in his true colours, as Napoleon's ally, he rudely refused to become a spy, or *mouton*. Was this because Napoleon had paid him? Octave Aubry is in no doubt about this. He says that Napoleon gave the doctor a substantial sum of money in September 1817, and later remarked, 'The doctor was never so devoted to me till I began giving him money'.

Napoleon had said, 'The English can all be bought'; and in his opinion O'Meara was at Longwood House for the money. This sounds lamentably like Napoleon's cynical character. He always believed that everyone had his price, and in St Helena he kept up his old attitude. He actually tried to suborn Count Balmain, the upright Russian Commissioner, and the stupid old French Commissioner, the Marquis de Montchenu, whom he despised. Montchenu wrote in a letter to the Duc de Richelieu, that Montholon had been deputed to approach him, and ' . . . looking straight at me he said, "The Emperor knows how to buy. A man can be useful to him and he gives six millions".'

In seeking at the outset to make Dr O'Meara a salaried official

I

of his household he was clearly trying to 'buy' him, as he later tried to 'buy' Dr Verling and probably Dr Stokoe. O'Meara, with his admiral's support, refused the offer of pay. If he did later succumb to the blandishments of the despot of Longwood, as everyone else in the house was doing, he naturally did not mention it. He did record receiving a parting gift of 'a superb snuff-box and a statue of Napoleon himself'. I think he earned these gifts.

After leaving St Helena he probably received money from members of the Bonaparte family, and made quite a lot of money from his writings and from publishing a memorial of the 1815 campaign, given to him by Napoleon. Against a nineteenth century background all this does not seem too reprehensible. After all, O'Meara's career was first interrupted and finally wrecked by his association with Napoleon, which had not been his own choice.

Admitting that he accepted money, what did he do for it? What was the spying of which he was accused? Almost anything to Lowe's suspicious mind; and also to another even more complex mind, one which had always been ready to believe the worst of fallible human nature, and to play upon its weaknesses to secure his own designs — Napoleon's. Napoleon trusted no one. Though he liked O'Meara he expected that he would betray the secrets of the bedside, and he once remarked to Gourgaud, '*Si O'Meara écrit jamais un journal il sera fort intéressant. S'il donne la longueur de mon c . . . ce ne sera que plus intéressant.*' He did O'Meara an injustice. O'Meara betrayed none of his patient's confidence; and it was not from him that the world was to learn the spicy details of Napoleon's curious gynandromorphic body.

During most of his time in St Helena O'Meara could pass freely between Longwood and the outside world, the only British subject with any personal knowledge of Napoleon who could do so. A cheerful, sociable, rather garrulous young man such as he was, naturally gossiped about what went on inside the 'prison camp', and brought into it welcome tittle-tattle from outside. The residents in Longwood were particularly avid for any news, including reports from Europe, or in the newspapers, which could have a bearing on their own fate.

When O'Meara was sent home he smuggled out of the island letters for the Bonapartes and others. This heinous crime, as it seemed to Government supporters, was a fairly natural expression of the concern and sympathy which he felt for his patient. It is hard to blame him if he thought that it was an unduly harsh and oppressive measure to deprive the prisoner of the right to send uncensored letters to his relatives. Wellington agreed with this viewpoint, and so must any modern humanitarian. Hudson Lowe, the gaoler who had kept back a bust of Napoleon's son in case it contained a hidden message, and had forbidden anyone to carry letters to or from Napoleon, regarded the smuggling of letters as treachery. I find it harder to condemn the warm-hearted doctor, paid or not, who took risks to befriend the patient whom he was leaving with reluctance and apprehension.

Maitland was not the only senior naval officer who had a high opinion of O'Meara. In an article in *The Edinburgh Review*, 'Buonaparte and the Elba Manuscript', published in September 1818, a month before O'Meara reached England, there is a reference to 'Mr O'Meara, the respectability of whose character is beyond all question', citing in support of this opinion, not only Captain Maitland but 'Dr Ferguson, a gentleman high on the Medical Staff'. It is plain that O'Meara's brother officers liked and respected him, and no word of criticism is heard from patients, whom he treated with tenderness, as Maitland testified.

Doctors who identify themselves with their patients easily 'let their hearts run away with their heads'. A case in point is the release from detention, on the advice of psychiatrists, of dangerous psychopaths. It may surprise some readers to learn that psychiatrists have called the great Napoleon a psychopathic personality. But in St Helena his power to harm others was limited. What was not completely lost was that overwhelming personal magnetism, the almost hypnotic power to charm, which had enslaved so many victims.

O'Meara, a tender-hearted young Irishman, was a natural victim for that powerful personality. Unquestionably he became 'an indiscreet partisan' of Napoleon, as his colleague, the shrewd Dr Walter Henry observed. Henry found O'Meara charming and gentlemanly, but remarked that he 'sometimes became more animated in defence of Napoleon than was prudent or proper under existing circumstances; but the subject was never introduced wantonly or offensively by O'Meara'. Dr Henry admitted that O'Meara had been 'cajoled and fascinated — I will not say corrupted, into the admirer, adherent, agent and tool of Napoleon'.

All O'Meara's brother officers, indeed everyone he met in St Helena, were eager to be told anything about Napoleon. It was the same thing in Europe. There was a universal thirst for details which he was in a unique position to satisfy. It might have turned most men's heads. As for his partisanship, I should suspect a young man who did not feel deeply for such a patient in so terrible a situation of being too stony-hearted to be a really kind doctor or good psychiatrist.

Opposition to authority is an activity in which, in appropriate circumstances, a medical officer in public service may glory. Napoleon's case was an appropriate one for such an activity. I believe that his detention was necessary and probably just, but it could not be necessary or just to make it unduly punitive and harsh, and certainly not to the extent of prejudicing his health. To make the condemnation of O'Meara seem just and proper various allegations were added to the real cause of offence, which was that he embarrassed His Majesty's Government and their representative on the spot – the trouble-spot, the prison-isle on which the eyes of the civilised world were fixed.

Many of these prying eyes were those of busy-bodies and opponents of the Government. All governments must learn to live with such critics. That nineteenth century government could not feel complacent, however hard they had tried to ensure that Napoleon's health was properly cared for. They cannot be blamed for the absence of any French doctor, for they tried hard to dissuade Dr Maingault from selfishly deserting his post. They could not have anticipated that the quarrel between Napoleon and Lowe would stultify their plans for the calling in of consultants if his health gave cause for alarm.

By pure chance Napoleon chose, with Maitland's advice, a good doctor, who cared for him devotedly and earned his confidence to a considerable degree. That doctor should have been free to express his honest opinions about Napoleon's health and the treatment he needed; and these opinions ought to have been heeded.

O'Meara's departure was a severe blow to Napoleon, who missed his chatter, his amusing company and his loyalty, whether bought or not. He was very depressed, still felt ill, and did not feel equal to the struggle to win the allegiance of another British doctor. Lowe hoped to appoint Dr Baxter but he was the last man whom Napoleon would accept, so in the end the Governor had to settle for the posting to Longwood House of an attractive and popular young Irishman, James Roche Verling, surgeon to an artillery regiment.

This was in fact an excellent choice, and one more indication that Lowe really did try to accommodate Napoleon and the French. Verling spoke good French, and Napoleon had met and liked him on board *Northumberland*; but on principle he resolutely refused to see him, so Verling had to be content with looking after the other French residents of Longwood, and Mme Bertrand at nearby Hutt's Gate, a difficult and hypochondriacal patient.

From the interesting diary which Verling kept during his stay in Longwood House (from July 25th 1818 to September 23rd 1819) we learn that one of the servants told him that the Emperor was looking 'old, pale and sallow'. Verling wrote that he himself throughout his stay 'was never brought into personal contact with him', but 'thought from the slight view I had occasionally that he looked very ill'. In due course he reported his opinion to Dr Baxter, who encouraged him to go on trying to catch a sight of 'the old Imposter', as Baxter, still imbued with the conviction that Napoleon was shamming, called him.[5]

In January 1819 Napoleon had an alarming seizure and as he still refused to see Verling Bertrand was allowed to call in Dr Stokoe, because 'he was the person in whom the Emperor chose to place confidence'. Stokoe, who was an acquaintance of O'Meara, had had a brief meeting with Napoleon when he visited O'Meara at Longwood House. Bertrand had consulted him and recommended him to Napoleon.

Before describing the experiences of Dr John Stokoe, the second 'stiff surgeon' to be broken on the wheel of political pressure in St Helena, we must take a look at the senior naval officer who was to be his chief inquisitor.

Rear Admiral Robert Plampin arrived on June 29th, 1817, on board his flagship *Conqueror*, to take over from Admiral Sir Pulteney Malcolm as naval commander-in-chief. Napoleon liked Malcolm, whose conduct towards him had always been courteous and gentlemanly, and he was delighted by rumours that he was to become Governor instead of Sir Hudson. These hopes were dashed by the arrival of Plampin, who at first adopted a reasonable attitude towards Longwood House. Soon, however, he found it essential to his own peace of mind and hopes of advancement to become a subservient adherent of the Governor.

The particular reason for this was a dishonourable one. After sailing from Plymouth *Conqueror* had taken on board, off the Isle of Wight, a lady, at first assumed to be the admiral's wife. She proved to be his mistress and he installed her in The Briars, where he lived in St Helena. It did not take long for gossip to get to work, and eventually the self-appointed guardian of the island's morals, the Reverend Richard Boys, denounced the erring admiral from the pulpit, beseeching him 'to put away from him the accursed woman and to flee from the wrath to come while there was yet time'. Hudson Lowe put a stop to the persecution of the Admiral, who became his servile supporter.[6]

In some books the Admiral is incorrectly called Sir Robert Plampin. In 1820 he made direct application for the K.C.B. in acknowledgment of his services in St Helena. Lord Melville, Secretary of State for the Navy, politely brushed aside this improper approach, and everyone who had been in St Helena would have applauded his action. Everyone disliked Plampin from the Allied Commissioners to the naval officers who suffered under his command, and deplored his becoming the Governor's toady, whereas Admirals Cockburn and Malcolm had been his equals. Adjectives used about Plampin include 'timid' and 'obsequious'; and he is preserved like a fly in amber by Napoleon's description of him: 'He reminds me of one of those drunken little Dutch schippers that I have seen in Holland sitting at a table with a pipe in his mouth, a cheese and a bottle of geneva before him.'

Dr John Stokoe arrived in St Helena in June 1817 as surgeon to Admiral Plampin's flagship. He was then 42 years old and, after some twenty years service, was expecting soon to retire with a pension. Like every newcomer to the island he hoped to get a sight of Napoleon and one way was to cultivate an acquaintance with O'Meara, whose friendship with those at Longwood earned him many a dinner.

After O'Meara had dined several times on board *Conqueror* he invited Stokoe to visit him in his quarters at Longwood, and on his second visit Stokoe had the good fortune to meet Napoleon. The interview went well and Napoleon liked the doctor, partly because he wrongly imagined that Stokoe was courting Betsy Balcombe, a young girl of whom Napoleon was himself very fond.

In accordance with standing orders Stokoe reported his conversation with Napoleon to Plampin, who severely reprimanded him saying: 'You needn't have bothered being polite to him. I have enough trouble with the Governor as it is.'

Next Stokoe had to see Lowe, whose attitude left him in no doubt about the dangers of meeting Napoleon. When O'Meara's position was becoming intolerable Napoleon refused to accept Dr

Baxter in his place but said he would like Stokoe to be appointed. Stokoe, who had seen how O'Meara was treated, begged to be excused. Admiral Plampin said that he must bear any consequences of this refusal himself; and Hudson Lowe demanded his reasons in writing. To conceal his real reason, which was fear of the Governor, Stokoe said that he could not take on the responsibility without colleagues to consult. Plampin tried to twist this into an expression of disapproval of O'Meara, and lost his temper when Stokoe refused to fall in with this. This did not save O'Meara from dismissal; it only infuriated the Admiral.

The ill-temper shown by Lowe and Plampin warned Stokoe of the delicacy of his position among these sly scheming senior officers, and after O'Meara's departure he dreaded a summons to Longwood. When news reached St Helena that Cardinal Fesch had despatched Dr Antommarchi to be Napoleon's doctor, Stokoe was much relieved; but not for long. Soon after daybreak on Sunday, January 17th, 1819, a letter from Count Bertrand appealing for medical aid for Napoleon was brought to *Conqueror*. There was also a note from the Admiral's secretary for Captain Stanfell of *Conqueror*, requesting him to order Stokoe 'to go directly to Longwood and call on Dr Verling as Buonaparte is very ill'.

Napoleon had been seized around midnight by severe pain in the abdomen and shoulders, with fever, giddiness and brief unconsciousness. Bertrand's cry for medical help had arrived after a lengthy peregrination via Plantation House and The Briars, where the Governor and the Admiral were successively aroused, the latter from the arms of his mistress. The courier had then ridden to Jamestown and taken a boat to *Conqueror*.

By the time Stokoe had dressed and ridden the five miles to Longwood it was about 7 a.m. and Napoleon was asleep, having improved under the relaxing influence of his customary hot bath. So the first thing Stokoe was asked to do was to consider a request that he should become Napoleon's personal physician, to which end eight very reasonable articles had been drawn up, the last of which specified that Admiral Plampin's approval must be obtained. This formal request could have enabled Lowe to obey his orders from Lord Bathurst, to appoint a doctor acceptable to Napoleon.

The sequence of events just described was to prove important to Stokoe. The fact that he had not seen Napoleon immediately on his arrival at Longwood confirmed those idiots at Plantation House, Lowe and Dr Baxter, in their *idée fixe* that Napoleon was

shamming; and now he was trying to use Stokoe. Admiral Plampin
tried to deny that he had ever ordered Stokoe to go to Longwood.
Stokoe had the greatest difficulty in retaining the letter from the
Admiral's secretary, a facsimile of which is reproduced in M. Paul
Frémeaux's book *With Napoleon at St Helena*.

Stokoe, having told Count Montholon that, if the Governor
consented, he would accept the post of personal physician, was
taken in to see Napoleon, who was lying on a sofa, his features
drawn, still complaining of the old right-sided pain, from which in
fact he had never been quite free since he first told O'Meara about
it. It was never to leave him entirely. The slightest pressure over
the liver made him cry out. Stokoe diagnosed a chronic affection
of the liver and, when he was pressed by Napoleon for a prognosis,
the following highly significant exchange took place:—

> 'How long might a man live with such a complaint?' asked the Emperor
> at the same time requesting the doctor to answer him without
> evasion.
> 'There are instances of men living to an advanced period.'
> 'Yes, but is one as likely to live to that period in a tropical climate?'
> 'No.'
> 'What is the danger to be apprehended?'
> 'Inflammation, and possibly suppuration.'
> 'What would be the consequence of that?'
> 'If matter formed, and it broke into the intestines, he might be saved; if
> it pointed externally, he might be saved by an operation; but if it
> burst into the cavity of the abdomen, death must ensue.'
> *[from Stokoe's Memoirs edited by M. Frémeaux]*

It is plain that Stokoe had not merely diagnosed chronic hepatitis
but recognised the possibility of the development of an abscess of
the liver.

Stokoe visited Napoleon on and off from 17th to 21st January,
and his bulletins and verbal statements about his patient's illness
sealed his own fate. He had told Napoleon at the first visit, in
answer to a direct question, that continued residence in a tropical
climate would not benefit his condition. From his second bulletin
Lowe, who had contrived with Dr Baxter's help to fabricate false
versions of O'Meara's reports, was faced with the clear statement
about Napoleon's chronic hepatitis that 'in a climate where the
above disease is so prevalent it will eventually shorten his life'.

The bewildered doctor was now subjected to frequent interrogations by the Admiral and the Governor, designed to expose him
as a tool of the French. Plampin stormed at Stokoe with the sort
of unreasonable abuse which Lowe had used to O'Meara. Why had

he flouted the Governor's orders by referring to Napoleon as 'the patient', instead of General Buonaparte, as laid down? Stokoe could only reply that he had discussed this point with Bertrand and understood that it had been agreed with Hudson Lowe. Stokoe had been over an hour late for an appointment with the Admiral, because Napoleon had been ill and needed his doctor. Whose orders did he choose to obey; those of his admiral or those of a prisoner?

Stokoe, realising that Napoleon's illness had started some sixteen months before he saw him, had tried to elicit the story of those months by questioning Napoleon and others at Longwood. Innocent enough, any doctor might think; in fact an indispensable step in taking the history of a difficult case. But to the Admiral this was improper communication with an enemy, and it would in due course be one of the charges against Stokoe at a court martial.

Stokoe had not thought twice about handing to Bertrand written reports about his patient. To the Governor these were 'communications by writing' and thus a clear breach of his own Standing Order of July 1817, forbidding officers of the squadron to which Stokoe belonged 'to hold communication of any sort, by writing or otherwise, upon any subject with any of the foreign personages detained upon the island'.

Also under this heading came the articles drawn up by Napoleon's staff in their attempt to put Stokoe's attendance on a permanent footing. Stokoe had insisted that these must have the approval of Lowe and Plampin, but he was considered by them to have offended by even discussing them with the French before showing them to the Governor. This was to be the second charge at his trial. Caught in Hudson Lowe's tortuous coils Stokoe tried to avoid returning to Longwood House, despite his concern for his patient. Anticipating that it might be made impossible for him to see Napoleon he sent him a letter warning him of the dangerous nature of his hepatitis and urging him to continue treatment.

However Lowe, scenting some mysterious plot being hatched at Longwood, meant to let Stokoe have enough rope to hang himself, and others too if possible. His suspicions were expressed in the verbose rigmarole of letters which he sent to Plampin.

It all seems too childish, as though Stokoe were playing Alice to Hudson Lowe's Red Queen. But it was no game. In due course the absurd manufactured crimes were to be dressed up in legal jargon at a court martial, for the Red Queen was determined to have Stokoe's head. When the Governor was ready Stokoe was told by his captain that the Admiral intended to try him by a court martial 'for contempt and disobedience of orders'. Stokoe protested that the Admiral's positive orders had left him no discretionary power; but by now he knew what to expect from Admiral Plampin, whom at first he had regarded as his natural protector, as a naval officer.

A few days later Stokoe was advised to plead ill-health and told that he was to return home. 'I thought all my sufferings at an end,' he wrote. He sailed for England with a quiet mind, aware that though he might have offended against the local rules, invented by Sir Hudson as he went along, he was innocent of any offence against medical ethics. This was more than could be said for every British doctor in St Helena at the time. Hudson Lowe and Plampin, having deprived Napoleon of the doctor of his choice, seem to have given up the idea of a court martial quite happily; but at the Admiralty their Lordships, taking Lowe's report at its face value, decided to return Stokoe to St Helena to face trial. A medical board was unimpressed by his ill-health.

Although ordered to embark at very short notice, and wretchedly disappointed that he was not to complete the remaining months of his service quietly ashore, Stokoe feared no evil. He had not been told that he was to be tried. At the Admiralty he had met the kindly Admiral Sir Pulteney Malcolm and told him how very unpleasant it would be for him to serve again under Admiral Plampin. Sir Pulteney reassured him saying, 'Stokoe, you are a surgeon. You are more independent than any of us so long as you do your duty, but I think you ought to view your being sent back again as a proof that your conduct has been approved of.'

Any hope which Stokoe had that his 'tedious and disagreeable passage of 124 days' to St Helena would end in a prodigal's welcome was swiftly quenched. After being re-appointed surgeon to *Conqueror* he was told to consider himself under arrest pending trial by court martial. By failing to disclose what awaited him their Lordships had, as Stokoe wrote, 'deprived me of the favourable testimony I might have obtained from every officer I had previously sailed under'.

Far from having time to prepare a defence he had not been able to take leave of friends or to fit himself out for a warm climate. He could obtain no witnesses for his defence. His own commanding officer, Captain Stanfell, was President of the Court. Bertrand was ill and consequently Montholon was unwilling to leave Longwood; and in any case Lowe objected to the calling of witnesses who were foreigners and prisoners. Stokoe had to be content with cross-examining witnesses for the prosecution; and he did not do too badly; but his conviction was a foregone conclusion.

The charges against Stokoe are given in Note 7. The strange processes of the official mind whereby normal professional conduct was twisted into indictable offences have already been outlined. In Charges 1 to 5 and 9, we see how medical attendance on General Buonaparte could lead to a doctor being caught in the complexities of Hudson Lowe's regulations.

It became an offence, improper communication with the prisoners, to speak of anything not directly concerned with Napoleon's illness, to write a medical report for the patient (even to refer to him as 'the patient'), to take a careful history of his case or to refer to symptoms which the doctor had not personally witnessed, because this involved accepting as facts statements made by Napoleon and his friends.

Stokoe's pleas that he 'did not consider that any law could compel a medical man to deny his patient an opinion of his complaint', nor that the laws of the island about 'correspondence with the people at Longwood' could apply to a medical report, went unheeded. It was plainly scandalous to blame him for consulting the French about an illness which had begun months before he saw Napoleon. How else could he come to grips with a difficult case? Even today amoebiasis can be one of the most puzzling clinical problems in medicine.

Stokoe could offer no defence against the accusation that he had said that Napoleon was ill and might get worse. Time would show that he had been right; and not much time was needed. Just over eighteen months later Napoleon was dead, though, as M. Paul Frémeaux acidly observed, it took his 'death rattle' to convince the Governor that he was not in the best of health.

Two of the ten charges were unrelated to medical practice. One of these, the sixth, resulted from Stokoe's innocent involvement in a bit of intrigue left over by the more worldly-wise O'Meara. Because the Governor had been having O'Meara's correspondence secretly examined, Mr William Holmes, O'Meara's agent in London, had been sending packages to him under a false name.

Entirely on his own initiative Holmes had sent some packages to Stokoe and to a Mr Fowler, believing them to be friends of his client. When he realised that he had landed Stokoe in serious trouble he bombarded the Admiralty with lengthy explanations, insisting on the complete innocence of Stokoe whom he had never met. Holmes made no secret of the fact that his object had been to supply Napoleon with newspapers; and he showed his ignorance of the St Helena atmosphere by naively asking how this could be arranged. No attention was paid to his protestations of Stokoe's innocence.

The seventh charge implied that Stokoe had believed the story about Lowe trying to poison Napoleon, and had repeated it in Longwood. To these two charges Stokoe could only say that this calumny, as well as the Governor's interception of books and papers intended for Napoleon, had been common topics of conversation in the island, to which he had added nothing on his own part.

The eighth charge, a trivial one, concerned Stokoe's failure to keep an appointment with the Admiral 'without justifiable cause'. His patient's illness and need of a doctor was not accepted as a justifiable cause.

The tenth and final charge, like a blast from a scatter-gun, revealed the underlying cause for complaint against the luckless doctor. He had put the interests of his patient and the French prisoners before 'the intentions and regulations' of his Admiral.

The four day trial culminating in Stokoe's dismissal from the Service was a manifestly unfair and irregular one. Witnesses were afraid of the Governor or of the Admiral, or of both, and tended to evade Stokoe's questions. Honourable exceptions were Captain Stanfell, who, though President of the Court, declared that if Stokoe had refused to visit General Buonaparte on the 17th January he would have regarded it as an act of direct disobedience; and Dr Verling and Captain Nicholls, who agreed that it would have been impossible for Stokoe to have confined his conversation to Napoleon's health. They both said that they had discussed all manner of things with the French prisoners when they met them.

Such admissions, in Hudson Lowe's island, amounted to courageous demonstrations of friendship. These statements, favourable to Stokoe, were omitted from the official report of the trial, which can be seen in the Public Record Office.

Admiral Plampin, determined to have Stokoe convicted, gave his evidence in such violent and intemperate language that the Court dared to suspend the hearing, and request him to be more moderate. In cross-examination he evaded Stokoe's questions, launched into interminable digressions, and perjured himself about his attempt to make Stokoe surrender the letter ordering him to attend Buonaparte. Realising this, he had the report of the proceedings falsified.

According to Count Balmain, the Russian Commissioner, Stokoe's judges and the audience were moved by compassion. If they were, it did him no good, for they did their duty to the tyrants of St Helena by convicting and sentencing him.

In Count Balmain's opinion Stokoe could 'only be regarded as a man who was weak, imprudent and unfortunate'. Unfortunate he certainly was; prudent he tried to be by seeking to evade the call for help from Longwood, but his conscience and sense of duty as a doctor prevailed. But weak? His portrait suggests a kindly, gentle individual. In 1795 when serving on a Russian hospital ship, he had cured himself of typhus by drinking two full bottles of wine at a sitting; and in 1819, when heroic measures were again required, he defended himself with spirit and ability, though deprived of legal aid. After hearing the verdict Napoleon sent a note of encouragement and sympathy, but Lowe would not allow it to be delivered to Stokoe.

People in St Helena were puzzled that Stokoe had been brought to trial for conduct which seemed to them to be far less offensive to the Governor than O'Meara's had been. The general opinion was that Lowe had been slightly wary of the combative young Irishman, but now felt more sure of himself, in St Helena at least, despite the stir which O'Meara had raised in England.

The treatment of Stokoe was outrageous, but Lowe and Plampin contrived to sweep the awkward affair under the carpet, and there it remained so far as English historians were concerned. Lord Rosebery overlooked Stokoe. Sir Walter Scott mentioned him only briefly. J. Holland Rose, for long a leading authority, though writing after Stokoe's memoirs had been published, merely remarked that he was cajoled into disobeying British regulations. Cajoled — well it has to be admitted that in 1912 the indefatigable Frédéric Masson unearthed and published a note from Napoleon to Joseph authorising him to pay Stokoe £1000. French historians have commented that it was lucky for Stokoe that this note remained secret before his trial; but of course they have not hesitated to stress that any doctor who said that Napoleon was ill risked instant dismissal.

Smoke from the fire in which Stokoe was suffering was observed by some English newspapers at the time. *The Morning Chronicle*, ever watchful for evidence of harsh treatment of Napoleon, sniffed the scandal on Stokoe's first return to England.

On April 2nd, 1819, Stokoe's arrival in England was reported and it was stated that he had been given the choice between court martial and invaliding. In a leading article, commenting that Sir Hudson Lowe had forced the only doctor whose visits Napoleon would allow, to quit the island the moment his services were required, the Editor of *The Morning Chronicle* warned the nation of the imputations which it would suffer if Napoleon should get worse or die, deprived of medical attention.

At this time Stokoe's only offence, known to *The Morning Chronicle*, was that he had discussed with the French the retention by the Governor of newspapers sent to Napoleon. If they had known that the most serious complaint against him was that he had said that Napoleon was ill their fulminations would have been more forcible.

Strangely enough after Stokoe had been secretly hurried back to St Helena, tried and sentenced, it was without comment that *The Morning Chronicle* published a letter from him dated December 20th, 1819, with which he enclosed his reply to an article in *The Times* of 17th December. *The Times* had printed the charges against Stokoe and said that the sentence had been 'both proper and humane'. In a personal interview in the editorial office Stokoe could get no redress, beyond an undertaking to publish the minutes of the trial if he could obtain a copy.

Stokoe's early attempts to have his case reviewed aroused some sympathy and a little official disquiet; so much so that Hudson Lowe felt compelled to write to Lord Bathurst about 'infamous falsehoods' circulating in England. The members of the court martial which sentenced Stokoe must have had misgivings, for they recommended to the Admiralty that he should be granted half-pay. As he was no longer an officer, this was not possible, but he was given a pension of £100 a year from the Civil List, and a further £300 additional pay for his time in St Helena. This generosity, so different from the treatment of O'Meara, naturally encouraged him to hope for restoration of his rank, and he kept up the fight for many years. There certainly does seem to have been some official uneasiness about the case.

When Admiral Plampin returned to England, Stokoe was there to greet him at Portsmouth, and he made some sort of scene, about which Plampin kept quiet, perhaps feeling that he did not stand on very firm ground.

In 1829 an eminent lawyer advised Stokoe that, despite many irregularities in the proceedings at St Helena, he could do little, as there was then no appeal against the sentence of a naval court martial. When Sir George Cockburn became First Sea Lord at the Admiralty in 1841, Stokoe, realising that he must know all about the case, had one last try. Sir George went so far as to say, 'I have always considered the errors attributed to Dr O'Meara and you have proceeded from your having been placed in so trying a position'; but, though he personally acquitted them of any intention to oppose the Government, he could only conclude that he much lamented their severe misfortunes.

The half-ashamed generosity of the British Government to its discarded servant was eventually matched by the Bonaparte family, when they realised how much Napoleon had valued *'son chirurgien Stokoe'*. When Stokoe returned to St Helena in August 1821, Napoleon, not realising that he had been brought back to be punished, sent three urgent letters begging for his attendance. In the delirium of his terminal illness it was for Stokoe that he called.[8]

Stokoe's memoirs never became a second *Voice from St Helena* to rouse Europe's conscience. He was a very different type of man to O'Meara, and it seems likely that he was deterred from rushing into print by fear of losing his pension, and by hopes of rejoining the medical service of the Navy, for which he was still applying twenty two years after his dismissal.

It was a Frenchman who first gave Stokoe's memoirs to the world. M. Paul Frémeaux found it impracticable to publish the memoirs in full, for they were too diffuse, full of digressions and repetitions. An English translation by Edith Stokoe, a great-grand-niece of John Stokoe, appeared in 1902, long after all the furore aroused by O'Meara's revelations had died down. Stokoe is accordingly less well-known than O'Meara. He was better educated, more experienced, perhaps rather more of a gentleman, certainly less of a fighter than O'Meara. On what evidence there is I think he may have been a better doctor. I am not alone in believing that the grim prognosis which he gave to Napoleon in 1819 proved to be correct in 1821.

But, whether O'Meara and Stokoe were right or wrong, they were broken because they stuck to their diagnosis and identified themselves with what they conceived to be the best interests of their patient; who, unfortunately for them, was a political prisoner of unique importance.

I entirely agree with the pronouncement made by Sir Arthur Keith, in his Hunterian Lecture on January 8th, 1913: 'O'Meara and Stokoe were dismissed from the Navy by ignorant laymen because they were competent and truthful physicians.'

The medical service which Stokoe served faithfully for over twenty years, and for a further twenty years strove to rejoin, has since become the Royal Naval Medical Service, an autonomous service which has nothing to fear from laymen, ignorant or otherwise. It should not be too late for that Service to take steps to rehabilitate the memory of Napoleon's devoted doctors.

# CHAPTER VII

# Antommarchi and Arnott

Napoleon now knew exactly where he stood. The only two doctors who had examined him had told him what was wrong; and one of them had explained how it could kill him. But he would see no more British doctors. They could do nothing for him. They also knew exactly where they stood. The dangers of attending patients at Longwood, and particularly of making a diagnosis which was unacceptable to the Governor, were now clear. Napoleon summed up the situation with deadly accuracy. 'Hudson Lowe forbids anyone to suffer from liver complaints on this island. Any type of disease is permitted here except one — hepatitis.'

Napoleon had often been right in his premonitions. As a slender, almost emaciated young general he had forecast that he would be very fat at forty. He himself was the first to suspect that the liver was the seat of his trouble. Now, from Stokoe's prognosis, he felt sure that he could not recover if he had to remain in St Helena. He had said to Stokoe: 'I should have lived to eighty years if they had not brought me to this accursed island.'

Napoleon was right to put the blame firmly on Hudson Lowe. Lowe had wanted to appoint a British doctor to Longwood House. Lord Bathurst had told him to do so. Napoleon's stubbornness had wrecked his excellent plan to appoint Dr Verling, but nothing can excuse Lowe's refusal thereafter to appoint the man whom Napoleon wanted. His reason for refusing to agree to the choice of Stokoe was that the proposal had been discussed between the French and Stokoe before he had known about it. This was typical enough of the man, but his true underlying reason was even more disreputable. It was of course because Stokoe's diagnosis and prognosis meant that Napoleon was ill because he was in St Helena and would not get better if he were kept there. Lowe alone, and not in any way the Government, was responsible for refusing Napoleon's request for Stokoe and destroying this last chance of a happy ending to the story — a happy ending which would have been possible only if they had accepted Stokoe's advice, which in the light of Lowe's subsequent conduct is perhaps too much to hope for.

Napoleon was still not without hope that political pressure in Europe and a change of heart in London might bring an end to his exile. The French undoubtedly hoped to use Napoleon's illness to stimulate such a change of heart, and it was the suspicion that this illness was feigned or exaggerated, which led Hudson Lowe and his servile medical advisers to obstinate refusal to accept the diagnoses of O'Meara and Stokoe. Even if Lowe had been right, and these two had become partisans of their beguiling patient, he was not qualified to deride and disown their considered medical opinions. Napoleon's indignation was justified.

However, although Napoleon was convinced that he had hepatitis, it was from cancer that he expected to die, because his father had done so and he believed it to be hereditary. It was for that reason that he later ordered his last doctor, Francisco Antommarchi, to examine his body after death to see if he could discover anything which might save his son from the same fate.

This, at least, Antommarchi was well qualified to do for his unfortunate patient. He was an exceptionally bad choice for the post of personal physician, for he was not a physician at all. It has been said that he was one of the most gifted anatomists and dissectors of his day. After a varied experience he had become prosector, or assistant to a world-famous anatomist and pathologist, Professor Paul Mascagni at the hospital of Santa Maria Novella in Florence, attached to the University of Pisa.

The reason why such a singularly unsuitable doctor had been sent to join the household at Longwood was curious. Napoleon's mother and his step-uncle Cardinal Fesch, living in Rome, had been dabbling in spiritualism, and had allowed themselves to become convinced that Napoleon was no longer in St Helena, having been transported thence by angels. After Las Cases had left St Helena he was rather surprised to receive a letter from Fesch informing him that Napoleon had left the island, though 'the gaoler of St Helena' was keeping the glad tidings secret. As the deluded pair firmly believed in this rubbish no trouble was taken to select suitable candidates for the posts, when Napoleon asked them to find him a doctor and a priest. One of the priests, the decrepit old Abbé Buonavita, was useless for any purpose; but the other, the Abbé Vignali had studied medicine before becoming a priest and, although he is sometimes dismissed as having been only a medical student, he seems to have claimed to be a Doctor of Medicine of Rome University.

In his cruel disappointment over his relatives' choice of a doctor, Napoleon put it in a nutshell: 'I would give him my horse to dissect, but I would not trust him with the cure of my own foot.' Antommarchi himself candidly admitted, 'Up to the present I have had only corpses to deal with.' But he was not unduly overawed by the responsibilities of his position. He was a brash self-confident, almost aggressive young coxcomb, whose personality infuriated Napoleon. That he was a Corsican did not help at all, for Napoleon was quick to point out that he was the wrong type of Corsican, greeting him as *Capo Corsinaccio* — inhabitant of the Cape of Corsica, and expatiating upon the superiority of the inhabitants of his own more mountainous region. It was, as it were, a comparison between a Highland stalker and a Cockney, but Napoleon lacked the grave courtesy and politeness with which the stalker would have handled the relationship.

There is no doubt at all that Napoleon grew to detest his doctor, but Antommarchi's bland memoirs present a pleasing picture of the young Corsican accepting the appointment as an opportunity to render service and homage to the greatest of all Corsicans, who in turn treated his young admirer with paternal patronage. This idyllic relationship was a figment of Antommarchi's imagination, if it was not deliberate mis-representation. Perhaps his self-confidence enabled him to blot out memories of the less pleasant encounters with his patient.

All the memoirs of other residents of Longwood record the serious rows occasioned by Napoleon's dissatisfaction with the quality of medical attention which he was receiving from Antommarchi, which he bitterly compared with what he had been accustomed to in France. 'You come here,' he once said, 'as though you were paying a thirty sous visit.'

The flighty youth, as Count Montholon tolerantly observed, could not endure the boredom of life in Longwood House. He was often absent when Napoleon needed him, and his habit of taking long rides around the island annoyed the British authorities, who had to provide escorts. The most violent scene of all occurred when Napoleon urged Antommarchi to discuss the management of tropical diseases with some of the British doctors in the island. Antommarchi infuriated Napoleon by airily saying that he knew more than they did, and they could teach him nothing. The only possible source of this serene self-satisfaction was the discussions which Antommarchi had had with medical experts before leaving Europe.

Antommarchi's departure from Rome was considerably delayed because the Abbé Buonavita, the older of the two priests destined for St Helena, suffered a stroke which seriously affected his speech and locomotion. The delay was put to good use. Antommarchi attended a conference, called by Cardinal Fesch, at which some of the leading physicians in Italy discussed Napoleon's case, as presented in O'Meara's reports. They decided unanimously that the seat of the trouble was an obstruction of the liver. A régime of general medication was prescribed in a document which Antommarchi said was to be for him 'the law and the prophets', from which he must not deviate. A copy was given to the Abbé Vignali, which annoyed Antommarchi and led to a little misunderstanding in St Helena.

In London, where Antommarchi stayed for three months, he saw O'Meara almost daily and was shown copies of some of Stokoe's reports to Bertrand. He found that the name of Mascagni was a password to medical circles and he consulted several authorities with experience of medicine in the tropics, including St Helena. All of them agreed that the evidence pointed to hepatitis.

Antommarchi's activities in London aroused the suspicion of the authorities and he was summoned to the Colonial Office, where he saw Lord Bathurst, who instructed him to disregard all previous medical reports. From reports which he had himself received, he said, he could assure Antommarchi that Napoleon was 'perfectly well'. Officials at the Colonial Office were much perturbed about some anatomical charts in Antommarchi's possession. These were the work of Professor Mascagni which Antommarchi was preparing for publication. At the Colonial Office it was suspected that a chart of the lymphatic system was probably an escape plot in hieroglyphics. In such wise hands lay Napoleon's fate and the long-distance decisions about his health.

When Antommarchi and the two priests arrived in St Helena Napoleon had been without a personal physician for fifteen months, and had seen no doctor at all for eight months, during which his health had given rise to growing concern, expressed in letters from Bertrand and Montholon to his family. However Napoleon was in no hurry to see the new doctor and a day or two passed before he pronounced that Antommarchi and not Vignali was to take charge. If Vignali had really qualified as a Doctor of

Medicine of Rome, Napoleon may have made the wrong decision, surprisingly enough in view of his opinion of Antommarchi. Anyhow, Vignali passes out of the medical scene, to reappear when Napoleon, having decided to die a good Catholic, made his confession to the strange young priest.

Napoleon had steadfastly refused to see Dr Verling himself but he ordered Antommarchi to consult him about the treatment of tropical diseases, especially hepatitis.

Upholders of the theory that Napoleon's death was from cancer rightly point out that Antommarchi, a man without clinical experience, arrived in St Helena strongly prejudiced in favour of a diagnosis of hepatitis. Perhaps he fitted into that expectation anything which he believed he learned on physical examination of Napoleon. Be that as it may, when he first examined Napoleon in a darkened room he found that the left lobe of the liver was hard and painful; and he thought that he could also feel a tense and painful gall-bladder.

Napoleon continued to complain of pain in the right hypo-chondriac region (just below the ribs) and vague pains elsewhere in the abdomen; 'a sensation of extreme uneasiness in the right shoulder'; and a general uneasiness and inability to rest, which kept him moving from room to room, from sofa to bed. He said to Antommarchi, 'I am attacked with a chronic hepatitis, a disorder endemic in this horrible climate. I must fall a prey to it.'

He then launched into a violent tirade against the *bourreau* (executioner or hangman) who was trying to hasten his death. In the English translation of Antommarchi's book the torrent of abuse is omitted, probably because Hudson Lowe had already tried to bring a libel action against O'Meara. However the omission is signalised by four and a half lines of asterisks, encouraging one to refer to the French text. On a later occasion a rude word used by Napoleon about Hudson Lowe was evidently too strong for anything but asterisks in the French as well as in the English version.

Some time in November 1819 there was a development which was pleasant for Napoleon, reassuring to the British authorities, and of some significance to my later discussion of the true nature of his illness. The symptoms attributed to chronic hepatitis died down and Napoleon enjoyed excellent health for about eight months – and 'enjoyed' is happily the right word. Antommarchi had urged him to take more exercise, and he now threw himself enthusiastically into really hard labour in his garden, working on major improvements, rising early and calling at the windows of those still in bed. Making light of blistered hands and aching limbs he vowed that he would bend his body to his will. Antommarchi could hardly claim that his prescriptions had done the trick, for Napoleon refused to take medicine, true to his determination never to be *un homme à potions*. Napoleon's improvement was accompanied by much bantering and the usual ear-pulling, which rather surprised his *dottoracio*.

But even this welcome period of remission was not entirely free from an occasional stomach upset and a migrainous headache. Antommarchi was therefore not unduly optimistic and, in an interview with the Governor which he had requested at Napoleon's prompting, he pressed for the removal of some restrictions and spoke of the evil effect of the climate.

The ignorant layman, who had not set eyes on his prisoner for months, confidently scoffed at the doctor's fears. 'General Bonaparte enjoys excellent health notwithstanding all he says', boomed the Governor. 'This is the healthiest climate that I know, and it has been chosen for that reason. Undoubtedly, undoubtedly!' This was 'the law and the prophets' to Hudson Lowe, whatever Antommarchi's precious document might forebode.

During Napoleon's last Indian Summer of reasonably good health the entries in Antommarchi's journal, like the bulk of those in O'Meara's, are concerned with Napoleon's political philosophy, accounts of his old campaigns and discussions on various subjects – often anatomy and physiology. The human body and its ailments had always fascinated him; a fascination which helped to earn him a not wholly undeserved reputation of being a hypochondriac. He liked to give his symptoms an exact anatomical location. *'Oh mon pylore, mon pylore'* he would cry when gripped by severe abdominal pain. I have never heard of any other patient invoking his pylorus. He may have been a little adrift when he complained to Antommarchi of cramp in his spleen, though that organ is the target of more than one tropical infection. But he was probably right on the mark when, in the early summer of 1820, he began again to complain of 'deep-seated pain in the liver'. Napoleon's terminal illness had begun.

Dr S. Abbatucci, the chief protagonist of the liver abscess theory of Napoleon's death, in his book written in collaboration with the Belgian doctor A. de Mets, explains that his own convictions on the subject were initially inspired by Napoleon himself; by his denials of having ever suffered from stomach trouble, and his insistence on the liver being affected. Abbatucci quotes one of the occasions on which Napoleon assured Marchand that he knew he had liver disease, and that it was there that sharp razor-like stabs were cutting into him. (*C'est là. C'est la foie — une larde de rasoir qui me coupe en glissant.*') The knife-like quality of the pain deserves particular attention, for it is not characteristic of cancer.

On 28th April, 1821, within a few days of his death Napoleon remarked, 'It is worth noting that I have always had a stomach of iron: I have only recently suffered from it.'

On 18th July, 1820, Antommarchi wrote to the Chamberlain to Napoleon's mother, the Chevalier Colonna, to say that the emperor was suffering from 'chronic hepatitis of the most serious nature'. He had diagnosed this, he said, when he first saw Napoleon; some improvement had followed his treatment, but now he feared that recovery was impossible whilst the Emperor remained in St Helena.

All the old symptoms recurred; and in October and November the pain in the liver became increasingly severe. In March 1821 Napoleon was able to go out in his carriage but was becoming very careless about his appearance, and Antommarchi urged him to tidy himself up. Napoleon's pathetic reply — *d'un ton penetré* — must surely have shaken the brightly patronising young man — 'When I was Napoleon, I dressed quickly and with pleasure; but now, what signifies it whether I look well or ill?'

Napoleon may have been something of a hypochondriac and a very difficult patient. This last fact is often stressed by those who seek to excuse the medical mismanagement of his last illness. But it is impossible not to feel the deepest sympathy and admiration for the conduct of this once-great man, convinced that he was dying, and convinced too that for this his enemies were at least partly to blame. Knowing as we now do that the nasty medicines, emetics and so on, pressed upon him by Antommarchi could be nothing but useless irritants, we can only commend Napoleon's rejection of them. Denouncing drugs, he said that he knew his own constitution and preferred to trust to Nature; 'I will not have two diseases — that with which I am afflicted, and that which you would inflict upon me.' He could still joke with the doctor about his precious pills; and once, consenting to swallow some medicine, he did it with an air — one might say, with a toast — 'When a man has been guilty of irreverence towards Galen, it is thus that the sin must be expiated.'

The suffering stomach into which the young anatomist was so
eager to pour his emetics was causing his patient increasing
discomfort, with flatulence, frequent eructations, nausea and lack
of appetite. The pains in the right side became sharper, compared
by Napoleon to the thrusts of a knife or razor. Antommarchi felt
that he must write still more strongly to the Emperor's family; and
on 17th March, 1821, he wrote again to Colonna:

> The Emperor' s situation is growing daily worse; the hepatic functions
> are no longer performed; and those of the digestive organs are entirely
> suspended. . . . In order to exculpate myself from all responsibility I
> declare to you, to all the Imperial Family, and to the whole world, that
> the disease under which the Emperor is labouring is an effect of the
> nature of the climate, and that the symptoms it exhibits are of the most
> serious kind.

He ended that, if not removed from St Helena, the Emperor would
'soon be no more'.

Antommarchi's understandable desire to share the awful responsibility which he had at first so lightly assumed was at last
gratified. He was allowed to call in consultation an experienced
and well-qualified Army doctor, who was acceptable both to the
Governor and Napoleon. Dr Archibald Arnott, surgeon to the 20th
Foot, had attended the Bertrand family and the general warmly
commended him to Napoleon. Perhaps by now some of the fight
was out of the exhausted patient, and he may even have still
hoped to find a doctor who could help him. He gave his consent
without much ado, saying, *'Je ne sais pas si celui-ci est bon
médecin, mais il a bonne tenue. Je le reçevrai.'*

Arnott was a member of an old Scottish family of which many
members then and since served with distinction in the Army, and
in its medical service. The extent of his active service was attested
by no less than ten clasps to his Peninsular medal. In 1815 he had
'proceeded M.D.' as the expression has it, at Edinburgh University,
so should have satisfied the requirement of *bon médecin.*

The *bonne tenue* can be discerned in his portrait and he was by
all accounts a kindly, likeable man, and a thorough gentleman,
who could never have referred to his patient as 'The Old Imposter'
as Dr Baxter had done. Arnott was no 'stiff surgeon', indeed it
may not be too unjust to call him a pliable physician – a puppet
of Plantation House, prepared to produce a political diagnosis. His
conduct as a doctor is hardly to be understood unless one assumes
that he went to Longwood House under the influence of the view
prevailing in official circles that Napoleon was malingering in order

to obtain some amelioration in the conditions of his custody.

Arnott was an older man than Antommarchi, O'Meara or Stokoe, being only three years younger than Napoleon, who soon took a liking to him. He gave Arnott a snuff-box, variously described as being of gold, silver or silver-gilt; but, whatever the material, its value was enhanced a hundredfold by the letter 'N' which the dying man scratched upon it with scissors. When Napoleon instructed Antommarchi to examine his body after death he adjured him to let no English doctor see his body, except Arnott. Seldom can a patient's confidence have been more misplaced.

On March 25th, 1821, Arnott had his first discussion with Antommarchi, during which he praised the climate of St Helena, and said that there was no illness among the troops stationed there, which was simply not true. He saw Napoleon for the first time on 1st April and thereafter saw him sometimes twice daily until his death on May 5th. From some accounts it might be thought that he saw Napoleon infrequently, but his own book supports Octave Aubry, who mentions the regular visits. By March it was of course much too late for Napoleon's life to be saved by such remedies as existed at that time. Nevertheless Arnott deserves the condemnation first pronounced by Dr Arnold Chaplin, in 1913, that he 'stands convicted of culpable negligence'.

After his first visit Arnott said that, although Napoleon had a 'gastric intermittent fever', he was probably suffering from hypochondria. Hudson Lowe and Dr Baxter had always maintained that Napoleon was shamming. Arnott fell into step with The Establishment and marched behind them until eight days before his patient's death. In early April a conference to discuss Napoleon's case was held by Dr Thomas Shortt who had succeeded Baxter as principal medical officer. Dr Shortt suggested marasmus; Dr Burton a tendency to dropsy; and Dr Mitchell pyloric obstruction.

None of these amount to a proper diagnosis, though Mitchell came near to the mark. Only Dr Livingstone had the courage to say that the condition was probably aggravated by the climate.

Arnott, the only British doctor who had actually seen the patient, continued to maintain that Napoleon was not really ill, that it was all 'probably more mental than any other'.

Napoleon later agreed to Dr Shortt and Dr Mitchell attending a conference at Longwood House, in Antommarchi's room, saying that he agreed to it to please others, not himself. The only tangible result of this meeting was a recommendation to bathe his loins with eau-de-cologne. Bonaparte poured scorn on 'the mighty conference' which had produced such a piffling recommendation.

On 17th April Arnott stated that he was 'more and more convinced that the disease was hypochondriasis'; and even as late as 23rd April he reported to Hudson Lowe that Napoleon was a case of 'hypochondriasis having many digestive symptoms' but that he 'saw no symptom of danger about him'. Meanwhile his patient had been feverish with profuse drenching sweats; toxaemic, often delirious, often in severe pain, which he had told Arnott was 'a sharp piercing pain that cuts into me like a knife'. Vomiting had been persistent, at first of watery matter, then undigested food. For some time he had had a good appetite but now he was eating nothing but bringing up a chocolate coloured substance. Marchand, the *premier valet-de-chambre*, had heard Napoleon, chatting to Arnott over cups of coffee, telling him that he was sure they would not understand his illness until they examined him after death — *lorsque l'on m'aura ouvert*. However, on 26th April he asked Arnott for an opinion, and Arnott said that he thought that the symptoms indicated 'some derangement of the digestive organs'. Was ever a diagnosis more vaguely non-committal? But on the very next day Arnott, at long last, became anxious and told Hudson Lowe that the disease was serious. One week later Napoleon was dead. Octave Aubry, understandably merciless to Arnott, insists that even five days before the end Arnott still suspected the French of mis-representing the facts, for, when he was told that Napoleon had persistent hiccups, he said, 'I consider the symptoms very serious, if the thing is true.'

Towards the end, instead of reassurances about Napoleon's illness being 'more mental than any other', Lowe was bombarded with bulletins on a note of belated alarm, although to the last Arnott seemed to hope that the hypochondriac might yet pull through. The day before his death Arnott's note said: 'He appears better than he was two hours ago'; but in less than twenty four hours he had to admit 'He is dying'.

The day before Napoleon died Arnott ordered an enema to be given, though Antommarchi protested that Napoleon was much too weak. Arnott, however, insisted, not only, as he said, for the patient's sake but 'for the sake of my own reputation'. This is positively the only indication that he felt himself in any way culpable.

It is hardly surprising that Arnott's reputation has received a severe mauling at the hands of many historians, most of whom comment on the difference between his reports to Lowe whilst Napoleon was alive, and the opinions expressed in his book after he had left St Helena. His most recent critic is also the most severe. M. Gilbert Martineau, in his book *Napoleon's St Helena*, writes of Arnott: 'His responsibility for the Emperor's end was grave, for he was as ignorant as Antommarchi but much more malevolent.' He alleges that Arnott persistently stressed the diagnosis of hypochondria in order to get into the Governor's good graces. Montholon, in his verbose memoirs, states that quite early in his attendance on Napoleon Arnott told him, Montholon, that he took a grave view and spoke of gastritis. In view of what Arnott was reporting to Lowe this is hardly credible, but if true would fully justify M. Martineau's strictures. Arnott strikes me more as a man who, having absorbed the Plantation House view of the case before seeing Napoleon, failed until nearly the end to open his mind to the possibility of serious organic illness. He was like the legendary chairman of a committee who said: 'My mind is made up. Please do not confuse me with the facts' — a highly reprehensible attitude in a doctor, certainly, but hardly malevolent.

It is not quite so easy to determine if Arnott can fairly be called ignorant. He certainly ought not to have been, for he had recently proceeded M.D. at Edinburgh, a qualification then regarded as one of the highest distinctions in medical education. He was well versed in the advanced medical practice of his day. This point was stressed in 1903 in an article in the *British Medical Journal* by Sir W.H. Broadbent.

Arnott was the only doctor to make a record of Napoleon's temperature, which he gave on 3rd April as '. . . heat 96'. Commenting on this, Broadbent remarked that, 'clinical thermometry, while practised by a few advanced physicians for some years previously, did not come into general use till after the publication of Wunderlich's treatise of 1868.'

The strongest justification for the use of the word 'ignorant' is the fact that this well educated experienced doctor was unable — for it is too terrible to believe that he was really unwilling — to recognise a dying man, as the young anatomist had done months before.

Arnott's own book does virtually nothing for his reputation. Until a week before his patient's death he had clung to the belief

that there was no physical basis for his illness. One might suppose
that some explanation was called for when a patient had died of
hypochondria. Wisely perhaps Arnott offers none, but takes the
simpler course of a straightforward report on the case as he saw it,
in the archaic medical language of the day; studiously refraining
from offering any diagnosis — not even man enough to admit he
had been wrong.

If he really did not feel that he had anything to be ashamed of
perhaps he was ignorant after all. If he deliberately evaded any
reference to his mistaken diagnosis, malevolent may not be quite
the word, but one could think of more severe adjectives. By
inference he shifts the responsibility on to the shoulders of
Antommarchi, to whom he refers in his book, though nowhere
else, as 'Professor' Antommarchi! Stressing Napoleon's refusal to
accept treatment, he wrote that Napoleon said 'that he was
convinced medical aid could be of no avail to him, and that he was
labouring under a fatal disease'.

Arnott, preoccupied with Napoleon's constipation and the need
to clear out what he called the *primae viae*, relentlessly pressed
purgatives and enemas on his victim; and at the very end 'that
nothing should be left undone, although *moribundus*, sinapisms
were applied to the feet, blisters to the legs and one to the
abdomen'.

We need not be too critical of Arnott's crude treatment.
Napoleon was eating nothing and there was nothing to clear out of
his *primae viae*; but in Arnott's day the evils of constipation were
a subject about which even intelligent doctors loved to be
pompous and busy. It was a field in which it was easy to appear to
be achieving something — however useless and uncomfortable it
may have been to the dying man.

If there is any attempt at self-justification in Arnott's book it is
presumably in the concluding section entitled — 'Remarks', and
the attempt must be pronounced a failure.

Claiming that cancer, from which he now felt sure that
Napoleon had died, was very difficult to diagnose, he expressed
surprise that it should have existed in a man of Napoleon's
temperate habits. 'I have seen the disease before, but it was in men
addicted to ardent spirits — decided dram drinkers.'

It is hard to believe that this view represented intelligent
opinion in the mid-nineteenth century. As it had been suggested
that the endemic dysentery of St Helena might have played a part
in Bonaparte's illness, Arnott pointed out that dysentery among

troops was due to the fact that 'they do not take care of themselves . . . and are also prone to intemperance.'

No doubt the troops did drink a lot in St Helena where there was little else for them to do; but the young Irish doctor O'Meara showed evidence of profounder thought about the dysentery and hepatitis which afflicted them than Arnott with his stupid preoccupation with strong drink.

In Arnott's mainly unenlightened speculations there does shine one gleam of constructive thought which I would like to think derived from an essentially kindly nature. Discussing Napoleon's cancer he asks, 'Might not the depressing passions of the mind act as an exciting cause' in a person with some hereditary pre-disposition to the disease? In due course I intend to suggest that 'the depressing passions' of Napoleon's mind may well have played an important part in his fatal illness. Meanwhile it is enough to credit Arnott with having shared in that sympathy with the poor sick prisoner which was felt by O'Meara and Stokoe.

Napoleon, who usually disliked doctors, certainly found nothing malevolent about Arnott. He was within a few weeks of death when he first saw Arnott, and the aggressive spirit in which he usually received doctors may have weakened; but he probably soon began to feel as much at his ease with this older man as he had done with the kindly Stokoe.

At his first visit Arnott was only allowed to see Napoleon in a completely darkened room; and he wrote:

I could not see him, as he would not permit a light to be brought into the room, but I felt him — or another.

There are indications that Napoleon's reluctance to see British doctors was partly because he did not want them to notice and perhaps talk about his physical imperfections. Even the likeable, patently trustworthy Dr Verling, though living in Longwood, was not to be allowed to come near him, unless he would consent to be bought. As I have said, Napoleon misjudged O'Meara when he thought that he might reveal a patient's secrets. The only British doctor who revealed this particular secret was Dr Henry. Napoleon had never been his patient, and he saw him only after death.

Antommarchi was also only allowed to see Napoleon in a darkened room, at first; but, when Napoleon had decided that he was to make a post-mortem examination, he exposed himself to the young Corsican almost defiantly. Stepping from his bath and throwing aside his sponge, he said, 'See doctor, what lovely arms, what smooth white skin without a single hair! Breasts plump and rounded — any beauty would be proud of a bosom like mine. And my hand — how many amongst the fair sex would be jealous of it.'

Arnott does not refer to having to examine Napoleon in the dark after his first visit, so it is likely that, as he gained his patient's confidence, this was not insisted upon. Napoleon may have said that only Arnott was to see his body after death because he already knew all about it.

The dying Napoleon was without the solace of man's traditional ministering angel. His second wife, Marie Louise, had deserted him after his first abdication and was living with her paramour Count Neipperg, by whom she had had two illegitimate children. Whilst drawing up his will Napoleon had been heard to cry out: 'To be a Corsican — and to forgive such an outrage'.

His first wife Josephine, herself not noted for fidelity to either of her husbands, had died whilst he was in Elba. Her physician, Dr Horeau, told him that she had grieved for him, and that, unlike Marie Louise she would have driven through occupied France to comfort him. According to one account her name was the last word he spoke. His first sweetheart Desirée Clary, married to Bernadotte, was now Queen of Sweden, and his last, Marie Walewska, much the nicest girl in his life, had been dead nearly four years. His devoted sister Pauline, even his ageing mother, would certainly have joined him in St Helena had the Powers permitted it.

Albine de Montholon, the notoriously loose-living wife of the senior member of the Household living in Longwood, had shown some willingness to comfort the exile, but she had left the island with her children in the summer of 1819. The wife of General Bertrand, living at Hutt's Gate, just over a mile away, had also wanted to escape to Europe, but had postponed her departure when it seemed that Napoleon might be mortally ill. Napoleon had never really liked her, because he knew that she had tried to persuade her husband not to accompany him into exile. Still he felt hurt when he learned of her intention to leave with her children.

Fanny Bertrand was not the kind of woman who would have made a good nurse and, in any case, her position at Longwood would have been impossible. Napoleon had formed the remarkable delusion that she was a prostitute, and he coarsely abused Dr Antommarchi for refusing to help him to make her his mistress.

Her husband recorded Napoleon's foul-mouthed attacks on her character in his Journal calmly and without comment, just as he recorded the Emperor's cruel rejection of his own services.

The duties of nursing the dying man devolved upon the male members of The Service; not perhaps the most satisfactory solution, but more satisfactory than might be supposed by those who have never seen the tenderness with which the toughest of young soldiers cared for comrades wounded or dying in battle. Not that Napoleon's young men were particularly tough. If anything rather the reverse.

Mlle Avrillon, Josephine's ladies-maid, and others, described how Napoleon, who had a particular liking for handsome youths, used to select his valets, pages and footmen personally. Often, like his most famous valet, Louis Constant Wairy, they had already served an apprenticeship with Josephine. Constant and the famous Mameluke Roustam deserted the Emperor at the time of his first abdication, and their places were taken by Louis Marchand as *premier valet-de-chambre*, and Louis Etienne Saint Denis as first Mameluke. Saint Denis was known as Ali, and often dressed in Oriental clothes.

During Napoleon's last illness these two shared the very exhausting night duty, and towards the end they were assisted by Montholon. Occasionally Pierron, the major domo, or the elder Archambault was called upon for help with the heavy lifting. The groom Noverraz was himself ill at the time, with a second attack of liver trouble, and Napoleon, in all his own misery, spared a kind thought for this young Swiss giant who had fought off the peasants who tried to attack the fallen Emperor in 1814. Napoleon ordered that he must be sent home, saying, *'Je ne veux pas que ce brave garçon périsse, victime de cet affreux climat.'*

By the end they were all worn out. The brunt fell on Marchand, not only because he was the senior valet, but because his services were particularly acceptable to Napoleon, who would often send for him even when he was off duty. He had been in the Emperor's service since 1811 and he retained to the end a high sense of the dignity of his position, and devoted deference to his exacting master. It was he who strove to correct Antommarchi's almost deliberately boorish behaviour, and to teach this denizen of the dissecting room how to conduct himself 'at Court'; how to address an Emperor, however low he had fallen.

Marchand was twenty four when he came to St Helena, a good-looking, vivacious, pleasant young Frenchman. He buckled

down to all the intimate, even sordid duties of a nursing
orderly – the turning, changing of clothes and sheets, baths,
frictions, enemas, with skill and patience, and apparently without
expectation of reward. His reward took his breath away when he
learned of it. Testifying that 'His services were those of a friend',
Napoleon made him an executor of his will, created him a Count,
and gave him the diamond necklace which Queen Hortense had
given to her step-father on parting.

Ali, stretching himself out on the carpet at the foot of
Napoleon's bed, was no less willing but must have been too clumsy
or unintentionally rough for the sickroom, for he found Napoleon
'uncertain in temper'. His attempts to help were often rejected and
Marchand was sent for. This was the main reason why Montholon
eventually had to take Ali's spells of night duty.

General Bertrand, who was usually in attendance by day, made
several attempts to take a turn in the more tiring night-duty. The
manner in which his offers were brusquely rejected reflects no
credit on Napoleon. The fact that the final and most crushing
rejection is reported more fully in Montholon's memoirs than by
anyone else reflects still less credit on Montholon himself. His
version, with all its emphatic italics and block letters is as follows:

> *I have already told you that Montholon suffices me; it is your fault that*
> *I have become so accustomed to his services, which are those of a son;*
> *and now I will have no other's.* IT IS HE WHO SHALL RECEIVE MY
> LAST SIGH: THIS SHALL BE THE REWARD OF HIS SERVICES.
> *Say no more on the subject.*

The name of Henri Gratien Bertrand was for generations a byword
for fidelity. He had served as Grand Marshal of the Palace since
1812. In St Helena, where the pretentious title was retained, he
was the senior member of Napoleon's last little Court, and was the
patient arbiter of all their petty quarrels, able to remain a little
aloof from it all since he and his family did not live in Longwood
House. It is believed that Napoleon turned against Bertrand
because he had planned to send his family to Europe.

Montholon, who had spared no pains to worm himself ever
deeper into Napoleon's confidence, slyly played upon the extent
to which Napoleon would feel abandoned if he permitted Bertrand
to accompany his wife in order to settle her affairs in France.
Behind Napoleon's outwardly generous permission for the Grand
Marshal to go with his family could be detected the suggestion
that if he went he need not bother to return. The plan was

Dr. Francis Burton                  Dr. Walter Henry

Dr. James Verling                   Dr. Thomas Shortt

*Left:* Dr. Alexander Baxter

Baron Corvisart
*From an engraving by M. Blot after a painting by Gerard,* 1809

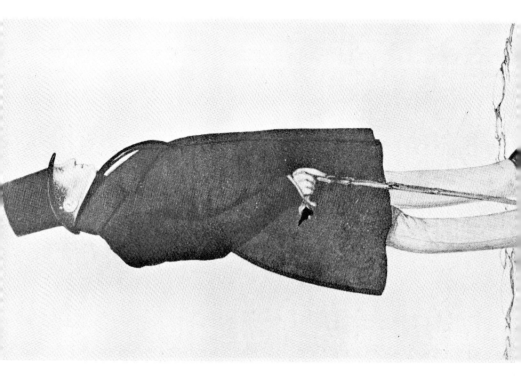

abandoned but the harm was done. Napoleon's withdrawal from Bertrand, however, probably grew from deeper roots. He may have been a hero to his valet, but was too shrewd an observer of human nature to fail to detect that he was no hero to the man who knew him better than any valet — his Grand Marshal.

Bertrand's disillusionment with Napoleon and his reading of his self-centred character, is apparent from his conversations with Gourgaud and others. How profound his disillusionment was, and how near he must have come to hating Napoleon, can be deduced from his diaries. Napoleon knew all about the diaries being kept in Longwood House itself. If he suspected that another pen was scratching away at Hutt's Gate he was too good a psychologist to overlook the possibility that it might be dipped in acid which could corrode the bright surface of the Legend.

But Bertrand throughout his life never complained of his treatment. He neither said nor did anything which could tarnish the Legend, or impair his own reputation for faithfulness. His plain unvarnished reporting of Napoleon's words and deeds would have been enough, but it was all in cipher. Even when it was at last painstakingly deciphered by M. Paul Fleuriot de Langle in 1946 there was in Bertrand's *Cahiers* no hint of what his feelings may have been when he had to record foul abuse of his wife, or comments on himself, such as this:

> The grand marshal is a blockhead [un bêta]. He is no use to me. He did not come here out of attachment, but because he would have perished like Labédoyère and Ney.[1]

In his notebooks Bertrand recorded his daily observations of the dying Emperor with the diligence of one aspiring to become a trained nurse — every groan, every sigh, every hiccup, and all the usual details of a nurse's report. His accurate reporting, far more effective than the florid and rather journalistic outpourings of Antommarchi, Ali, Marchand and Montholon, enables us to share the vigil of the little group throughout the closing weeks of Napoleon's life.

They were all much affected by the sight of the man, who for so long had dominated his surroundings, now reduced to complete dependence on them. At first he made determined efforts not to give in. His last excursion outside Longwood was a visit to the new house which Hudson Lowe, with the best of intentions, was having built for him. He would have none of it because the quarters for his valets were too far away from his own; which he thought was typical of English carelessness about providing decent accommodation for servants.

In a last despairing attempt to take exercise he had a see-saw made, and used it for about a fortnight. The end opposite to Napoleon's, usually occupied by Montholon, had to be weighted to compensate for his bulk.

Shortly before he was compelled to take to his bed more or less permanently Bertrand saw him looking with a pathetic air at Marchand, who was helping him. 'Poor me – my limbs no longer support me,' he said. But, though clearly alive to the pathos of his situation, he wasted very little time on self-pity. Recognising more clearly than any of them, including Dr Arnott, that he had not long to live, he set about preparing for death. He personally gave instructions about the construction of a *chapelle ardente* to receive his body.

In the protracted process of drawing up his will he contrived to forgive everyone against whom he felt he had grievances, including the British people; but not their hated rulers. 'I die prematurely, assassinated by the English oligarchy and its hired killer; the English nation will not be slow in avenging me.'

To his absurd suspicions of the 'hired killer's' attempts to poison him he now added the conviction that he had been supplied with poisoned snuff.

Mme Bertrand was not the only woman whose character he besmirched. Among those whom he claimed to have seduced he named his first sweetheart, Desirée Clary, whom in fact he had cruelly jilted. He convinced himself that Dr Antommarchi, having deprived him of the chance of seducing Fanny Bertrand, had seduced her himself and was leading a life of extreme sexual licence. Napoleon had always tended to use the coarsest of barrack-room language, and to use it in inappropriate company; and his dismissal of Antommarchi was expressed in language which could only be recorded in Bertrand's secret cipher.[2] He took another look at his will, in order to leave Antommarchi enough money to buy a rope to hang himself; and expanded yet again on the young Corsican's inadequate care of him, compared with what he had expected in France.

All Napoleon's filthy talk, and what Maximilien Vox calls frightening sexual rancour, one must charitably assume to have been a symptom of the toxaemia of his mortal illness, poisoning his mind as well as his body. I think Bertrand must have realised this. He knew the worst as well as the best of the Emperor, having served him personally for nearly ten years. Now it brought tears to the honest grand marshal's eyes to see the once all-powerful autocrat humbly and gently begging again and again for a spoonful of coffee, obedient as a child.

On 9th April Antommarchi went to Plantation House where he saw Hudson Lowe and the Marquis de Montchenu, and demanded an immediate passage to Europe. Bertrand, forgiving as usual, despite Napoleon having proposed that he himself should procure his wife for him and force her if she proved stubborn, quietly sought a reconciliation. On 15th April he found Napoleon in a quieter mood, saying that, although he had fallen out of the habit of receiving Mme Bertrand, he knew that she was an excellent woman.

But he was failing fast by then. In contrast to his corpulent body his limbs were beginning to get emaciated, and his face, which had for some time been of a curious yellowish, sallow and earthy colour, became noticeably thinner. He told the doctors that anything he ate came up instead of going down, but they assured him that this was all imagination. However he could eat nothing except a little jelly, lemonade and orgeat (a syrup made of almonds, sugar and orange-flower water). For some futile reason the doctors would not allow him any coffee, though he begged for some, pathetically but never angrily. The only thing which now made him testy, apart from poor willing Ali's clumsy ministrations, was the buzzing of swarms of flies.

What made night-duty so arduous was the need to change the patient's vest, and usually also his sheets, as often as seven times in one night, because of the drenching sweats which exhausted him.

Even before he began to get ill the observant young British officer, Lieutenant Basil Jackson, had commented on his unpleasant habit of spitting without regard to where it might fall. Now he coughed and spat a lot, 'and what he coughed up looked like coffee-grounds with a rather reddish tinge, like chocolate', as Ali wrote. Bertrand noted that towards the end, when he had barely the strength to spit, his vest was stained by a reddish spittle — *son gilet couvert de crachats rougeâtres qui n'ont pas la force d'aller plus loin.*

Upholders of the liver-abscess theory of his death consider that this chocolate-like matter might have been the detritus from a liver abscess which had perforated into the stomach — or into the lungs.

Towards the end Napoleon was often delirious, which probably accounts for the differing versions of his last words.

Bertrand, who wrote that on the night before his death Napoleon asked twice what was his son's name, and was twice answered — *Napoleon* by Marchand, gave his last words as '*à la tête de l'armée.*' In other versions the words are less coherent. Montholon thought that he twice made out words like — '*France — armée — tête d'armée — Joséphine.*'

Soon after muttering these words Napoleon, with a sudden convulsive movement, clasped Montholon and bore him to the floor where he held him so tightly that he could not even cry for help. Archambault, Bertrand and Antommarchi came in and they got Napoleon back into bed.

The end, when it came, was peaceful — three sighs at long intervals, and he stopped breathing a little before 6 p.m., on May 5th, 1821, just after the firing of the sunset gun.

# CHAPTER VIII

# Coroner's Inquest

On the question of what really caused Napoleon's death I propose to ask for a verdict of 'Not Proven', a convenient finding which is possible only under Scots law. A more accurate title for this chapter would therefore be Procurator Fiscal's Enquiry, but that could puzzle English readers who might not be aware that in our happy land North of the Border the procurator fiscal replaces the English coroner. Somehow our Scottish officials do not 'hit the headlines' as do their English counterparts who, from their uniquely privileged position, tend to pontificate about the pet bees in their bonnets, and to direct the harsh light of publicity upon private griefs which in Scotland can more often be curtained in kindly privacy.[1]

On the morning of the 6th May, 1821, the Governor went to Longwood House to pay his last respects to the great prisoner on whom he had not been able to set eyes for some four years. 'He was the greatest enemy of England and of myself also; but I forgive him', said Hudson Lowe. Smug and trite though the words sound, they were spoken with some emotion and respect. Sir Hudson then ordered that an autopsy should take place immediately, as if he could hardly wait to discover some convincing reason for the unexpected death of the man who, he had so confidently asserted, had really been in excellent health.

The French, although Lowe did not realise it, were equally determined to have the examination made, because the Emperor had wished it; but they seem to have been innocent of any thought of making political capital out of the findings whatever these might be. All they wanted was an end to their exile. However, they protested against the Governor's almost indecent haste, and secured a postponement until 2 p.m.

They wanted the examination to be made in secret, but Hudson Lowe would have none of that. He was determined to be more of a coroner than a procurator fiscal. He had never witnessed an autopsy and was uncertain about how he would react to the gruesome spectacle, so he arranged to be represented by his Deputy Adjutant General, Sir Thomas Reade, who was accompanied by two staff officers, Major Charles Harrison and Captain William Crokat, and seven British doctors, all of whom were well aware of the political implications of the procedure which they were about to witness.

The French were represented by Bertrand, Montholon, Marchand, St Denis and Pierron the butler. Thus the total number of people who crowded into the small billiard room,* fifteen by eighteen feet, poorly lit by two side windows, amounted to seventeen — ten British, five French and two Corsicans, the Abbé Vignali and Dr Antommarchi, who performed the post-mortem examination — not at all the scene envisaged by Napoleon, who had directed that Dr Arnott was to be the only British doctor permitted to see his body after death.

The billiard table on which the body was laid was adequate for its purpose, but in every other respect Antommarchi's task cannot have been easy. In the post-mortem rooms of Europe he had been accustomed to a good deal more elbow-room, a supply of running water and considerably better light. When the examination ended at 5.45 p.m. the light in that small green-painted room must have been most inadequate. The sunset gun had just been fired, and in that latitude darkness falls swiftly with only a brief twilight.

The official report was prepared by the principal medical officer, Dr Thomas Shortt, who had detailed Dr Walter Henry to 'minute down the appearances'. In 1823 Dr Henry used his notes made at the time to compile a detailed report at Sir Hudson Lowe's request, and he incorporated this report in his book *Trifles from my Portfolio*, published in Quebec in 1839. In a later book, *Events of a Military Life*, published in London in 1843, he described the findings in more general terms.

Dr Antommarchi wrote two reports, one on the 8th May, 1821, and a somewhat different one in his book, *Les Derniers Moments de Napoléon*, published in Paris in 1825. There are thus four reports, or five, if one includes, as does Dr Paul Hillemand, the copy of the official report which Sir Hudson Lowe, tenacious to the end, compelled the weak Dr Shortt to amend. With so much material I must try, like Dr Barry O'Meara, not to 'tire the reader with the detail of a medical journal'. Some details which might be

* Some accounts say it was the drawing-room. Marchand, in his *Mémoires*, wrote *le billard*.

thought to belong more appropriately to a text book of pathology must be included. Those who want fuller reports can refer to the sources which are listed in Note 2.

The most complete account of the external appearance of Napoleon's body is given by Dr Henry. Because of its bearing upon Napoleon's problems in the sexual sphere it is quoted in my first book.* In his memoirs Dr Henry, who had accepted the official version that cancer had caused Napoleon's death, commented that Napoleon remained mysterious and inscrutable to the end, in that,

> notwithstanding his great sufferings and the usual emaciating effects of the malady which destroyed him, the body was found enormously fat . . . Over the Sternum, or breast-bone, which is generally only thinly covered, there was a coat of fat an inch and a half thick and on the Abdomen two inches — whilst the Omentum, Kidneys and Heart were loaded with fat.

If the stoutest of readers will press a finger upon his or her breast-bone an immediate impression may be gained of the burden of fat which poor Napoleon had had to carry.

In the abdominal cavity, grossly overloaded with fat, two organs were the objects of special interest — the stomach and the liver, especially the latter, because the controversy about Napoleon's hepatitis, a source of conflict between the French and the English, had spread beyond the confines of St Helena and threatened to involve other countries. In 1817 Napoleon's mother had been told of the unhealthiness of St Helena. More recently Antommarchi, Bertrand and Montholon had all written to Napoleon's relatives in much more specific terms, and they knew that he was said to have hepatitis which could only get worse if he remained in the tropics.

The European sovereigns, meeting at the Allied Congress in Aix-la-Chapelle, had returned no answers to the dignified and moving appeals sent to each one of them by Napoleon's anguished mother. Presumably they accepted the British assurances that in St Helena the old enemy was not only safe but well cared for and in good health. Now it had become essential to our country's good faith that this opinion should be sustained. As we shall see, it would not be Hudson Lowe's fault if it was not. Above all else he had to make sure that there should be no suggestion that Napoleon's death could be attributed to any illness actually acquired in St Helena.

This was quickly and triumphantly achieved with the publi-

---

* *Napoleon: Bisexual Emperor.* Kimber 1972.

cation in May 1821 of the official report, followed in 1823 by Dr
Henry's report. No one could possibly be blamed for the death
from cancer of the stomach of a man with a familial predisposition
to that disease; or so it seemed in 1821, and for many years
thereafter. Today we might be a little less cocksure.

The official report stated:

> The stomach was found the seat of extensive disease, strong adhesions
> connected the whole superior surface, particularly about the pyloric
> extremity to the concave surface of the left lobe of the liver, and on
> separating these, an ulcer which penetrated the coats of the stomach
> was discovered one inch from the pylorus sufficient to allow the
> passage of the little finger. The internal surface of the stomach to
> nearly its whole extent was a mass of cancerous disease or scirrhous
> portions advancing to cancer, this was particularly noticed near the
> pylorus.

The diagnosis of cancer was, of course, based purely on what we
call macroscopic examination — that is to say, it was not confirmed by the study of portions of tissue prepared for examination
under a microscope. The opinion that certain portions were
'advancing to cancer' can only be called guess-work. The guess was
probably that of Dr Walter Henry, the note-taker, for in his own
report he wrote of 'scirrhous thickening fast advancing to cancer'.

Antommarchi, the trained pathologist who had performed the
examination, was less dogmatic; but he rather failed to present a
very clear picture, one way or the other. In his first report, written
in St Helena, he supported the view that there was an extensive
cancerous ulcer in the stomach, with an area of scirrhous
thickening. This was the only report which the French accepted at
the time, and from it they were able to derive some satisfaction
from the reflection that Napoleon's death had been unavoidable,
and that it was not hastened by the conditions of his captivity. It
is possible that Antommarchi, who had experienced Hudson
Lowe's malignity, agreed with the official view in order to save
himself trouble, if not actual harassment; for on his arrival in
Europe he began to tell a different tale. He let it be known that it
was the English doctors who had insisted on the diagnosis of
cancer. He stated openly that Napoleon had not, in fact, died of a
hereditary disease but from a condition acquired in St Helena,
which he described as 'gastro-hepatitis'.

Antommarchi refused to sign the official report and this has
been taken as an indication that he disagreed with some of its
findings. It has also been said that he refused to sign because it was

written in English, or because Bertrand ordered him not to sign because Napoleon was referred to in the report as General Bonaparte.

In 1932 a Belgian doctor, A de Mets, alleged that Antommarchi refused to sign the report because he did not want to associate himself with an attempt to clear Great Britain of blame for having exposed Napoleon to the rigours of a tropical climate. Dr Walter Henry was the first to state a similar view. He wrote that Antommarchi had been on the point of signing 'when he was called aside by Bertrand and Montholon'. Henry attributed Antommarchi's refusal to sign to his unwillingness to contradict the diagnosis of hepatitis.

Antommarchi himself later explained his refusal by saying: 'I had made the autopsy, it was for me to report upon it', which seems very reasonable.

It may have been Antommarchi's refusal to sign the report which led Dr Hillemand to assert that Antommarchi 'did not open the body'. He refers to him throughout his book as 'Antonmarchi'; and is the only writer to make this curious assertion. He does not tell us who else may have performed the postmortem examination if Antommarchi did not do so. By 1825 Antommarchi seems to have concurred with the almost universal acceptance of cancer as the cause of Napoleon's death, although his second report, written in that year, does not paint the picture of an instantly recognisable cancer so graphically as does the official report. He now wrote:

> The stomach appeared, at first sight, in a perfectly healthy state; . . . but, on examining that organ with care, I discovered on its anterior surface, near the small curve, and the breadth of three fingers from the pylorus, a slight obstruction, apparently of a scirrhous nature, of little extent, and exactly circumscribed. The stomach was perforated through and through in the centre of that small induration, the aperture of which was closed by the adhesion of that part to the left lobe of the liver.

Later in the report, after remarking that there was an extensive cancerous ulcer in the stomach, he recurred to the perforation, which, he wrote, formed 'a kind of canal, which, but for the adhesion of the liver, would have established a communication between the cavity of the stomach and that of the abdomen.'

When Antommarchi turned to the examination of the liver interest intensified, and necks were craned to see if O'Meara and Stokoe, and indeed Antommarchi himself, would be vindicated or confounded. Antommarchi took out the organ and heated arguments erupted about its condition. Dr Shortt considered that it was definitely enlarged; Arnott agreed that it was large but not unduly so for a man of Napoleon's bulk; others disagreed.

Sir Thomas Reade, the senior representative of the Governor, saw that he would have to take a hand, and he pressed Antommarchi to make a particularly careful examination. In his own report Reade wrote:

> Upon my appearing desirous to see it close he took his knife and cut it from one end to the other, observing to me 'It is good, perfectly sound and nothing extraordinary in it'. He observed at the same time that he thought it was a large liver.

Sir Thomas then contributed a shrewd observation, remarking: 'There is a wide difference between a large liver and a liver being enlarged.' Finally, after much debate, a sentence agreed to by all was adopted and the report read: 'The liver was perhaps a little larger than natural.'

The doctors could have spared themselves the trouble of arriving at this cautious verdict. Sir Hudson Lowe pounced upon the point and compelled the weak Dr Shortt to erase that sentence and to substitute: 'With the exception of the adhesions occasioned by the disease in the stomach no unhealthy appearance presented itself in the liver.' Really, one is almost compelled to admire that man's persistence and the cunning with which he could twist things to suit his book. The spineless principal medical officer tamely submitted, though he did keep the original copy, which he annotated in his own hand: ' "The words obliterated were suppressed by the orders of Sir Hudson Lowe," signed Thomas Shortt.' It was said that he never forgave the Governor for thus compelling him to sin against medical ethics.

So much for the size of the liver. What about its condition? Antommarchi held the liver in one hand and cut across it. According to Dr Henry's report, Antommarchi

> expected to see a flow of pus from the abscess which had been anticipated in its substance, but no abscess, no hardness, no enlargement, no inflammation was observed.

This satisfactorily robust statement of the British 'party line' was not supported by Antommarchi, who may have been the worst physician among those present but was certainly the most experienced pathologist; in fact he was the only one. In his report on May 8th, 1821, he confined himself to the brief statement that 'The liver was congested and larger than normal.' When he came to write his longer report four years later he may have felt it necessary to reconcile in some way the opinions expressed in his first report with his subsequent statements that he had yielded to pressure by the English doctors, and had suppressed his real opinion that Napoleon had acquired his fatal illness in St Helena.

Anyway, his second report went a good deal further in the direction of incriminating the liver, although there is some inconsistency between some of its sentences. Thus, he begins by saying that the liver was hardened, very large and distended with blood, but adds that 'the texture of the liver, which was of a brownish-red colour, did not, however, exhibit any remarkable alteration of structure.' In the next sentence but one he states:

> The liver, which was affected by chronic hepatitis, closely adhered by its convex surface to the diaphragm; the adhesion occupied the whole extent of that organ, and was very strong, cellular and of long existence. The concave surface of the left lobe adhered closely and strongly to the corresponding part of the stomach, particularly along the small curve of that organ, and to the epiploon. At every point of contact the lobe was sensibly thickened, swelled and hardened.

One thing about the liver upon which all the reports agreed was the presence of the adhesions, which are a sure sign of disease in the organ or in neighbouring tissues. In the official report these adhesions were attributed to disease in the stomach, but curiously enough this point is made only in the amendment to the report which was dictated by Hudson Lowe, who had not been present. We have already seen the lengths to which he could go in suppressing the opinions of his medical advisers, (and Dr Shortt certainly chose the right word when he wrote 'suppressed'); but presumably Lowe must have discussed his own contribution to the report with one or more of the doctors who had been present.

The firmness with which Lowe had had to intervene to quash any mention of liver disease is indicated in a letter which he sent to Lord Bathurst on the subject, in which he wrote:

> Dr Arnott has appeared to me to have conducted himself as a perfectly upright and honest man in not encouraging the desire evinced to ascribe the disease to the liver, and showed his judgment also in having an opinion to the contrary. Dr Shortt, however, thought the disease proceded from the liver, without having even seen the patient alive, but he feels a little ashamed, I believe, of the opinion he has expressed.

So there *had* been a desire to attribute Napoleon's death to liver trouble. Lowe did not of course remind Lord Bathurst that three doctors who *had* seen the patient alive had all 'thought the disease proceded from the liver'.

From the evidence of the Governor's secretary, Major Gideon Gorrequer, the most assiduous spy in St Helena, we learn that Hudson Lowe had had trouble, and a lot of trouble, not only with Dr Shortt but with other doctors, before he succeeded in twisting the post-mortem report to conform to his policy. Gorrequer always maliciously enjoyed reporting any difficulties encountered by the Governor, for whom he usually used the nickname 'Mach' in his diary. His entry for the 7th May, 1821, included this sentence:

> Mach worried Dr Shortt and Dr Arnott to make them alter the report of the dissection, and the whole of the doctors concerned, who after much noise and much rage on his part, did alter it.

From this one might fairly deduce that Lowe concocted his own bogus contribution to the official report after discussion with one or more of the doctors; probably with Dr Henry or Dr Rutledge, neither of whom had signed the report. Both of them adopted a somewhat contemptuous and hostile attitude to Antommarchi, especially Rutledge. According to Gorrequer, Lowe also badgered Shortt and Arnott into giving him letters to be attached to the report, indicating that Napoleon would not have lived so long had it not been for the adhesion of the liver to the stomach.

The somewhat pained tone of Lowe's letter to Lord Bathurst may have reflected the shock of finding that Dr Shortt had dared to state an opinion which he knew would displease the Governor. Hitherto he had seemed to realise that in St Helena 'a perfectly honest and upright man' was one who agreed with the Governor. Lowe, who had personally chosen his former associate Dr Baxter to be his principal medical officer, had resented Baxter's successor being chosen without his approval.

No doubt it would have been proper of Sir James McGrigor, the head of the Medical Department of the Army, to have consulted the Governor, but he had very good reasons for making the choice personally. He had complained that he received Dr Baxter's reports only through Hudson Lowe, and he had deliberately chosen a man who was unknown to the Governor, but well qualified for the post. Sir James must have suspected that Baxter had been under Lowe's thumb.

When at last the worm had turned and it was Baxter's turn for one of those stormy interviews in the Governor's office, one of the complaints which he made, in a spirited attack on Lowe, was 'that he had lost the protection of his chief' [Sir James] on account of his unwavering support of the Governor of St Helena. He particularly expressed his resentment about the part which he had been compelled to play in the preparation of the bulletins about Napoleon's health. Lowe had frequently refused to accept even Baxter's fabrications without many alterations. Now, in the final quarrel, Baxter indignantly alleged that 'his name had been slandered in consequence of the share he [Lowe] had made him take in the Bulletins'; and he hinted broadly that he thought Lowe was afraid that he might tell his story to His Majesty's Ministers.

Dr Shortt had begun well — even a little too well. On February 2nd 1821, in one of his verbose outpourings to Lord Bathurst, Lowe somewhat contemputously complained that Shortt had gone almost too far in expressing views which he knew would please — praising the remarkable healthiness of St Helena; roundly condemning O'Meara. Soon, however, Lowe began to suspect that Shortt was sending to Sir James McGrigor different opinions to those which he gave verbally to the Governor. Not man enough, it seemed, to have a mind of his own, he was the last man from whom Lowe expected such an insult as an honest professional opinion. But when Sir Thomas Reade submitted his report, Lowe learned that Shortt had held strongly, and for a time stubbornly, to his opinion that the liver was indeed enlarged.

Arnott, who at first agreed with Shortt, had capitulated, but, if he had stuck to his opinion, fifty percent of the signatories to the report would have been supporters of that unacceptable view. Only four of the seven British doctors signed; Thomas Shortt, Archibald Arnott, Charles Mitchell and Francis Burton. Henry and Rutledge were debarred from signing as they were only assistant surgeons, and Dr Thomas Livingstone had been sent out of the room by Dr Shortt before the examination was completed. The suspicious mind of Hudson Lowe fastened on to this point, and he easily persuaded himself that Shortt had been trying to reduce the opposition to his views about the liver.

Lowe was quite right about Thomas Shortt being ashamed of himself, but time would show that he was ashamed, not of having expressed an opinion which was unwelcome to the Governor, but of having weakly followed Arnott in capitulation. Of course they both had good cause to feel thoroughly ashamed of themselves. Both had disgraced, even if only briefly, the good name of British medicine and the honoured Edinburgh medical school.

The adhesions which bound the liver to the stomach below and to the diaphragm above are very important, and their existence was denied only by young Dr George Henry Rutledge, whose part in the proceedings is briefly described in Note 3. He later wrote a paper refuting the views expressed by Antommarchi in his book. In the book Antommarchi, who had referred to the adhesions briefly in his first report, went into greater detail as I have quoted on p. 171.

His opinion of the toughness of the adhesions was supported by Dr Henry, who wrote that the separation of the adhesions between the liver and the diaphragm was only done 'with very considerable difficulty'; and, in fact, Antommarchi had had to use a scalpel as well as his fingers.

Rutledge, however, claimed to have thrust in his own finger and easily separated the organ.

In a brief biography of Rutledge in Dr Arnold Chaplin's *St Helena Who's Who*, there is no mention of any special experience in pathology, and in fact Rutledge's paper, included in the Lowe Papers, does not indicate outstanding educational qualifications. One sentence reads: 'These trifling matters adds to the number of mistakes which Antommarchi's book are complete with'. Disliking pedantry, I usually refrain from that contemptuous little sniff — *sic* — by which authors demonstrate the superiority which they share with their readers, but it does seem abundantly justified here.

In Dr Henry's opinion:

> The small adhesion of the convex surface of the left lobe to the Diaphragm . . . appeared to have been a continuation and a consequence of the adjoining adhesion between the Liver and the Stomach.

Antommarchi, however, does not call it a small adhesion, but speaks of extensive adhesions which were strong cellular and long-standing. Since these were associated with chronic hepatitis it seems reasonable to associate them with some disease of the liver rather than of the stomach. They indicate the presence, at some time, of inflammation all round the liver (peri-hepatitis). Adhesions caused by cancer of the stomach would not have been 'of long existence', since that disease has a short course; unless the cancer developed in an old ulcer. But gastric ulcer could hardly have been the cause of the adhesions between the liver and the diaphragm.

The strong adhesion between the liver and the stomach near its outlet (the pylorus) was penetrated by that 'kind of canal' described by Antommarchi. Dr Shortt, in his letter of the 8th May, 1821, written at Lowe's special request, said:

> Had the edges of the ulcer which penetrated the coats of the stomach near the pylorus not firmly adhered to the liver death would have been sooner as part of the stomach contents would have escaped into the abdomen.

This point was elaborated as strengthening the British viewpoint, since the liver, far from being the cause of Napoleon's death, actually seemed to have postponed it by acting as a plug for the perforation. No one considered the possibility that this 'sort of tunnel' could have been an opening from the liver into the stomach. Naturally enough no one ventured to recall John Stokoe's prognosis. No one mentioned the fact, probably not realised at the time, that this is a most unusual site for a perforation of the stomach.

What happened after the post-mortem examination, about which there is the usual confusion and conflict of evidence, unfortunately did much to frustrate attempts in the future to evaluate the findings by the use of modern methods.

Napoleon had wished his heart to be removed and sent to his second wife, Marie Louise, who would have been much embarrassed by so awkward a memento, for she was living with her paramour Count Neipperg, to whom she had presented two children. The heart and stomach were placed in separate silver vessels in which they remained overnight. Bertrand and Montholon begged to be allowed to take the heart to France. Antommarchi wanted to take the stomach, and it was assumed that he hoped to use it as evidence that no treatment could have saved his patient's life.

The Governor however ordered that these organs must be buried with the body. He refused to allow embalming of the body, which, according to the evidence of Marchand, was therefore treated with some sort of *liqueur aromatisée*, said by some to have been *eau-de-Cologne.* Two Frenchmen who have not believed that Napoleon died of cancer have alleged that Lowe insisted on the stomach being buried with the body in case the cancer theory might later be disproved. They are Dr Hereau who wrote in 1829 and Surgeon General Abbatucci in 1938. Dr Hereau assumed that the dampness of the climate of St Helena and other factors would lead to the rapid decomposition of the body. He was proved wrong in 1840, when the body was exhumed and found to be in a remarkable state of preservation.

Those who have come to believe that Napoleon was killed by arsenical poisoning have suggested that it was arsenic which preserved the body. A more likely explanation is that its condition was due to the method of burial. The body was hermetically sealed in an inner casket of tin which was enclosed in three more coffins, two of mahogany and one of lead, and placed in a kind of stone sarcophagus inside a well-constructed vault with thick stone sides, excavated in the lava and black rock of the wind-swept Geranium Valley.* The sealing of the coffin was the duty of Armourer Sergeant Abraham Millington. Both Antommarchi and Rutledge claimed to have sealed the vessels containing the heart and stomach. (The point is unimportant, but Rutledge's version, along with a description of the grave by Lieutenant Duncan Darroch is given in Note 3.)

Although Lowe's conduct was enough to justify the suspicions of Hereau and Abbatucci it seems more likely that his refusal to allow the removal of the heart to France was due to his habitual tendency to say 'No' to any request, and perhaps a desire to hinder the establishment of any sort of shrine for the growing cult of Bonapartism.

He had Napoleon's body guarded during the night before it was placed in the coffin, after lying in state to be viewed by respectful crowds of British residents as well as the sorrowing French.

According to one account Sir Thomas Reade appointed Dr Rutledge to watch over the body; other accounts say that the responsibility was assigned to Dr Arnott. Probably the duty was shared by them and by other officers. Saint Denis wrote that Dr Arnott 'exercised the utmost vigilance in order that no part of the Emperor's body should be removed'; and that until the coffin was sealed down he and an orderly officer were always present. Marchand also wrote that Arnott was given the task of guarding and never leaving the body, especially the two vases containing the heart and stomach.

Arnott himself described his grisly night vigil to the famous Edinburgh professor, Sir James Young Simpson. He had gone to bed with pistols under his pillow, ready to repel a possible attempt by the French to get possession of the specimens, which he had put in a basin of water. Hearing a splash he jumped up but found 'it was only rats trying to get at the flesh' — easily the nastiest of all the stories of the Longwood rats, two of which had once

* Later re-named Valley of the Tomb.

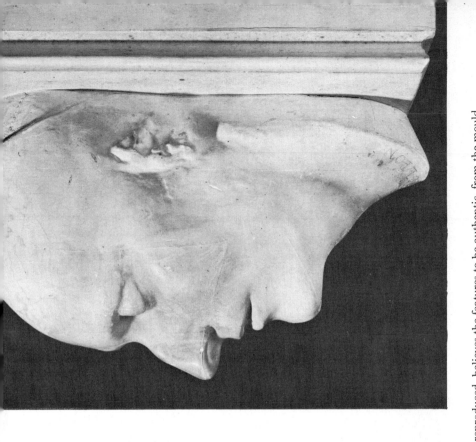

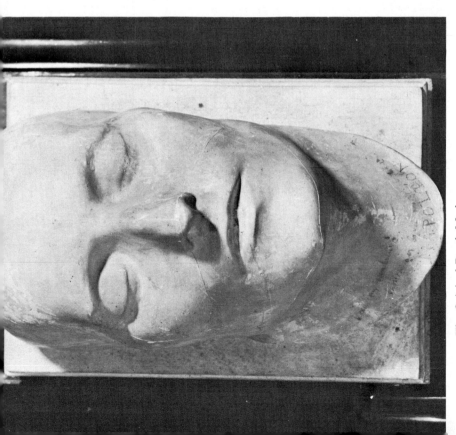

The Original Death Mask

Baron de Veauce, with whose permission these photographs are reproduced, believes the features to be authentic, from the mould taken by Dr. Burton soon after Napoleon's death. The rest of the head was modelled at a later date by Antommarchi. The emaciation of Napoleon's face during his last illness seems to have restored the sharp features of the young Corsican general of the late 18th century.

Napoleon's Lying-in-State at Longwood. The Madame Tussaud impression taken from the Antommarchi death mask.

jumped out of Napoleon's hat as he was putting it on.[4]

Despite the strict vigilance imposed by the suspicious Governor it is almost certain that Antommarchi contrived to take away from St Helena two small portions of Napoleon's body. Two small pieces of intestine, believed to have been given by Antommarchi to Dr O'Meara, were given by him to the great English surgeon, Sir Astley Cooper, who placed them in the Hunterian Museum of the Royal College of Surgeons in London, which he had founded.

The specimens disappeared when the building was damaged by bombing in the Second World War. They had long been an object of interest and photographs of them can be seen in several books and articles dealing with Napoleon's death.[5] Sir Astley Cooper, according to Lord Brock, considered that the specimens were cancerous tissue. Sir Arthur Keith, who when Conservator of the Royal College of Surgeons of England* made a detailed study of these specimens, was one of the authorities who accepted them as genuinely part of Napoleon's body.

Some, who did not believe this, held that it would have been virtually impossible for Antommarchi to have removed them under the watchful eyes of Sir Thomas Reade and nine other British observers. Perhaps these critics were visualising the conditions in a normal post-mortem room, with the pathologist more or less isolated from the spectators. In the small, overcrowded and poorly-lit billiard room at Longwood House very little sleight of hand would have been needed by Antommarchi to remove and secrete those small pieces of gut. This could hardly be said, however, about another kind of specimen which, according to the valet Saint Denis, was taken by Antommarchi at the request of the doctor-priest, Angelo Vignali. It seems that Vignali wanted a relic of some sort, possibly more on account of his interest in medicine than out of reverence for Napoleon, and Antommarchi removed two small pieces of rib. Even if these pieces were cartilage ('gristle') the effort required to detach them would have made concealment difficult. Possibly Ali was using a euphemism to veil a more intimate and reprehensible 'body snatch', which has been the subject of some speculation. Antommarchi cannot have foreseen the rich financial harvest which would one day be reaped by the possessors of this relic.[6]

His motives for removing even the piece of intestine are obscure. It was generally assumed that he thought the pieces were

* He is incorrectly referred to as President, by several authors.

M

cancerous tissue which would help to confirm the diagnosis of cancer. This assumption is completely at variance with everything which Antommarchi said or wrote. It is moreover inconsistent with his undeniable knowledge of anatomy, for when the specimens were microscopically examined some ninety years later they proved to be small patches of lymphoid tissue known as Peyer's patches, which are normally present in the intestine.

Detailed examination of these specimens was ultimately to give strong support to the opinion expressed by Antommarchi, when he wrote to the Chevalier Colonna: 'I declare to you, to all the Imperial Family and to the whole world that the disease under which the Emperor is labouring is an effect of the nature of the climate.'

Microscopic examination of the specimens showed evidence of chronic inflammation which, together with the clinical course of Napoleon's illness, led Sir Arthur Keith in 1913 to conclude that he had suffered from 'an endemic fever with symptoms of inflammation of the liver'. Although Sir Arthur accepted the likelihood that 'his father's disease, cancer of the stomach' had finally killed Napoleon, he pointed out that 'There is no kind of cancer of the stomach, nor of ulcer of the stomach, unless that ulcer is part of a general infection, that can give rise to such attacks of fever as Napoleon suffered from in the first three years of his illness.'

After discussing the case with Sir William Leishman, a noted authority on tropical diseases, Keith surmised that the endemic fever from which Napoleon clearly suffered was probably what was then called Malta Fever or Mediterranean Fever, which today we call Brucellosis. Sir William Leishman pointed out that goats had been imported to St Helena from Malta, for the sake of their milk, long before Napoleon's arrival there. This point, though interesting, is unimportant since Brucellosis is now known to have a wider geographical distribution than was then recognised. It is a condition which can mimic various other diseases, and even today, like amoebiasis, can pose a clinical puzzle.

Another suggestion to account for the feverish course of Napoleon's illness was that he might have suffered from 'paludism' or malaria. This theory, advanced by Sir Frederick Eves and by the Belgian doctor, de Mets, was dismissed by other writers on the grounds that there are no mosquitoes in St Helena. Special climatic conditions must exist for these insects to transmit malaria, and it seems that these do not exist in St Helena. But, whether there are malaria-carrying mosquitoes in St Helena or not, malaria is not a likely explanation for Napoleon's last illness; although it is said that he suffered from it in Corsica in early life.

Sir Arthur Keith, although he did accept cancer as probably the final cause of Napoleon's death, had made a small breach in the ramparts of the British official defences. Napoleon may have died from 'his father's disease', but he did suffer from some disease which he would not have acquired if his place of exile had been in England or America. This small breach would not be widened for a considerable time, and it might be said that it would never be widened by Englishmen, who with true-blue stubbornness have stood shoulder-to-shoulder in closing it, or preferably in ignoring suggestions that it might exist.

In 1961 the American author, Ralph Korngold, wrote:

> Modern pathologists consider it practically certain that Napoleon did not die of cancer.

If he had expressed that opinion in *The Lancet, The British Medical Journal*, or even in *The Sunday Times*, as I have done, he would have been denounced as a mentally unbalanced heretic, in tones of contemptuous indignation, not unmixed, or so it has seemed to me, with a trace of hysteria.

When Lord Moynihan, the President of the Royal College of Surgeons, showed the Napoleonic specimens in the Hunterian Museum to a French professor, René Leriche, in 1927, he did so, if we can believe Leriche, with a great show of secrecy. [See Note 5.] Leriche thought that they showed dysenteric perforations, and he wrote that Lord Moynihan then assured him that Napoleon had not died of cancer, but Great Britain had encouraged that belief in order not to be held responsible for his death. The renegade! But why the secrecy? Did even so eminent and respected a surgeon still feel bound to toe the old nineteenth century party-line? (A more likely explanation is that possession of the Napoleonic relic had led to some unpleasantness in the past, and it had been less prominently displayed and unlabelled. [See Note 5.])

It would obviously be overstating the case to suggest that it has been mainly national feelings which have influenced the firmness with which British doctors have rejected any challenge to the cancer theory; whilst the French have sought to prove that their hero's death was directly attributable to the conditions of his exile.

Nonetheless, from the outset many Frenchmen were inclined to suspect that this was so. Shaken by the premature death of the man for whose return to France many had lived and prayed with emotions comparable to those of Scottish Jacobites — 'Will ye no' come back again' — their first reaction was to suspect murder, probably by poison. After all O'Meara had assiduously prepared their minds for such suspicions, with his tales of the Governor's evil intentions.

The poisoning theory was revived in 1961, with the publication of a book, *Who Killed Napoleon?*, by a Swedish dental surgeon Dr Sten Forshufvud, which I would describe as a brilliant piece of detective fiction. Heavy concentrations of arsenic in hairs, known to have been taken from Napoleon's head at different times between 1816 and 1821, were demonstrated by modern scientific methods in Glasgow, by Dr Hamilton-Smith and Dr Lenihan. Drs Forshufvud, Wassen and Hamilton-Smith pointed out that many of the symptoms and signs of Napoleon's last illness, which many people have agreed were quite inconsistent with the diagnosis of gastric cancer, can much more plausibly be attributed to arsenical poisoning.

The finger of suspicion is pointed, not at some agent of the Governor, but at the man who had become Napoleon's most trusted companion, Count Tristan de Montholon, presumably acting as an agent in the pay of the Bourbons. According to Forshufvud, agents of the Bourbons had been administering to Napoleon small doses of arsenic for many years, dating from as far back as the Battle of Leipzig in 1813.

At that time Napoleon was still a hero to many Frenchmen but he was no longer the spoiled child of Victory. His insatiable ambition and many failures had drained France of blood and treasure, and no doubt many Frenchmen were prepared to remove him, as the German conspirators attempted to remove Hitler in 1944. But if Bourbon sympathisers had really been able to begin poisoning him in 1813 it is hard to believe that they would have waited until 1821 to complete the process, by adding arsenic to his medicines, which was a classic eighteenth century French method of poisoning when superimposed on previous small doses of arsenic.[7] With Napoleon securely held by the Allied Powers the Bourbons had no need to encompass his death, and it really does seem unlikely that Montholon would have resorted to poison, however ardently he may have longed for Napoleon's death, bringing his own exile to an end.

Those who have believed that arsenic is a likely cause of his

death have suggested several possible sources of accidental
arsenical poisoning. Arsenic in the soil, in the water, in medicines
— it was in common use as arsenious oxide for stomach
disorders — are some of the suggestions. The most popular is that
the green curtains round Napoleon's famous little camp-bed could
have been dyed with 'Paris Green' (copper aceto-arsenite) from
which, in the damp atmosphere, arsenious vapours were released
whilst Napoleon lay for several hours each day in the small space
enclosed by the green curtains.

It might be incautious, at this distance in time and without the
hope of scientific proof, to dismiss any possibility within the wide
range of medicine. It is, however, a scientific fact that the finding
of arsenic in the hair does not warrant a diagnosis of arsenical
intoxication, because arsenic is widely distributed in nature and
the arsenic in the hair may reach a kind of equilibrium,
independent of the amount of arsenic passing through the body.

To dismiss the suggestion of murder by poison is not to say that
no one was to blame for Napoleon's death at the comparatively
early age of fifty two, even indeed if one accepts the diagnosis of
cancer. This point must be considered later.

Many writers have dwelt with compassion upon the doomed
Emperor suffering, at Waterloo and even long before that, from
the agonising pain of the cancer which was to kill him years later.
Doctors know that the natural history of cancer of the stomach is
a matter of months rather than years, and some have therefore
speculated if it could have been upon a painful liver that the
famous hand thrust inside the waistcoat was pressing. Liver disease
could be one explanation of Napoleon's piles, for that condition
sometimes points to a disorder of the blood supply of the liver.
What might have caused this hypothetical liver trouble? Schistosomiasis was the guess of Professor Wardner Ayer, who mentions
Napoleon's enlarged and tender liver among the signs pointing to
that infection. (See p. 88) Alcoholic cirrhosis? Certainly not.
Napoleon was not a drinking man. Half a bottle of Chambertin
well diluted with water was his daily ration — nowhere near the
level of an alcoholic in any country. He hardly ever touched
brandy, whatever one might deduce from those famous and
seductive advertisements. We know from his valet that although
the Mameluke Roustam carried a silver flask of brandy Napoleon
hardly ever had recourse to it. Not one of the Emperor's
detractors could even hint that the great mind was ever bemused

by drink. Syphilis? Well, someone always has to make the insinuation, but I am convinced that in Napoleon's case the so-called evidence is manifestly insufficient to support the allegation. (See p. 89.)

Plainly, the possibility most deserving of serious consideration is that the liver was the seat of hepatic amoebiasis, probably with abscess formation. After all, three of the four doctors who examined Napoleon during his last illness diagnosed hepatitis. The only exception, Dr Arnott, thought that there was nothing wrong with the dying man. The conference of eminent Italian doctors who scrutinised the evidence in 1819 concluded that it could point only to hepatitis.

Baron Hippolyte Larrey, the son of Napoleon's most famous surgeon and himself an army surgeon, wrote in 1892 that Napoleon's real malady had been the chronic hepatitis which was endemic in St Helena. He considered that if there was an ulcer of the stomach it was secondary to the liver disease, and was not cancerous. Paul Triaire, the biographer of Dominique Larrey, declares strongly in favour of hepatitis, but, although he says that Larrey was deeply affected by Napoleon's death, it is not clear if he was one of those who blamed the conditions of the Emperor's captivity for his early death.

Somewhat surprisingly, the next doctor to come out boldly in support of this diagnosis was an Irishman, Dr J. Knott. In 1913, in a verbose article full of rather ponderous banter at the expense of Dr Arnold Chaplin, whose book about Napoleon's illness and death had just been published, Dr Knott stated his belief that Napoleon had died of hepatitis of long standing, which he designated 'St Helena Disease', underlining his statement that it was endemic in the island. Although by 1913 the *Entamoeba histolytica* had been identified and its association with dysentery and hepatitis recognised, Knott did not refer to that specific infection.[8] He believed that Antommarchi's opinions had been treated with too little consideration.

This view was expressed much more strongly and in greater detail in 1931 by Dr A. de Mets who in 1938 was co-author of a book with Dr S. Abbatucci.[9] Dr Tailhefer believed that de Mets was moved to defend Antommarchi because the Corsican doctor was an ancestor of his. A sponsor of the book, M. A.F. Vincentelli, President of the Chamber of Commerce of Antwerp, where the book was published, was also a descendant of Antommarchi.

Dr de Mets blamed Frédéric Masson for his scathing attitude

towards Antommarchi and proved that he had been quite wrong
to dismiss him as an ignorant 'barber-surgeon' of a type long out
of date. Unfortunately, he said, Antommarchi was too much a
'man of the laboratory' to get on with Napoleon. For Masson
Napoleon's dislike of Antommarchi would have been enough to
condemn him unheard. O'Meara and Stokoe are also commended
as men who knew all about the endemic hepatitis. Dr Abbatucci,
later to become *Médecin Général* of the French Colonial Army,
wrote that, in common with most people, he had always been
accustomed to think of Antommarchi as an ignorant inefficient
doctor, but, having discovered the extent of his experience and the
excellent training which he had received from the world-famous
Professor Paul Mascagni, he felt bound to accept him as a very
knowledgeable anatomist and pathologist. If this is so he was
certainly the only one in St Helena in May 1821.

Surgeon Lieutenant General Raoul Brice, a strong supporter of
the liver abscess theory, in his book *The Riddle of Napoleon*
(1935) wrote: 'The credit of giving the precise diagnosis rests with
Surgeon Colonel Abbatucci, of the Colonial Army'; but Abbatucci
himself wrote in 1934 that Dr Pullé, of the Medical Society of
Rome, had stated in 1932 that Napoleon died of an amoebic liver
abscess. Curiously enough Brice heads his chapter on the subject
'The St Helena Disease', the expression used by Dr Knott in 1913.

Generals Brice and Abbatucci had much experience of tropical
diseases; in Abbatucci's case chiefly in Morocco, where he treated
many cases of amoebiasis. They point out that amoebic dysentery
was endemic in the island and severely affected the British
garrison. Napoleon's whole household, including Dr O'Meara,
suffered from it from time to time, and the major domo, Cipriani,
died of it. I should point out that we are only entitled to say that
these people had dysentery. It could have been bacillary dysentery
which does not affect the liver. It is interesting to note that early
in the twentieth century a considerable outbreak of diarrhoea and
dysentery followed the arrival in St Helena of large numbers of
Boer prisoners of war. This was attributed at the time to scarcity
of food compelling the islanders to resort to tinned foods to which
they were unaccustomed. (*British Medical Journal*, vol. 2, p. 445,
1903.)

Careful consideration of the writings of Abbatucci and Brice has
convinced me that they have proved their case. They wrote in the
1930s. The increased knowledge about amoebiasis which has
accumulated in the '60s and '70s serves to strengthen their case. It

can be said with complete justice that accounts of Napoleon's illness from about the middle of 1817 fit with perfect accuracy the descriptions of amoebiasis, with involvement of the liver and abscess formation, given in leading textbooks of pathology, tropical medicine and general medicine (Sir John Conybeare's twelfth edition is a good example). It is all there — the remittent fever with drenching night sweats; the feeling of heaviness and discomfort below the ribs on the right side, with referred pain in the right shoulder; the palpable, tender liver.

Amoebiasis is very common in the United States and an American pathologist, Dr L. Schiff, devotes sixteen pages of his textbook, *Diseases of the Liver* (1963) to hepatic amoebiasis and amoebic hepatic abscess. Every one of the symptoms and signs which he mentions were present in Napoleon's case.

Two diagnostic points of importance in Napoleon's illness seem to have escaped the attention of previous medical writers. One, relatively minor but still significant, was the colour of his skin; the second, of great importance, was the nature of his pain.

A muddy, sallow-looking skin is typical of hepatic amoebiasis, in which true jaundice seldom occurs. Napoleon always had a rather striking olive complexion like old marble, which many people thought added to the classic distinction of his features. Legend, or perhaps myth, ascribes this to the fact that as an infant he lived for a time in a mountain village with his nurse, who fed him on olive oil when the supply of goats' milk ran out. In St Helena an increasingly unhealthy-looking earthy sallowness was remarked upon, not only by those who saw him there for the first time, but by people who had known him long before he went there.

Schiff's detailed description of the nature of the pain and tenderness, which he calls the earliest and most common manifestation of hepatic amoebiasis, exactly matches what Napoleon told his doctors, and what they found when they examined him. In particular Schiff describes the pain as 'ranging from a dull aching discomfort to a sharp stabbing pain'. It will be remembered that Napoleon at first complained of dull discomfort making him want 'to lean or press his side against something'. Later he suffered from sharp stabbing pains like a knife or razor going into him. Now, such pain is not at all characteristic of cancer of the stomach, of which it has been said: 'Pain as an early symptom is unfortunately absent in about one half of the cases of cancer of the stomach' (Boyd). The pain, when present, is described as 'dull and distressing but not acute' (Price).

The referred pain in the right shoulder is very suggestive of liver trouble. Dr J.J. Groen and Dr R. Turner, an English pathologist who contributes a section about Napoleon's illness to M. Gilbert Martineau's book *Napoleon's St Helena*, suggest that this referred pain might have been caused by adhesions between a callous ulcer of the stomach and the liver (Groen) or between the liver and the diaphragm (Turner).

Several experts have stressed that an illness of some four and a half years with a cessation of symptoms of from eight to ten months is most unlike the course of a case of gastric cancer; and also that signs of infection are not normal in the final stages. In Brice's opinion this 'period of remission' is particularly typical of liver abscess. In justice to 'The Opposition' it should be said that the end of that period of remission, in about September 1820, could perhaps have been the start of an entirely new illness. A gastric cancer beginning then and ending fatally some eight months later would represent a not uncommon course in that dreadful illness; though we are still left with the absence of wasting and the doubts suggested to many doctors by the bouts of fever.

Then we have that curious 'red spittle' like reddish chocolate, which for Abbatucci and Brice is highly suggestive of the detritus (it is not correctly called 'pus') from a liver abscess, which they believe had ruptured into the stomach. Later, if we accept their theory, it was to perforate the stomach and cause generalised peritonitis and death. Bertrand's words were *crachats rougeâtres*, and it is possible that the lung may have been the source, for the rupture of a liver abscess into the lung, with 'anchovy sauce sputum', is rather more common than rupture into the stomach. The tough chronic adhesions between the liver and the diaphragm, above which lies the lung, could point to that route for discharge of the abscess, rather than through the tunnel described by Antommarchi between the liver and the stomach. Dr Turner considers that the reddish spittle could have been an agonal discharge of fluid from the congested lungs, at the very end, and of little significance in determining the cause of death. The accounts of Bertrand and Saint Denis do not seem to support this view. Surgeon General Abbatucci believes that the abscess ruptured on the 21st March, 1821, when Napoleon brought up some such substance. This was the day on which the alarmed Antommarchi wrote his last letter warning the Imperial family of

Napoleon's impending death. I have invoked the toxaemia of whatever condition may have been killing Napoleon to explain his strange mental state towards the end; the delusions about Mme Bertrand; the unsavoury allegations against former friends; the savage outbursts about Antommarchi and even about the faithful Bertrand. Another possible explanation is that all this was a manifestation of the so-called Hepatic Encephalopathy, resulting from grave liver damage, in which may occur euphoria, drowsiness, mental confusion and, an expression particularly applicable to Napoleon, 'defects of behaviour'. (See *British Medical Journal*, 4 viii 73, page 279.) This condition, however, is associated with destruction of liver tissue much more extensive than was found in Napoleon's liver.

In the chain of evidence which sustains the theory of Abbatucci and Brice a missing link is Antommarchi's failure to find an abscess in the liver at the postmortem examination. It is undeniably a most important link to be missing. Schiff states that there are no anatomical changes in the liver which can confirm a diagnosis of hepatic amoebiasis, which can only be done with certainty by finding an actual abscess. Whilst this explains the absence of gross changes in the substance of Napoleon's liver, it need not entirely rule out the possibility of an abscess. There may, in such cases, be a single large abscess or more than one small abscess. It is reasonable to suppose that an abscess large enough to rupture into the stomach or lung should have been discernible, though it could have collapsed after the discharge of its contents, and thus be easily missed. Abbatucci holds that there was probably a small abscess which had emptied itself fifty days before the autopsy, and so was not seen. It will be remembered that Walter Henry wrote that Antommarchi failed to find an abscess, though he had expected to do so. How thorough was his search? It seems that Antommarchi made only one cut into the substance of the liver and had to be urged even to do that. Only Henry wrote of Antommarchi's 'first incision', implying that he made others. A hint of cynicism or sarcasm is discernible in that part of Henry's report, and it may well be that when Antommarchi came to examine the liver he felt a little over-awed, even hampered by the tension and slight hostility with which the ten British observers awaited his opinion about the liver.

As I have said, the theory of Abbatucci and Brice can be supported by recent advances in our knowledge about the complex and varied clinical pictures which amoebiasis can present.

I have found that some recent critics of the theory, such as Ganière, Hillemand and Turner, appear to have paid little attention to the enlarged knowledge which is available, and do not seem to be fully conversant with modern trends of thought about this perplexing and deceptive disease.

Much ink has been wasted in discussions about whether Napoleon ever had dysentery and whether amoebic dysentery really did occur in St Helena, imported it is suggested by Chinese labourers. Dr Turner asserts that amoebiasis was not endemic in St Helena, though imported cases did occur. It is now known that it occurs all over the world.

The question of whether Napoleon had dysentery or not is in fact completely irrelevant. Dysentery is the exception rather than the rule in amoebiasis. The invading organism wants to live undisturbed in the body of its host — man. An attack of dysentery represents the outbreak of hostilities — man's attempt to expel the invader. Schiff reminds us that a liver abscess may develop in a patient who has never had dysentery; an important fact which he thinks is not sufficiently understood. This point is clearly expressed in the following quotation from the *British Medical Journal*:

> Infection by *Entamoeba histolytica* usually produces no symptoms. Less commonly it causes diarrhoea, sometimes recurrent, and least commonly it produces dysentery. The majority of patients with proved amoebic liver abscess give no recent history of bowel upset and often no such history at all; when the abscess is diagnosed *E. histolytica* is infrequently found in the stools. (p. 178, 17 vii 71)

That one paragraph stultifies pages of criticism of the theory that Napoleon could have suffered from amoebiasis.

Dr Ganière conceded that there is much evidence to support a diagnosis of amoebiasis, but thinks that Napoleon probably had an 'episode' of dysentery with hepatitis, which ended in spontaneous cure. Spontaneous cure of a liver abscess may indeed occur with the rupture of the abscess into the stomach or intestine; but that would not necessarily cure the underlying amoebiasis. Here we may remember, with considerable admiration I think, that rupture of the abscess into the intestines, with hope of spontaneous cure, was the first possibility mentioned by John Stokoe, in reply to Napoleon's direct question.

Dr Ganière's opinion about the specimens in the Hunterian Museum is a curious one. He thinks that Great Britain would not have preserved these specimens if they supported the politically unacceptable diagnosis of dysentery. But the specimens were at first thought to be cancerous tissue. Surely by 1913 the fires of political controversy had died down; and we are not, I hope, invited to suppose that two men of the standing of Sir Arthur Keith and Lord Moynihan would have allowed their professional opinions to be swayed by thoughts of 'My Country — Right or Wrong'.

It has been said that 'You choose your disease when you choose your doctor'; and it may well be that doctors who have examined the evidence have tended to interpret it according to their own chosen theories. The theory of amoebiasis was at first exclusively ventilated in countries other than Britain, and in books and articles not likely to have been widely read here. Curiously enough, in 'A Literary Letter' in *The Sphere* of 1st February, 1913, the editor, C.K. Shorter, stated that Napoleon did not die of cancer but of a liver complaint endemic in St Helena; and he disclosed the political motives which had led to the truth being suppressed. This bold statement seems to have attracted as little attention as did Dr Knott's article a little later in the same year. The translation into English of General Raoul Brice's book, in 1937, introduced the theory to a wider public; and it has been discussed in one or two books recently.

In the most recent medical biography of Napoleon, which contains many curious errors,[10] Dr Paul Hillemand accuses Antommarchi of having gone to St Helena with his mind made up in favour of hepatitis, and having fitted all that he subsequently found into that preconceived idea, based upon what Hillemand calls 'O'Meara's mistaken diagnosis'. There is certainly some truth in the accusation as applied to Antommarchi, though the same could not be said of Stokoe. But it seems to me that Dr Hillemand has himself fallen into the kind of error which he condemns in Antommarchi, by his own interpretation of what he regards as 'evidence' supporting his belief that Napoleon had a gastric ulcer for many years, despite Napoleon's own repeated and strenuous denials that he had ever suffered from any kind of stomach trouble. Hillemand does not appear to deploy any specialised knowledge of tropical diseases to justify his assertion that O'Meara was mistaken.

An acknowledged authority on tropical diseases, Sir Philip Manson-Bahr, observing that amoebiasis 'may simulate many other diseases, including cancer', reports a case in which an amoebic ulcer was actually taken for cancer. Amoebiasis can itself cause a kind of tumour called an amoeboma, most commonly seen in the large intestine. Sir Philip quotes Dr J.H. Walters, an experienced consultant in tropical diseases: 'Amoebic liver abscess continues to provide the greatest pitfall in clinical tropical medicine' (1970). Dr R.G. Hendrickse, of the School of Tropical Medicine in Liverpool, recently wrote that amoebiasis, which has a global distribution, is 'one of the most perplexing entities in clinical practice'; and he commented upon the extremely varied forms which the disease can take in different populations.

Surely we should feel considerable admiration for the efforts of O'Meara, Stokoe, and Antommarchi to get to grips with a problem which can puzzle the modern clinician armed with so many aids to diagnosis which they lacked. They had, of course, never heard of *Entamoeba histolytica*, but each in his own way was groping towards the truth about a case which might have defeated many a doctor today. O'Meara clearly recognised the connection between the dysentery and the liver troubles which were prevalent in the island. If Napoleon really did have hepatic amoebiasis then the prognosis which Stokoe gave him was brilliant; whilst Antommarchi's expression for the endemic disease, from which he felt sure Napoleon was suffering, showed his flair for pathology — he called it 'gastro-hepatitis'.

Despite my declared intention to follow the example of Barry O'Meara and not to 'tire the reader with the detail of a medical journal', I have found it necessary to include rather a lot of text-book material and professional argument (not, I hope, too indigestible for non-medical readers) in order to justify asking for a verdict of 'Not Proven' on the question of what really killed Napoleon. One essential piece of evidence is lacking. Hudson Lowe ensured that the alleged cancer could never be histologically examined; and he did so, in the opinion of some Frenchmen, deliberately. The verdict, as is so often the case, must depend upon circumstantial evidence. Of course the supporters of the cancer theory can always claim that they need not rely on circumstantial evidence but upon the demonstration of an advanced cancer at the post-mortem examination. But should this be an inquest in which no one cross-examines the doctors giving expert evidence?

Dr Shortt could easily have been broken down. He would probably have confessed at once his sin of allowing the Governor to alter his report. This reprehensible deed is seldom mentioned. One recent commentator, a Fellow of the Royal Society of Canada, Charles Mitchell, who believes that the hepatitis was invented by the French who hoodwinked O'Meara into supporting them, wrote that the alteration of the report was done 'no doubt for a political motive'. No doubt! But what would a modern jury make of that wickedness in high places? No one has cross-examined that delightful 'hunting-shooting-and-fishing' Irishman, Walter Henry, a splendid raconteur with a gift for writing, not matched, as is often the case, by an ability to spell.[11] Hardly anyone has shared Henry's surprise that the body of a man dying of so notoriously wasting a disease should have been upholstered in inches of subcutaneous fat (which usually disappears entirely in the late stages of cancer) with an apron of fat — the omentum — inside the abdomen in which the organs were cushioned in further layers of fat.

Worse still, in the days of histology and the microscope, no one has asked how Henry, Shortt and the rest, looking at specimens in Antommarchi's hands without actually handling them, could pontificate, probably in all sincerity, about 'scirrhous portions advancing to cancer', and so on. How did they know? They didn't because they couldn't. Such considerations, apart from the suppression of facts which displeased the Governor, and without calling the only expert witness, Dr Antommarchi, to explain his doubts, should be enough to make us very cautious indeed in accepting the statements in the official report which during the past hundred and fifty years have been repeated in countless books and articles in many languages, and have, not surprisingly, become ineradicably fixed in men's minds and accepted un-questioningly. It has not been unknown for erroneous statements to have been transferred from one history book to another; and the same thing has occurred in medical text books. (I recall a case in point in which an oft-repeated error was exposed in the first edition of Bailey and Love's *Short Practice of Surgery*.)

Some of the lone voices which have sounded out against the parrot chorus about Napoleon's cancer deserve to be mentioned. The first, and he was very early on the scene, was the Frenchman, Dr J. Hereau who, in a book published in 1829 with a dedication to the King of Rome dated 1827, bluntly stated that Napoleon did not die of cancer but of chronic gastritis aggravated by the climate and the vexations to which he was subjected. We should remember that the term 'gastric ulcer' had not yet been invented. Unwilling

to accuse the British Government of deliberately causing
Napoleon's death, Dr Hereau said that it was enough to send him
to St Helena; the climate, the doctors and the Governor did the
rest.

Baron Hippolyte Larrey in 1892 was the next to throw doubt
on the cancer theory. In 1895 an American, Dr E. Andrews, saw
no alternative to accepting it, but observed that the terms in which
the condition of the stomach was described were ' . . . obscure . . .
the facts badly observed and badly reported.' In terms of 1895,
and even more in terms of 1974, this criticism is certainly
justified; but we should be wary of judging those doctors in St
Helena by the standards of a hundred and more years later. In
1901 Dr Marcel Baudouin diagnosed gastric ulcer, aggravated by
nervous influences. In 1912 and 1913 the first British rejections of
the cancer theory were heard in a long-winded note by G.L. de St
M Watson, editor of the journal of Captain Piontkowski; in C.K.
Shorter's blunt statement quoted on p. 188 of this book; and in the
mocking voice of Dr Knott from Ireland. Dr A. de Mets in 1931
wrote that his own disbelief in the cancer theory was shared by
two doctors who had for many years made detailed studies of
Napoleon's case, Dr Hartmann and Dr Erasmus Paoli. Dr de Mets
was not even convinced that Napoleon's father had died of cancer
and said that the report about it was very vague.

After Abbatucci had declared strongly for amoebiasis a Polish
doctor, V. Binger, in 1934 offered the diagnosis of intestinal
granulomatosis (Hodgkin's Disease). Raoul Brice meanwhile had
exposed what he called 'The Myth of Cancer', and in 1936 Dr Paul
David wrote from Lille in support of Abbatucci's views.

In 1952, in a book published in Oklahoma, Dr P.M. Dale
roundly declared 'Certainly the Emperor did not die of cancer of
the stomach as is commonly asserted'. He voted for a perforated
peptic ulcer, and so did Dr Guy Godlewski in 1957. It has been
suggested that such a perforation might have led to the formation
of a subphrenic abscess (below the diaphragm) which could
perhaps account for the adhesions above the liver. Godlewski
considered that the ultimate perforation of the ulcer was due to
undernourishment in an exhausted and mentally depressed
subject. He quoted Dr Marcel Dunan as holding this view.

Napoleon was unquestionably depressed and often exhausted in
his long battle of nerves with Hudson Lowe; but if he was
undernourished it was no fault of the Governor. The tables at
Longwood House, on both sides of 'the green baize door', were

generously supplied, much more so than those of most of the inhabitants of St Helena. All his life Napoleon treated his stomach badly, but mainly by the irregularity of his meals and the speed at which he ate them. He was no gourmet but we know from Bertrand and others that during his last months he often asked for special delicacies, roast chicken and other meats, which he ate with a good appetite almost to the end.

On 13th December, 1816, Baron Stürmer, the Austrian Commissioner, mentioned in one of his reports that Napoleon had an extremely good appetite and was growing fatter; and in 1817 his good appetite was commented on by Clarke Abel, who accompanied Lord Amherst on his visit to Longwood when returning from his embassy in China. Abel wrote that Napoleon seemed to be in excellent health and putting on weight, although 'At the time he was at the point of dying, as he has been ever since of an incipient hepatites (sic)'. This was published in *The Quarterly Review* for 1819, (page 90) and, as that magazine was strongly pro-Government, we may suspect a touch of cynicism at Bonaparte's expense; but it is also evidence that it was already known in Government circles that there was anxiety in St Helena about the prisoner's health, and that the anxiety arose from that controversial diagnosis of hepatitis. A local resident who saw Napoleon a few months before his death described him as being 'as fat and round as a china pig', and sketches made of him before he took to his bed confirm this description.

Writers who have mentioned the features of Napoleon's illness which did not conform to the picture of a case of cancer have naturally mentioned the absence of wasting, but have not drawn attention to his good appetite. This is in fact a strong argument against cancer of the stomach, for a marked lack of appetite, and sometimes particularly a distaste for meat, is an early characteristic of that disease.

In the 1960s the allegation that Napoleon's death was due not to cancer but to arsenical poisoning was a favourite subject for debate in the national newspapers as well as in medical journals, to which Dr D.C. Wallace contributed an opinion from Australia that the arsenic was probably administered as medicine.

It can be seen that, until the suggestion was made that Napoleon might have been poisoned, and by a Frenchman at that, virtually no British voice was raised to challenge the British diagnosis of cancer. Apart from Lord Moynihan's cautious, even secretive, admission to Professor Leriche in 1927 and Dr Knott's

somewhat light-hearted contribution, British medicine has resolutely supported the decision which absolved our country from
blame for the great man's death.

In a foreword to Abbatucci's book Professor Tanon, Professor
of Medicine in the University of Paris, stated that the diagnosis of
cancer, which conveniently cleared England of the suspicion of
having allowed the distinguished prisoner to die from the effects
of the murderous climate, 'had never satisfied anyone'. This is a
somewhat surprising claim in view of the chorus of agreement with
that diagnosis which had been, and still is, heard all over the
world. Professor Tanon's sweeping assertion found no echo until
1961, with the statement, already quoted, by the American
author, Ralph Korngold that 'modern pathologists consider it
practically certain that Napoleon did not die of cancer'.

Soon after that, however, two modern pathologists, after full
discussion of the case for amoebiasis, came down on the side of
cancer — Turner in 1968 and Hillemand in 1970. But of course
they could base their views only upon the 'obscure . . . badly
observed, badly reported' opinions of men who could do no better
than use the knowledge and methods of the nineteenth century in
attempting to interpret pathological appearances which we now
know cannot possibly be evaluated without the use of a
microscope.

Without a microscope those eight doctors in Longwood House
could do no more than surmise that Napoleon had had cancer. The
hundreds of doctors who have discussed the case in the subsequent
century and a half have been able to base their opinions, however
wisely and confidently expressed, only on surmises about the
surmises of those eight doctors. I can do no more than support the
few who have dissented from the views of the majority and have
proposed what I consider to be a more convincing alternative.
That alternative certainly cannot now be proved, any more than
the diagnosis of cancer can be proved; but, in calling for a verdict
of 'Not Proven', I am not required to prove a valid alternative, but
only to create reasonable doubts in the minds of the jury. The
only evidence on which pathologists might possibly have based
unchallengeable opinions was sealed up in Napoleon's coffin. I
have briefly examined the possible motives of the shifty witness
on whose orders this was done.

I have also questioned the only competent expert witness, Dr
Antommarchi, who quite probably has been maligned when his
evident disagreement with the British doctors has been set aside as

N

the worthless opinion of a stupid opinionated young man, possibly paid by Napoleon to advance views which the Governor considered tendentious. He was, on the contrary, a trained, experienced pathologist, and the only one there. If he did come to St Helena expecting to find that Napoleon had hepatitis that expectation was solidly founded upon lengthy discussions with many leading medical men of the day about the reports of the only two doctors who had examined Napoleon. He had also discussed the case in great detail with one of these doctors, Barry O'Meara.

It is accordingly with considerable confidence that I would invite a jury to consider whether succeeding generations of doctors have perhaps accepted too readily the official report on the examination of that grossly obese body, carried out in an overcrowded, badly lighted room without proper facilities for washing the specimens, and above all without our modern knowledge of cancer which would caution us against accepting such a diagnosis without microscopical examination.

Have British doctors for too long huddled round Hudson Lowe's spineless medical advisers, like rugger players when a man loses his shorts? Perhaps a peep at the vulnerable areas of their case is overdue.

We must now consider the question which might have been asked at my hypothetical inquest by lawyers representing the Bonaparte family. Was anyone responsible for Napoleon's death? If amoebiasis was the real cause of his death then it must follow that the decision to send him to St Helena was indeed, as he himself had vowed, his death warrant. Though he could have been infected before going to St Helena there is absolutely nothing to suggest that he was.

But is it conceivable that His Majesty's Government sent him there in order to encompass his death, as some have alleged? I think not. St Helena was chosen as a secure place of exile. Admittedly Lord Liverpool hoped that in that isolated spot in the Atlantic Ocean Napoleon would soon be forgotten; but I cannot believe that he also hoped that he would soon die. No one had then heard of the amoeba which would tear at the liver of this Prometheus chained to his rock. The study of statistics concerning the healthiness of Britain's growing possessions was not a normal function of any department of the Government. Lord Liverpool and his colleagues possibly put some trust in Wellington's opinion that St Helena was really a very pleasant place. But surely, as time passed, reports of the high incidence of dysentery and hepatitis in the inflated garrison, who were dying in noticeable numbers, must have begun to reach London and ought to have been noted.

The early diagnosis of amoebiasis is important today because we have specific treatment by which it can be cured and the development of such complications as liver abscess prevented. In Napoleon's day all this was still not possible, and, once amoebiasis had taken a hold, cure was unlikely, though it is possible that its relentless progress might have been arrested if the repeated pleas of his family for his removal to a temperate climate had not been brushed aside. Of course if his illness was a gastric ulcer, or even a localised cancer (and no secondary growths or enlarged glands were seen at the autopsy) then modern surgery might have benefited him. But operations to remove part or all of the stomach lay far in the future.

Even if Napoleon's illness was incurable by methods available in his day, this does not entirely absolve Britain from blame. If a doctor cannot cure it is still his duty to alleviate, support and comfort; and I certainly cannot include under this heading the futile, almost ritualistic, irritations, the blisterings and purges inflicted upon the dying man by Dr Arnott, admitting, as he did, that he had to think of his own reputation. Even if he felt that he must leave nothing undone his conduct deserves censure under the humane dictum — 'Thou shalt not kill, but need'st not strive officiously to keep alive.' (From A.H. Clough's poem, *The Latest Decalogue*).

Napoleon was a difficult patient and must share some of the blame, on account of his obstinate refusal to see any British doctor, if he could not have O'Meara or Stokoe. Young Dr James Verling might have helped, though if he had tried to do so he could well have suffered for it, as they did.

No blame can be sufficiently severe for the official refusal to pay any attention to the opinions and recommendations of the doctors who had examined Napoleon; to say nothing of the disgraceful treatment of the doctors themselves, for expressing opinions unwelcome to the Governor. Here of course was the real nigger in the woodpile.

The unrelenting hostility of Napoleon to Hudson Lowe stultified any steps which the Government might have taken to alleviate his condition. Lord Bathurst wrote to ask Hudson Lowe to assure Napoleon that the King and his Ministers were not indifferent to his declining health and earnestly wished him to have all the medical help he needed. This was not just a belated gesture. The Government had made provision for such requirements in their regulations for Napoleon's incarceration. But the ridiculous situation in which these two had become inextricably entangled in their *folie à deux* made any help offered through the Governor completely unacceptable.

The comfortable assumption that Napoleon's death from cancer of the stomach, 'his father's disease', absolved Britain from all blame for his death can no longer be accepted without reservations.

Professor Sir Stanley Davidson, writing about the cause of cancer (its aetiology) says this: 'Nothing is known of its aetiology, though there is a striking hereditary influence'. Professor R.A. Willis, commenting upon the predisposition of the Bonapartes to cancer of the stomach, mentions the early death from that disease of Napoleon's father and his sister Caroline; whilst his sisters Elisa and Pauline 'almost certainly' and his brother Lucien 'probably' also died of it.

It is thus easy to see why upholders of the cancer theory have agreed with Dr Thomas Shortt, who said at the time that Napoleon would have died when he did 'on the throne of France as well as in St Helena'. Today we know that our knowledge of the causes of cancer must be incomplete, and that in every case more than one factor is probably at work. Dr Flanders Dunbar of Columbia University writes: 'There seems to be an X factor which is partly physiological and partly psychological'. We cannot be sure that men like the sixteenth century doctor and philosopher Jean Fernel (Joannes Fernelius) were barking up the wrong tree in asserting that a state of melancholy could produce bodily changes, even up to the ultimate disaster of cancer.

Clearly it would be too bold to assert nowadays that there could have been nothing in Napoleon's environment in St Helena, his diet, the many stresses and frustrations of his lonely life and wretched situation, which might not have been present in a climate and country to which he was accustomed, and which could have contributed to the start, or influenced the course, of his illness — even if it was cancer. And of course if it was cancer developing in an old ulcer, or simply a chronic gastric ulcer which perforated, then no one could doubt that the emotional stress of his last sad years must have contributed heavily to the origin and progress of his illness. Everyone knows about the influence of psychological or emotional factors in causing peptic ulcers. Terms such as 'business-man's ulcer' are commonplace.

It is beginning to look as if there are only two theories which can free our country from a major share in the blame for Napoleon's death. These are the belief of Dr Forshufvud that he was poisoned by the French themselves; and Professor Ayer's theory that all his illnesses can be traced to schistosomiasis acquired during his Egyptian campaign.

Even if Napoleon all his life was 'an ulcer personality', as Dr Ganière points out; even if it takes two to make a quarrel and Napoleon contributed far more than his share to the strife with the Governor, his worst enemies must surely feel deep sympathy for him and wish that the wonderful story could have been given a happy ending.

I have been unable to refrain from severe criticism of the professional conduct of a fellow Edinburgh man, Dr Archibald Arnott, though I have said that he was a kindly well-educated doctor. The balance can now be slightly redressed. Arnott was ahead of his time in the use of a clinical thermometer and perhaps also in his perception of the possibility of some psychosomatic influence in the case. He told Hudson Lowe that he could not anticipate a happy result of his treatment because 'the patient could not be given the one thing he most desires, liberty'. In his book, shining through his obstinate preoccupation with intemperance as the cause of illness, including cancer, there is that startlingly modern shaft of light — 'Might not the depressing passions of the mind act as an exciting cause?'

The perceptive younger doctor, O'Meara, commended by Maitland for his tenderness, had seen the same light. He had written to Bertrand, after leaving St Helena, about his apprehensions over Napoleon's health:

> . . . two years of inactivity, a murderous climate, mean and ill-ventilated apartments, outrageous treatment, lonely and forsaken, with all that can destroy the spirit acting in concert to aggravate his illness, and to make one fear the worst.

Arnott's medical treatment offended against one of the clauses in the Litany of a great physician, Sir Robert Hutchison; 'From making the cure of the disease more grievous than its endurance; Good Lord Deliver Us'. But much may be forgiven him if his kindly and certainly impressive personality earned him the trust and even the affection of his lonely patient, as the Arnott family have believed, and as that snuff-box, on which the dying man scratched the letter 'N', attested. It has never been hinted that Arnott expected, let alone asked for, any reward for his attendance on Napoleon, or that he hoped eventually to profit from it, as it has been alleged O'Meara, and even Stokoe, did. It is a reassuring reflection, if we are entitled to indulge in it as I hope we may be, that at this lowest ebb of his fortunes Napoleon received some disinterested service and even friendship from a Scottish professional gentleman. That kind of personal service and friendship had not often come his way and no man ever needed it more than he did in St Helena. The most abiding impression of Napoleon's exile is his terrible loneliness, starved of all true affection. This at least can never be laid wholly at Britain's door. Not one of the great men of Napoleonic France chose to share the fallen Emperor's exile in Elba or St Helena; and, what is more regrettable, neither did any of the leading doctors of France.

No man ever had more devoted servants but, although they gave him loyal service, they could hardly give him friendship. Between them and the officers of the Household hovered the mysterious Pole, Captain Piontkowski, who had given up his rank and served as a private in Napoleon's small army in Elba. On board *Bellerophon* he was a perfect nuisance, pestering everyone to get permission to go to St Helena as a domestic servant, repeatedly shouting 'I renounce my rank'. Eventually he was allowed to follow the exiles to St Helena, where he was disliked and distrusted by them all. Napoleon thought that he was probably a spy and did not regret his departure after little more than a year.

Some of the officers of the Household would themselves have been in peril in France during the White Terror. There had been no question of allowing the two loyal and dashing generals, Savary and Lallemand, to stay with Napoleon. To the British they were little more than gangsters; Savary not much better than Heinrich Himmler in 1945.

With the possible exception of General Henri Gratien Bertrand, the members of Napoleon's last little court were nonentities whose names are known to history only because they shared his captivity — The Faithful Few, though 'long-suffering' might be a more appropriate adjective. It was inconceivable that they could become his real friends. To them he was still the Emperor, the autocratic, self-centred man who had said such things as 'Friendship is only a name; I love nobody: I am not made for love. The heart-felt emotions, so-called, have no share in my organisation: I only care for people who are useful to me — and for so long as they are useful.' Was it too late for such a man, in Napoleon's terrible situation in St Helena, to find a true friend? Probably it was. Bertrand summed it all up when he said to Gourgaud: 'The Emperor is what he is. We cannot change his character. It is because of that character that he has no friends, that he has many enemies and indeed that we are in St Helena. It is also the reason why neither Drouot, nor those who were with him in Elba, or anyone else, apart from ourselves, would follow him here.'

Wearied by the bickering of the members of his court and their jockeying for position in the favour of their capricious master, Napoleon turned more and more to that lively conversationalist Dr Barry O'Meara. But he was a British officer and Napoleon found it impossible to trust him implicitly.

Frédéric Masson may have been unfair in his denunciations of Antommarchi, but his opinion that most of the troubles of the captivity arose from the fact that there was no French doctor in Longwood House was probably an eminently sound one. Fortunately here again our country cannot possibly be blamed. Every effort was made to persuade Dr Maingault not to abandon Napoleon, but if that seasick, unadventurous and obviously selfish young man had gone to St Helena he might have been unable to stand up to the Governor and his venal medical advisers. Baron Corvisart, a physician of international repute, no doubt belonged to a wider stage than Longwood House but, if he had gone himself instead of selecting Maingault, he could have rendered a very great service to Napoleon, to his country and indeed to ours. He understood Napoleon perfectly and knew well how to deal with him in his various moods. So indeed did Baron Yvan, who had left Napoleon after his first abdication. Yvan's son, Alexandre Napoleon Yvan, said that his father had regretted for the rest of his life having abandoned the great man who had been like a father to him; and had wished that he had died with Napoleon in a foreign land.

I doubt whether Baron Larrey, mentioned in Napoleon's will as the most virtuous man he had ever known, was much troubled by similar regrets. He was a Gascon, traditionally a boastful people, and his habit of lauding his own undoubted surgical skill when actually soliciting for decorations, honours and promotions, together with his too frequent querulous references to the inadequacy of the financial rewards given to him by generals whose lives he had saved, combine to make him less than a wholly admirable figure to an army medical man. I suspect that the virtuous Larrey might have been as bored and almost as tiresome in Longwood House as Gourgaud.

All the Bonapartes were proscribed and banished from France. Napoleon's mother, living with her half-brother Cardinal Fesch in Rome, had said that she would give her last farthing to the Emperor. Her letter to the Allied Powers begging to be allowed to join her son was not answered. Just as well perhaps, for there would have been little room for her in Longwood; but she would certainly have kept them all on their toes. Napoleon himself said that his mother had the head of a man on the body of a woman. She refused to be unduly impressed by the fantastic success of her second son; remarking drily: *'Pourvu qu'il dure* — If only it lasts'.

Claude Manceron judged that 'You could put the whole history of their relationship under a microscope and still not find a trace of tenderness'. Perhaps so; but the formidable matriarch of this extraordinary family had one golden rule — the child she loved the most was the one who at the time was suffering most. There is no doubt which of Mme Mère's children needed her most in 1819, when Napoleon had served four years of his sentence and his terminal illness was just beginning. This then is the happy ending which I wish our country could have arranged for the saga of Napoleon. He had been out of the current of European affairs for four years; the old energy had waned; and if he had been allowed to live in the Rinuccini Palace in Rome, which his mother had bought in 1818, he could hardly have been a serious threat to the peace of the world. I doubt if his mother could have refrained from occasionally murmuring the nanny's age-old saying: 'I always said it would end in tears'; but such passing irritations could have been soothed by Pauline's generous brother-worship.

Any such happy ending was not to be. The reality is not pleasant to contemplate. Napoleon was dying without the comforting presence of anyone who truly loved him for himself. The remnants of his drab little court stayed out of duty and self-interest. Some of the domestic staff — The Service — come best out of it, with their devoted attendance on the dying man. They had all grown up during the Napoleonic era and oculd hardly conceive an existence without the Emperor to be served.

The loneliness and sadness in which 'the incomparable meteor had ended its course upon the earth' leads me to just one last theory about the cause of his death — and a pretty strange one it may seem.

M. Gilbert Martineau, the French consul in St Helena and a
leading authority on Napoleon's life there, commenting, in a letter
to *The Times* on 11th December, 1962, on the suggestion that
Napoleon was poisoned, wrote that in fact he died of boredom.
This apparently bizarre theory was first suggested in 1823 by
Count de Las Cases, one of Napoleon's companions during the
first year of his exile. Much the same thought is expressed by
another authority on Napoleon, Dr Felix Markham, who writes:
'discussion of the physical cause of Napoleon's death is academic,
the real cause was despair and frustration.'

What can a doctor say about such interesting theories? A
coroner might raise his eyebrows over a death certificate in which
the cause of death was given as 'Boredom', or in Arnott's words,
'the depressing passions of the mind'. Although we have moved on
a lot since Arnott's day we have perhaps not moved on quite as far
as that. But the day may come. For several years doctors have
been writing about the so-called 'Gold watch Syndrome', resulting
from the boredom of retirement; though it is not normally
regarded as a fatal condition.

However, in a report of the abstruse discussion of a difficult
case, published in *The British Medical Journal* of 15th June, 1968,
the patient's family doctor was quoted as having summarised the
psychosomatic influences which had affected his patient's life. He
ended by saying: 'I feel that he died because all that he lived for
had somehow come to nothing,' an exact description of
Napoleon's last days on earth. Even in Elba, before making his last
fling, Napoleon, with his usual genius for hitting the nail on the
head, had said: 'On a small island once one has set the mechanism
going, nothing is left but to die of boredom — or in some heroic
venture to escape from it.'

It would be a hard enemy indeed who could fail to be a little
shaken by the terrible pathos of Napoleon's quiet rebuke of the
intolerable General Gaspard Gourgaud, who had been bleating
away as usual about the dreadful boredom of life in Longwood
House:

'Do you think that I have no bad moments when I lie awake at night and
think what I was — and what I am now.'

Epilogue

# When Did He Really Die?

Three leading characters in the Napoleonic story were believed at the time to have, as it were, survived their official or apparent deaths. These were the Tsar, Marshal Ney and the Emperor himself.

People have often been surprisingly unwilling to believe reports of the death of those who have been greatly admired, loved or hated. Martin Bormann, Hitler's 'Brown Eminence', who was never actually seen to have killed himself or been hanged, like his fellow war-criminals, is thought by many to be still alive and available for vengeance. The occasional arrests and interrogations of false Bormanns have parallelled the efforts after 1858 to get hold of Dhondu Pant, the infamous Nana Sahib, who was generally believed to have been responsible for the treacherous massacre of British troops at Cawnpore on 26th June, 1857 and the subsequent butchering of their wives and children a day before the arrival of General Havelock's force. The Nana had been allowed to take refuge in Nepal by the ruler Jang Bahadur, who had been a strong supporter of the British and had sent his Gurkha troops to help in suppressing the mutiny, which they did with a ferocity which was, alas, displayed by both sides in that time of tragic misunderstanding. Jang Bahadur informed the British Resident in Katmandu in 1859 that the Nana was dead, but for almost forty years false Nanas were frequently captured and questioned, until in 1894 the Viceroy ruled that such attempts could only stir up old passions which everyone wanted to allay.

Similar stories were widely believed in 1945 about Subhas Chandra Bose, the revolutionary chief of the Indian National Army, recruited from prisoners of war in Japanese hands. Although he certainly died after an air crash on 18th August, 1945, he was thought by many to be wandering around the hills and villages of India, a fugitive from justice long after the mild punishments awarded to his followers had been ended by their country's achievement of the independence from British rule for which they had campaigned, no doubt with sincerity but by methods unacceptable to the nations fighting against the Axis Powers.

Among those whose deaths were doubted for kindlier reasons have been the Prince Imperial, Sir Hector MacDonald, Lord Kitchener and Lawrence of Arabia.

The Prince Imperial, Napoleon Louis,* son of Napoleon III and hope of the Bonapartists, was killed on 1st June, 1879, at the age of twenty-three, whilst serving in the British Army during the Zulu war. The circumstances of his death shocked the French and shamed the British. He was with a patrol which was surprised by an overwhelming force of Zulus and, as he was struggling to mount his horse, ominously named Fate, a holster-strap broke and the scared horse bolted, leaving the young prince to die alone, 'fighting like a lion' as his assailants later related. Soon it was being said that not only Fate had been scared into bolting. Captain Carey, commanding the patrol, was accused of having galloped off without a backward glance, crying 'Sauve qui peut', according to French reproaches. He was cashiered by sentence of a court martial which was later set aside by the Duke of Cambridge, the Commander-in-Chief. The Empress Eugénie, the prince's mother, had appealed to Queen Victoria for clemency for Carey; and there had been some popular clamour on his behalf, because it was suspected that he had been sacrificed to divert attention from the failures of much more senior officers. Lord Chelmsford's campaign had certainly brought no glory to British arms, and this was the last straw. On the other hand there were murmurs exculpating all British officers from blame. The headstrong prince had been expressly forbidden to leave Headquarters, but had disobediently joined the patrol, in ardent quest for glory, like a true Bonaparte. The unhappy Carey, though restored to his rank, was shunned in the Army for the remaining four years of his life.

Grief in France over the loss of a fine young Frenchman was soon eroded by sinister rumours. The body, stripped and mutilated, had been difficult to identify with certainty; though the superstitious Zulus had not removed a chain of medallions round the neck, fearing that they might have magic properties. The British, it was said, had wanted to get rid of the Prince

* Napoleon Eugène Louis Bonaparte, usually called Louis; signed himself 'Louis Napoleon'.

Imperial and had virtually, if not actually, murdered him; or perhaps he was not dead at all but kept hidden for some sinister reason. No one seemed able to suggest any motive for such perfidy or trickery, whichever it was. But you know *Perfide Albion*, always up to something in the furtherance of Imperial infiltration.

Major-General Sir Hector Macdonald (1853-1903) was the son of a Highland crofter who enlisted in the Gordon Highlanders and won his commission in the field, after the future Lord Roberts had offered him the alternative of being awarded the Victoria Cross. Soon after taking up an appointment as a major general in Ceylon he was recalled to London to be told that charges of a disgraceful nature had been made against him. Lord Kitchener, who was himself addicted to the kind of conduct alleged against Sir Hector, sent him back to face the music but he committed suicide in Paris rather than be tried by court martial. His widow brought his body back for burial in the Dean Cemetery in Edinburgh. In the Highlands, and especially in his home town of Dingwall, no one would believe that their beloved 'Fighting Mac' could have killed himself, let alone done anything dishonourable. It was obviously a fabrication, probably by English generals, jealous of the fame and fighting qualities of the lowly-born Scottish soldier.

Indeed it was not only in the Highlands that it was whispered that Kitchener of Khartoum had brought about the downfall of the popular soldier, who was widely regarded as the true hero of the Battle of Omdurman, which had set Kitchener himself on the path to fame. The rumours rapidly proliferated. Sir Hector, it was believed, had chosen to disappear rather than have his private life investigated. He was still in France; and first reappeared, as General Kouropatkin, fighting for Russia against the Japanese. Next, at the Battle of the Somme, the French general commanding a neighbouring division was recognised by many Scottish soldiers as being really Hector Macdonald. But, in the hardiest of all the legends, he is to be found fighting not alongside but against the Army which had betrayed him, as the Prussian general Von Mackensen. John Montgomery, in his biography of Sir Hector Macdonald, discusses these extraordinary rumours and devotes an appendix to the von Mackensen story.[1]

When the truth is sad or even sordid it cannot compete with a truly inspired romantic lie of this description. Upholders of the most popular of the 'Fighting Mac' legends, easily able to overlook the grave in Edinburgh, are unlikely to inspect the register of births in Haus Leipnitz, Saxony, where on 6th December, 1849, some four years before the birth of Hector Macdonald, August von Mackensen was born. It was the start of a long and distinguished life, during which his military career brought him just once fairly close to the Scottish hero.

When he visited Palestine in 1898, as an aide-de-camp to the Kaiser, Hector Macdonald was also in the Middle East, fighting in the Sudan where, as a colonel, he commanded a brigade of Egyptian and Sudanese infantry at the battle of Omdurman. Von Mackensen's picturesque appearance in his Hussar uniform with the Death's Head of his first regiment grinning from his towering busby, captured the imagination of the British; but it was a surprise to see the nonagenarian Field Marshal, like a ghost of more respectable days, among the German generals supporting Hitler at many rallies of the Nazi Party.

If he had really been Macdonald he might, towards the end of his life, have encountered some of the soldiers of his old regiment.

As 15 (Scottish) Division advanced through Westphalia and Hanover we were vaguely aware of the presence of a number of elderly generals and members of the old nobility of Germany, several being in residence near the Steinhüder Meer. One at least qualified for favoured treatment, being the mother-in-law of the present Queen of the Netherlands. Field Marshal August von Mackensen was one of the old soldiers who watched the sands of Nazi militarism running out before the advancing tide of Allied power. General Sir Miles Dempsey sent Colonel Sir John Carew-Pole and Major Tim Lewis, Royal Scots Greys, who told me the story, to look for the old Field Marshal. They found him in a farmhouse near the old Hanoverian town of Celle, and he was soon explaining to them how he would have opposed our advance, leaving them in no doubt that he felt sure that he would have made a much better job of it than the Nazi generals. Although at the time we were all forbidden to 'fraternise' with enemy nationals the two British officers were proud to give their smartest salutes to the old Prussian who died just six months after the war ended, one month short of his ninety-sixth birthday.

Lord Kitchener was never seen again after H.M.S. *Hampshire*, taking him on a mission to Russia, blew up off Marwick Head in the Orkney islands, on June 5th, 1916. Although the explosion was assumed to be due to striking a mine, one of those known to have been laid by the German submarine *U.75*, commanded by Lieutenant Commander Kurt Beitzin, this has never satisfied everyone.

About four years after the loss of *Hampshire* I was on holiday in Pomona, the attractively named main island of Orkney, and found the islands still buzzing with the strangest rumours about Kitchener's fate. It had all been a plot by the Government to get rid of the obstinate field marshal, never an easy colleague for soldiers or civilians, and now past his best but unwilling to retire. So 'They' had blown up *Hampshire* – it had not been a mine at all. In case the Orcadians got wind of the evil scheme they had all been forcibly detained in their homes by 'the polis and the military', who thus prevented them from saving the lives of many poor sailors, who had dragged themselves up on the rocky shore, only to perish from exposure, victims of official secrecy.

Another popular theory maintained that what 'They' were concealing was the fact that Kitchener was really alive. One of the few survivors had seen him standing in the gunroom flat immediately after the explosion. Because news of his mission to Russia had leaked out, *Hampshire* was blown up so that he could slip off to Russia by another route. The Russians were holding him as a prisoner. Other stories alleged that he had been betrayed to the Germans and was now their prisoner; or he had been spirited away to a cave on some remote island in the Hebrides, whence he would one day return. All rubbish according to yet another school of thought – Kitchener was indubitably dead, but 'They' did not want the world to know this, hence the secrecy. This story was supported by one trump card of 'evidence'. Some weeks after the loss of *Hampshire* a noticeably tall corpse had been washed ashore and before it was removed some observant islanders had noticed that it lay rigidly 'at attention' – who else could it be but 'K of K', a soldier to the last.

The absurd fantasies multiplied readily in those days, when all around could still be seen the wrecks of the Kaiser's Grand Fleet which had been scuttled, and sank to the reverberations of rifle fire, whilst a terrified excursion of school children, circling the sinking fleet, thought that the war had started all over again. No wonder that Orcadians young and old were full of exciting stories; but Kitchener's survival was believed in by many many others, including his sister.

Belief in the survival of Lawrence of Arabia was kept alive in other countries, rather than in his homeland where people may have been puzzled by the strange devices by which he seemed to back into the limelight but sadly accepted the evidence of his fatal crash in a motor cycle accident. To suspicious foreigners, confident in their belief that his enlistments in the Army and the Royal Air Force were blinds drawn over secret service activities, his death seemed clearly to have been faked by the British; and long after his death they could suspect his clandestine finger in any Middle Eastern imbroglio.

In each one of these cases, except that of Kitchener, a body was buried; but a detail like that seldom deters the legend-makers, who, in the case of Highlanders mourning the death of 'Fighting Mac' could blandly ignore the indisputable existence of the genuine August von Mackensen, an apparently insuperable obstacle.

There is no such insuperable obstacle to belief in the legend about Alexander of Russia, indeed there is a surprising amount of evidence to suggest that the Tsar chose to disappear and live the life of a hermit, or rather a penitent, in some remote monastery in Palestine or Siberia. The astounding and macabre story is examined in great detail by Maurice Paléologue in his book *The Enigmatic Czar.*

In my first book I described the remarkable friendship, with strange homosexual overtones, which began at the dramatic and important meeting between Alexander I and Napoleon, alone on a raft anchored in the river Niemen at Tilsit, on 24th June, 1807. At the time of what can almost be called his love affair with Napoleon, from 1807 to 1809, Alexander was tall, handsome, with blue eyes and curly golden hair — much too pretty for a man. In fact he was rather effeminate. By the time of his visit to England after Waterloo he had become 'a little over-ripe' and one young girl described him as '*horridly* Pink and Pudding-like'. Lady Shelley called him a 'mincing dancing Dandy'. Wellington was her ideal man and she can hardly have approved of a message which the Tsar asked her to give to the Duke: '*Dites-lui que je l'aime comme ma mâitresse.*' But this was no doubt part of Alexander's 'insatiable desire to please' which worked its spell on a great many women and on men also. His soldiers, from their rather distant viewpoint, adored him. In his dealings with them, for all his genuine kind-heartedness, he could be a savage disciplinarian even by the standards of those harsh times. Alexander's personal magnetism, as is often the case with this indefinable quality, owed something to play-acting, for at heart he was timorous and unsure of his ability to achieve his great desire, to be loved for himself and not because he was a monarch.

Neurotic, impulsive, swinging erratically from charming gaiety to profound melancholy, he was recognisably a case of mental instability, not altogether surprising in a son of that vicious monster Paul I. Napoleon found him highly intelligent but admitted that 'there was a piece missing'. 'He had no roots', was how one of Alexander's mistresses put it. Increasing deafness may have contributed a little to his 'depressive melancholy complicated by gloomy mystical obsessions' (Paléologue). Another factor was a feeling of guilt over his part in his father's murder, although it was a passive part.

Such a man was a natural magnet for the kind of bogus mystic always on the lookout for followers, or dupes, preferably rich and influential ones. The best known of these in Alexander's life was the absurd Livonian, Baroness de Kruedener, *née* Barbe Julie de Wietenhoff, who was about fifty when she hooked him.[2] She liked to be regarded as an 'evangelical prophetess' and may or may not have believed that she 'bore within her heart the living Word of the Redeemer'. She certainly devoted her life to meddling in international politics with the aim of relieving suffering humanity; but her vaguely mystical, even if noble, nature made her erratic, unpredictable and, in the opinion of most statesmen, dangerous. Both the noble and the mystical sides of her nature appealed to Alexander; and the impressionable, imaginative emperor, who was himself forever elaborating similar vague humanitarian schemes, became her willing disciple. It was whilst he was under her influence that he became the moving spirit in the idealistic but woolly Holy Alliance.

Another and possibly more significant attachment was to a strange fanatical young monk called Photius, whose sinister influence seems to have foreshadowed the fatal fascination of Rasputin.

Alexander's officially accepted death occurred far from his capital, in Taganrog, a port giving access to the Black Sea via the Sea of Azov. It was a strange and, in many ways, most unsuitable choice for a seriously ill Tsar; and M. Paléologue believes that it might have been deliberately chosen in order that Alexander could be taken away in the yacht of an English lord, to end his days in a monastery in Palestine.[3] Alexander had spoken of being 'crushed beneath the terrible burden of a crown'; and had repeatedly declared his intention of laying it down by abdication.

The reason for the Tsar's decision to disappear, which is usually given by upholders of the legend, is not so much his increasingly disturbed mental state as a growing determination to devote the rest of his life to the expiation of the abominable crime of having participated in the murder of his father. Whilst Paul was being brutally done to death Alexander was on the floor below, pretending to be asleep and deaf to the yelling of his father.

Support for this theory is provided by the fact that of three people who would have had to connive in the faking of Alexander's death, two had been conspirators deeply implicated in the murder of Tsar Paul. These were Prince Volkonsky, who was one of the assassins, and James Wylie, Alexander's doctor, who had supported the official version that Paul had died of apoplexy, and had patched up the body for the lying in state, stitching wounds and using cosmetic arts to disguise the bruises on the face. The third person whose connivance was indispensable was the Tsarina, who, it was said, had been begged by her husband to help him in his design for 'saving his soul by devoting the end of his life to strict penances'. She remained in strict seclusion until she died of a heart-attack some five and a half years after her husband's death or disappearance.

Alexander's survival was widely believed in, even by members of the Imperial family, who knew that he had often spoken of abdication in favour of his brother Nicholas. No priest saw Alexander between 27th November, 1825, when he took communion, and his death four days later, which was an exceptional omission of the necessary observances at the death of a Tsar. Various inconsistencies in the report of the postmortem examination led to the belief that the body was not that of the Tsar, but was a soldier's corpse provided by a Dr Alexandrovitch.

The body lay in state for several days, during which many people alleged that the face did not resemble the Tsar. Two French doctors who had recently seen him agreed with this, and stated that decomposition was so far advanced that death must have taken place earlier than the date given as that of the Tsar's death. It is not pleasant to think what the condition of the face must have been more than three months later when the Dowager Empress viewed the body at Tsarkoe Selo near the end of the long journey to St Petersburg. However Marie Feodorovna had received some unrevealed confidence from Prince Volkonsky and she was moved to declare that the body was indeed that of her dear son. When the body reached Moscow on its journey from Taganrog troops had to be used to clear the Kremlin because the people wanted to see that it was indeed their beloved Tsar. The imperial tomb was subsequently opened twice, by Alexander II and by

Alexander III, and on each occasion was found to be empty.

Thirty nine years after Alexander's death or disappearance an old Siberian hermit or staretz (pilgrim of God) called Feodor Kusmitch, died near Tomsk. He used to speak of the campaign of 1812 and other events in Alexander's life, and at least one old soldier had identified him as the Tsar. Many Russians, perhaps preferring the legend of a death in Siberia to one in Palestine, have since believed that Alexander I died in February 1864 under the name of Feodor Kusmitch.[4]

Michel Ney, one of the most attractive and, in some ways, the most interesting of Napoleon's marshals, although a very different kind of man, shared one disability with Alexander — a tendency to mental instability. A superb leader, brave in battle, known throughout the army as 'The Bravest of the Brave', he also displayed high qualities of moral courage and endurance, which enabled him to become the unquestioned hero of the Retreat from Moscow. During those days of mounting horror Ney outshone them all. The Emperor, King Joachim Murat, princes, marshals and generals all came to rely on this one man; and he was never the same man after that exhausting experience.

'Exhausting' may be a mild word for what Ney endured but it is deliberately chosen, for I consider that after that campaign of 1812 Ney was progressively affected by what we now call 'Battle Exhaustion' — 'Shell Shock' of the First World War. A convincing case can be made for that diagnosis, but this is not the place in which to develop it.

Napoleon liked to say that Ney was mad, but I suspect that, with his knowledge of the human heart, he knew very well what had made this brave soldier unpredictable, undecided, yes even timid. Napoleon told Metternich in 1813 that he had no generals left, for the terrible cold of Russia had demoralised them all. 'Like a madman' is an expression which crops up repeatedly in contemporary accounts of Ney's conduct during The Hundred Days. He had always been a little excitable and difficult, but now he was unbalanced.

Inspiring though his leadership could still be during the desperate last moments of the Imperial Army at Waterloo, it was tinged with the clearest indications that he was seeking death in battle. Passing General Drouet d'Erlon he shouted, 'Hold on! If we are not killed here, you and I will be hanged by the émigrés'. Displaying every sign of madness — but who is not just a little mad in battle? — Ney had cried to his troops, 'Come and see how a marshal of France should die!' Knowing what lay ahead we can surely wish that the exciting career of that incomparable leader could have reached its fitting end there, on the field of Waterloo, in his tattered uniform, hatless, his powder-blackened face crowned by the glowing chestnut hair which had earned him his nickname *Le Rougeaud*, battering on British guns with his broken sword. But the soldier's death was denied to him and his high fever of excitement at Waterloo was succeeded by depression and apathy.

To most Royalists Ney was inevitably the supreme traitor, the man who had promised Louis XVIII to bring the Usurper to him in an iron cage, only to desert the King and rejoin the old master, who had made him the Prince of the Moskva. But much later, when it was too late, the embittered vengeful Duchess of Angoulême, daughter of the murdered Louis XVI, broke down and wept when they told her what Ney had done for France and just what he meant to Frenchmen.

Ney has meant a lot to the British too, so much indeed that many have found, and still do find, it impossible to forgive our own hero Wellington for failing to save the life of the French hero. The most recent expression of this deep feeling is that of my friend Major General Alastair MacLennan, a keen and strong-willed student of history. Reviewing Lady Longford's book *Wellington, Pillar of State*, he wrote:

> Wellington still appears a very cold fish to me. . . . I do not find it in my heart to forgive him for not lifting a finger on Ney's behalf. True he gives his reasons but they are so feeble as merely to indicate a sense of guilt and had far better been left unsaid.

I must refrain from offering here my own analysis of Wellington's character, beyond saying that I earnestly believe that he had, as Sir John Fortescue believed ' . . . actually an emotional nature which he kept, owing to early training, under so stern control as to forbid it any vent except upon very rare occasions.'

'Duty' was his watchword throughout his long life, which was governed to an exceptional degree by his fairly simple conception of what, in any circumstances, his proper duty ought to be. In 1815 it was his duty to refrain from interfering in matters of internal French politics, and he was always a stickler for the proprieties. Wellington shared the almost universal dislike of Louis, and he later gave it as his opinion that France would have done better to have kept Napoleon. He was ready to advise the

king on political matters, but Ney's case was something quite
different. The showing of mercy or withholding it was Louis' royal
prerogative. It was important that Wellington should not make the
king seem to be the puppet of the commander of the occupying
troops. He treated enemy generals courteously, but after Waterloo
he refused to see Generals Mouton and Cambronne because he
'thought they had behaved so very ill to the King of France'.

Surely some such thought must have been behind his much
criticised refusal to intervene and save Ney from the firing-squad,
despite moving appeals from Ney's wife, Aglae. Wellington may
have found these hard to resist but he had to do so, and the
eminent historian Sir Charles Petrie finds it 'difficult to blame
him'. Sir Charles adds that Ney's 'treachery had been of a
particularly heinous kind, for at the very moment that he set out
from Paris with the avowed intent of bringing Napoleon back in an
iron cage he was in secret league with Napoleon.' I doubt if this is
strictly fair for I believe that the underlying cause of Ney's
treachery in triplicate was the mental imbalance and confusion
which kept him swithering uncertainly almost to the last moment.

Keenly though we might wish that the story could have been
given a sentimental novelist's ending, with a magnanimous King
Louis, counselled by the Great Duke, restoring Ney to his wife and
family, it seems very likely from all we know of Ney's fiery
character that he would have hated to owe his life to the
intervention of an enemy general.

Ney was probably the last man whom the great majority of
Frenchmen wished to see fall victim to the vengeance of the
Bourbons. Louis himself ardently hoped that Ney would escape
and leave the country; but Ney chose to await his fate in apathetic
inertia. Could he possibly have known that, certain though his
conviction must be, France would never go through with his
execution? There is a legend that Ney's execution was faked. The
Royalists, according to this story, tried to make their revenge
sweeter by picking the firing squad from among Ney's old soldiers;
just the men who would want to spare him if they could. When he
made his flamboyant gesture, eyes unbandaged, giving the order to
the firing squad himself — 'Soldiers! straight to the heart — Fire!'
and struck his chest with his right fist, he burst a concealed bag of
red dye, whilst the soldiers fired over his head. He then appears as
Peter Stuart Ney, a schoolmaster in Georgetown, South Carolina,
who declared on his deathbed that he was Marshal Ney of France.
Supporters and opponents of this legend both produce evidence

which they regard as convincing.

The well-known English writer Cecil Roberts relates how Theodore Chaliapin, the son of the great Russian singer, once told him of his belief in the story of the Tsar's life as a hermit in Siberia, and the story is so well-documented that it is hard to dismiss. It is less easy to accept the romance of Marshal Ney's 'after life' as a schoolmaster in South Carolina, however fervently British and French alike might wish it to be true. As for the legends that the man who died in Longwood House on 5th May, 1821 was not Napoleon, I for one do not believe a word of them.

Among the thousands who found it hard to accept the report of Napoleon's death, some three months before his fifty-second birthday, there were two who were already mentally prepared to be assured that he was not really dead. Napoleon's mother and her half-brother Cardinal Fesch, who were living in Rome, had taken up spiritualism and fallen under the influence of an Austrian lady, Mme Kleinmüller, who specialised in visions of a vaguely religious nature. In one of these visions, as she told a delighted Mme Mère, she saw Napoleon being transported by angels from his island prison. Count de las Cases, after leaving St Helena, was assured by Mme Mère that she knew that the Governor's reports from St Helena were false, as her son was no longer there. So when Napoleon asked his mother to send a doctor to replace O'Meara and a priest to remedy the lack of a Roman Catholic priest in the island, she and Fesch did not greatly exert themselves to find suitable applicants for the posts.

Antommarchi's defects as a personal physician have already been described but the two priests were much worse represent-atives of their profession than he was of his. The Abbé Buonavita was a mumbling decrepit old man of nearly seventy, who seemed much older because of the effects of a recent stroke. His young assistant, the Corsican Abbé Vignali, had studied medicine as well as theology but has been described as very ill-educated for either profession.[5]

Napoleon was horribly disappointed; and resentful that his mother and Fesch, both well known for their parsimony, had so patently done things 'on the cheap'. He could not know that they had not bothered to find good men simply because they were convinced that Napoleon was no longer in St Helena to be harassed by an anatomist and a couple of bog-priests.

It would certainly have needed Mme Kleinmüller's squadron of angels to waft the best guarded prisoner in the world out of St Helena as Colonel Otto Skorzeny and his paratroopers abducted the ageing and rather reluctant Benito Mussolini from the mountain hotel in the Gran Sasso, where he was held prisoner by his own disillusioned compatriots. Napoleon's reluctance was more marked than that of the Duce and, though he was a younger man, he was prematurely aged. The eagle had moulted considerably since his last triumphant flight to the towers of Nôtre Dame.

The physical change in Napoleon mentioned in Chapter 4 was accompanied by equally significant changes in his personality. Generals and politicians alike had commented on an increasing indecision and a tendency to talk when the man of Montenotte and Lodi would have acted. An occasional flash in the pan during the Waterloo campaign produced no effective discharge of the old conquering energy. More and more, as Lazare Carnot had remarked in the early days of the Empire, the man of rapid decisions who resented the proffer of advice was replaced by one who talked instead of acting and asked opinions.

In St Helena he talked more and more, boasting of what he had done, had intended to do, and hoped he might yet achieve, for in the early days he was still sustained by the hope that changes in the political climate in Europe might result in his repatriation. But once this hope began to fade he was reluctant to take any resolute steps himself. Plans for escape was certainly being made, but those who hoped for success were disappointed by the apathetic attitude of the central figure in all their planning.

In St Helena itself after about the end of 1816 the possibility of an escape was gradually discounted; by Montholon and Gourgaud with some bitter comments that the Emperor had grown too soft, unadventurous and tired; and by Count Balmain in reports intended to reassure the Russian court. The French, who thought that Napoleon was too tired to undertake what would have been a daring and almost impossible venture, were probably right, for his last illness would soon begin to show itself.

For nearly a year, however, he seems to have toyed with thoughts of escape, or at any rate to have done nothing to discourage his more enthusiastic followers from scheming to that end. In particular he dropped broad hints about his hopes of help from his brother Joseph in America, who he said must be worth millions since he had got away with the Spanish diamonds. At his last farewell to Joseph in Rochefort in July 1815 he had entrusted him with important documents and a large sum of money, estimated at eight million francs. After Napoleon's death Joseph denied this, as well he might for the failure of the *Champ d'Asile* (referred to in Chapter Three) was chiefly due to lack of funds, which would need some explanation if Joseph Bonaparte really possessed a fortune.

In October 1816 Captain Piontkowski and three of the servants, Rousseau, Santini and the younger Archambault, were sent to Europe in order to reduce the expenses of Longwood House. The three Frenchmen were all entrusted with secret messages, and two of them, Archambault and Rousseau, went on to America to join the household of Joseph Bonaparte. Their arrival in that country gave a fillip to the plotting to rescue Napoleon which was being carried on there.

Long after 1817, indeed right up to the Emperor's death, ardent spirits in France, even in England and above all in America, nourished hopes not only of rescue but of restoration. In America, land of the free, in General Lallemand's *Champ d'Asile*, France's newest colony, those who were planning to rescue the Emperor and once again to fight under his eagles, could have looked to such soldiers as Marshal Grouchy, and Generals Vandamme and Lefebvre Desnouettes. An even more useful recruit to their cause was the French-American, Stephen Girard, owner of a trading fleet with a world-wide range. He was born in Bordeaux in 1750, went to sea as a cabin boy, settled in Philadelphia in 1776, and by 1812 had become both rich and influential.

In South America two Bonapartist officers, Generals Brayer and Latapie, planning a daring armed assault upon St Helena, had for their naval adviser a Scottish admiral, Lord Cochrane, future tenth Earl of Dundonald. Having left England in unmerited disgrace he was commanding the navy of Chile.[6]

Lord Cochrane was not the only British sailor who was prepared to aid the Bonapartist plotters. In Chapter Two I referred to the mutual admiration society which grew up between Napoleon and the Royal Navy. Rescue of Napoleon would have had to be more of a naval than a military venture and the suspicion that many sailors were eager to help, out of admiration for Boney or for gain, helped to give poor Sir Hudson many a sleepless night. It was not only sailors who were involved. Surgeon Henry accompanied the French party sailing home to Europe in the storeship *Camel* of five hundred tons, and he wrote that, now that secrecy was unnecessary, Mme Bertrand 'acknowledged that the Longwood people had found no difficulty in maintaining a clandestine correspondence throughout with their agents in London. She told us to our surprise, that two British Officers of the Garrison had been the chief agents in contravening the regulations of Government, and in forwarding letters and parcels to England'. Whilst English sympathisers smuggled unauthorised communications into the island the French sent clandestine appeals and papers for publication in Europe to help their cause.

Admiral Malcolm's opinion was that Napoleon could escape whenever he chose to do so and he ruefully admitted that the captains of the East India Company's ships were for the Emperor to a man. One naval officer, Captain Mackay of *Minden*, a ship of seventy four guns, who spoke French and was a fervent admirer of Napoleon, sent a message to The Briars offering to undertake commissions for Europe; and another sea captain offered to embark the Emperor in his ship for a thousand pounds. On H.M.S. *Favourite* taking O'Meara back to England in disgrace, Napoleon's doctor, already spreading his malicious tales of being asked by Lowe to help to dispose of the prisoner, found an interested and half-convinced audience of naval officers. No wonder Sir Hudson Lowe was in a permanent state of anxiety and that he disliked and distrusted naval officers especially. French sea captains were another worry. Many of them, if they could have approached the island, would have risked an attempt with no thought of financial gain. But on the sighting of a sail an intricate alarm system triggered off a state of maximum alert.

Did just one French vessel succeed in slipping past the tight cordon? Yes, if we can believe the strange tale told by an old merchant seaman, A. Chailly. When he was eight years old, the youngest and tiniest cadet in the Lycée Impérial, he was singled out on a parade by Napoleon, who made him a royal bursar. He was very envious of his old school friend, the young Las Cases, who was in St Helena with his hero, and in 1820 jumped at the chance of joining a ship called *Zénobie*, in which the master Captain Lépissoir was setting out to rescue Napoleon. Chailly claimed that they succeeded in landing on St Helena and met Montholon and Napoleon, who refused to leave because he felt death approaching; and indeed he was dead just six months later. The story of *Zénobie* and her strangely named captain is not the only remarkable anecdote in the memoirs of Chailly, which sound like the product of a fertile imagination aimed at getting money from Napoleon III, who was always generous to anyone with any kind of claim on the founder of the dynasty which he hoped to continue.

Gilbert Martineau, in a chapter on 'Plans of Escape', discusses some of the fantastic stories quite unsupported by material proof which have been propagated by 'leg-pullers, historical yarn-spinners and propagandists for the ideals of Bonapartism'; the latter being no doubt unwilling to believe that Napoleon could deliberately choose to end his days in captivity. Among other authors who relate some of these tales is Paul Ganière.

In the stories about Napoleon's alleged escape there are two contrasting themes, one involving the arrival on board *Bellerophon* of a bogus ex-Emperor, the other claiming that the real Napoleon went to St Helena and escaped from there.

According to the first theme Joseph Fouché, Napoleon's Minister of Police, had in about 1808 discovered a soldier, Rifleman Roubeaud or Robeaud, with a marked resemblance to Napoleon, and had used him as a 'stand-in' for Napoleon at some minor official functions and parades. It was therefore easy to substitute Roubeaud for Napoleon in 1815. Napoleon thus never left Europe and he turned up eventually as the proprietor of a spectacle shop in Verona. A romantic touch in this story makes it ideal material for a sentimental film. Napoleon secretly visits Vienna and, climbing a wall, watches his young son playing in the park at the Schönbrunn Palace. One version alleges that a sentry, noticing the suspicious behaviour of the intruder, shot him dead; and the date is actually given as 27th February, 1823. Some have believed that Tsar Alexander took Napoleon under his protection and allowed him to live secretly in a remote part of Russian Poland.

Fouché plays a more sinister part in a plot revealed only in a book published in the United States: *The Curious Story of Dr Marshall*, by J.W. Bailey. Dr Joseph Marshall, a shadowy figure employed as a secret agent by the Bourbons, became involved after Waterloo in a plot to smuggle Napoleon to England, disguised as his secretary. Although Dr Marshall was at the time in correspondence with Wellington, the escape was planned with Fouché's connivance; but Marshall backed out when he became convinced that Fouché intended to have his carriage attacked and both himself and his 'secretary' killed. Clearly Dr Marshall knew his Fouché.

The stories in which Napoleon is said to have gone to St Helena but escaped from there lack the sentimental touch but tend to be more exciting. Napoleon succeeds in getting to Brazil and thence to England by the Spring of 1819; later dying somewhere in

Europe in 1835. Another version presents him in 1840 as the ruler of a kingdom of Negroes — more in his line than selling spectacles. Paul Ganière tells us that an American author, Paul Ebeyer, has gone so far as to give the precise date of Napoleon's escape from St Helena, as 27th August, 1817.

Napoleon's games of hide-and-seek with Hudson Lowe and the orderly officers afforded plenty of opportunities for slipping Rifleman Roubeaud into Longwood House, in the extremely unlikely event of a soldier closely resembling Napoleon having made his way to St Helena unobserved; but the task of getting Napoleon off the island would have been virtually impossible. Perhaps it was not just to tease Hudson Lowe that Napoleon used to hide himself; and his insistence on doctors seeing him only in the dark could have had a deeper purpose than concealment of his curiously shaped body; but I do not think it was because Roubeaud was in Napoleon's bed. It is perfectly easy to believe that the part of Napoleon could have been played by a soldier who resembled him, even if only superficially. Many Frenchmen, even many of his soldiers, had never seen him at close quarters, and even those who had could well have been mesmerised by the familiar uniform topped by that unmistakeable hat. The owner of another unmistakeable variant of military headgear was successfully impersonated in Gibraltar in 1944, as part of the cover plan before the invasion of Normandy, by an Australian actor, Lieutenant Clifton James of the Royal Army Pay Corps who tells his entertaining story in his book *I was Monty's Double*.

But if the Roubeaud story really began in 1808 how did the soldier keep pace with the remarkable changes in the physique and appearance of the real Napoleon which were taking place at that time. Imagination wavers, indeed baulks, at the idea of faked family farewells at Malmaison and Rochefort, to say nothing of all those industrious diarists scribbling away to record the sayings, opinions and memories of a bogus Napoleon; and the pious pilgrims at the tomb in the Invalides filing past Rifleman Roubeaud.

It is highly improbable that when Napoleon III met Alexander II of Russia in Stuttgart in 1857 one of the topics of conversation was the Tsar's discovery that the tomb of his uncle was empty; or that Napoleon III was ever tempted to take a peep inside the most famous tomb in the *Invalides*.

In 1969, the year of the two hundredth anniversary of the birth of Napoleon, the question of the body in the tomb was raised yet again, and with quite a different theme to those which I have outlined. This time it is Britain which has effected the substitution. Napoleon really died in Longwood House and was buried in sight of all in Geranium Valley, which was later re-named The Valley of the Tomb. But at some time thereafter the tomb was secretly opened and the body of Cipriani Franceschi, Napoleon's major-domo who had died in February 1818, was substituted for that of Napoleon. *'Anglais, Rendez nous Napoleon'* cries M. Georges Rétif de la Bretonne, in his book with that title. England — Give us back Napoleon! Where do you think Perfidious Albion has been keeping him hidden? Where else but in that overcrowded repository in which, it may be recalled, Napoleon in an optimistic flight of fancy in 1815, had persuaded himself that he might end up in his own right — Westminster Abbey.

M. Rétif de la Bretonne, a journalist and collector of Napoleonic relics, must surely be allotted a high place in the ranks of those who seek to prove that generally accepted facts about Napoleon are not true. In 1960 he collaborated with his father, Commandant Rétif de la Bretonne, in a book proving that Napoleon's death-bed, presented by the Murat family to the Museum of the Invalides, is not the real one on which the Emperor died. It seems to be a work of supererogation to devote 338 pages and many illustrations, mostly irrelevant, to so unimportant a point. We know from Marchand, Lieutenant Duncan Darroch and others that Napoleon had two camp-beds in different rooms and, when it was feared that both would prove to be too narrow when he began to become very ill, Marchand bought a brass bedstead in the town, which was fitted up with green hangings like the most favoured of the camp beds. At first Napoleon found the new bed uncomfortable. The thought of the poor man, plagued by the fever and drenching sweats of his illness during the long hot tropical nights, going from one bed to another in search of sleep is sufficiently harrowing without worrying about which one he actually died on.

This matter of the wrong bed may be a purely French concern, but the possible substitution of Cipriani's body for that of Napoleon could be a further source of ill-feeling among Bonapartists against Britain; so it is as well that Rétif de la Bretonne's accusations, and his hopes that the Queen might authorise an investigation in the Abbey, appear to have excited as little notice as did the earlier book. Could there possibly be anything in all this?

Britain is not the only villain in the story. Cipriani himself figures as a spy of the English, a betrayer of his master and a suicide, all of which is probably quite unfair, although he was to some extent a man of mystery. Frédéric Masson, an acknowledged authority on almost every aspect of Napoleon's life, considered Cipriani to be the most interesting member of the Longwood staff, and indeed 'a romantic figure'. Gilbert Martineau calls him a thorough scoundrel, but finds him 'the most enigmatic of the servants'; and observes that a rumour that his death was due to poison could be cleared up only if his grave could be traced, adding that 'his tomb cost the Emperor a small fortune but it has vanished today — although there are plenty of tombstones of the same date in the cemetery at Plantation House'.

Cipriani Franceschi, the major-domo or *maître d'hôtel*, was certainly more than just a superior member of the domestic staff, for he enjoyed the complete confidence of Napoleon with whom he was often closeted for prolonged conferences. He was Napoleon's intelligence officer. He was allowed to visit Jamestown to get provisions and, being companionable, garrulous and bibulous, he made many contacts from whom he got information to take home to Longwood. He was a bit of a buffoon and easily made fools of the soldiers who had to guard him. He became expert in the age-old prisoner-of-war art of baiting his captors, even the Governor himself, whom he loved to tease and to confuse with arguments about what should be considered the essentials of life to a French household. It was Cipriani who supervised the ostentatiously public breaking up of the Emperor's silver, ensuring that the proceeding was witnessed by officers who were about to sail for England, and that they believed that it was made necessary by official meanness over the basic needs of the prisoners.

Cipriani was a militant atheist, outspoken against all forms of religious belief, and was also a rabid Republican and opponent of the concept of kingship. He made an exception in the case of Napoleon, to whom, says M. Martineau, he was 'fanatically devoted'. Being a Corsican he may have reconciled the apparent contradiction by regarding Napoleon as the head of a clan; and whilst he was with the Emperor in St Helena his son was in service with Cardinal Fesch and his daughter with Madame Mère.

Cipriani himself was first taken on the establishment of the Imperial household during the Hundred Days, but his connection with Napoleon dated from at least as early as 1794. He had known the Buonaparte family since his childhood and, like many other Corsicans, became a follower of the most successful and adventurous soldier their island had produced. He probably served in one of the Corsican battalions before becoming associated with another important Corsican, the lawyer Antonio Cristoforo Saliceti, a close friend of the Buonapartes, some twelve years older than Napoleon. Saliceti had become an influential man in Revolutionary France. He was one of the four Government commissioners at the Siege of Toulon and was later a commission- er with the Army of the Alps and the Army of Italy. These commissioners could be as dangerous to generals of the Revo- lutionary armies as we have been led to believe Soviet commissars could be to Russian generals.

Friendship with Saliceti helped young General Bonaparte, though in Italy he found Saliceti's ruthless looting of Church property for his own pocket little to his taste. Saliceti employed Cipriani Franceschi as a spy in Naples, and sent him to Capri, where he busied himself in subverting and bribing Corsicans who had taken service with the British.

At this time the Royal Corsican Rangers were commanded by Colonel Hudson Lowe, the future Governor of St Helena, who knew about Cipriani's activities but never met him and knew him only as Franceschi. This was why Cipriani dropped his surname which was never used in St Helena. Incidentally this explains why he is referred to in almost all books simply as Cipriani, and why his real position in Napoleon's confidence has been widely overlooked. The same lack of recognition clouds his true rôle when he was with Napoleon in Elba. Robert Christophe, for example, in his book *Napoleon in Elba*, dismisses Cipriani in half a sentence as 'another hot-blooded Corsican'; and refers to him in the index simply as 'Cipriani, (servant)'. But whilst Napoleon was in Elba he sent Cipriani as a spy to Vienna and his reports that the Allied Powers were considering sending Napoleon further afield, to some distant island off the African Coast, probably helped to sway Napoleon in deciding to return to France.

In Longwood House Cipriani's tale-bearing and the fact that he could always obtain lengthy private audiences with Napoleon, made him many enemies. General Gourgaud, always obsessionally jealous of anyone whom Napoleon seemed to favour, said that the Emperor 'would give us all up to keep Cipriani'. Napoleon certainly trusted him completely and even listened to his insubordinate criticisms of the undue luxury of the Montholons' apartments. He probably did not know that Cipriani had even presumed to criticise the Emperor himself, in whom he detected a growing tendency to believe in God. Cipriani pronounced this to be ridiculous in a man who had had so many men killed for his own ends.

It is hard to believe that any of those in Longwood House who disliked Cipriani would have thought of poisoning one who was unquestionably a loyal friend of the Emperor, which is what everyone believed at the time, just as responsible writers have believed ever since. I agree with Dr Ganière who dismisses as absurd the rumour that Sir Hudson Lowe, having discovered the story of Cipriani's role in Capri, had him poisoned. The Governor could quite easily have got rid of him without having to resort to murder. As for Rétif de la Bretonne's theory of suicide, one can only say that no one could have set about killing himself in a more inefficient and painful manner.

Cipriani's fatal illness began on 23rd February, 1818, with his collapse in agony whilst on duty in Napoleon's dining room. O'Meara, describing the illness as 'inflammation of the bowels', added that from the start it 'presented the most formidable appearances'. Cipriani was plainly critically ill; and 'It was soon evident that his life was in the most imminent danger.' As he was not responding to treatment Dr O'Meara called in the Principal Medical Officer, Dr Baxter and young Dr Henry, but no one could do anything and in less than three days Cipriani was dead.

O'Meara wrote that Cipriani had been unwell for a few days without complaining, and he had had attacks of dysentery in common with everyone else in the house. Only a few days before his death a chambermaid of Mme Bertrand and a child of a servant of the Montholons had died, so there may be cause to suspect some infectious illness, such as a fulminating attack of dysentery. Cipriani's illness however sounds more like the perforation of some part of the alimentary canal, and a ruptured appendix has been suggested.

Dr Henry expressed surprise that Napoleon did not visit his devoted servant during his last illness and did not attend the funeral. This point has been taken up by critics of Napoleon, as evidence of his cold heart. This is manifestly unfair. Walter Henry knew very well that Napoleon had wanted to visit Cipriani, and in fact the young doctor employed some of his Irish wit in deriding Napoleon's idea that such a visit might re-animate the moribund patient, as Bonaparte claimed to have rallied his wavering troops at Marengo and other battles. O'Meara had specifically advised that the sick man should not be subjected to the excitement of an imperial visit, and in his memoirs he verbosely expounded his reasons for giving this advice.

Cipriani was buried in the little cemetery of St Paul's near Plantation House. His funeral was well attended, not only by most of the Longwood House people but by British soldiers and civilians to whom he had been a well-known figure. O'Meara made it clear that, 'Had he been buried *within* the limits, Napoleon himself would have attended'. Even for so old a retainer he was not going to lower his colours, seeking Lowe's permission and submitting to an escort. His grief for Cipriani is, however, beyond doubt and, as we have seen, he paid for a handsome tombstone. Gourgaud wrote in his journal on the day of Cipriani's funeral: 'I rather think that His Majesty will miss Cipriani more than any of us. . . Will he ever be replaced?' Count Balmain reported to the Russian Government: 'Bonaparte is extremely affected, for he was greatly attached to him'. Baron Stürmer wrote in similar terms to Prince Metternich.

Napoleon had asked that Cipriani should be buried within the precincts of Longwood and it is not known why Hudson Lowe refused this request, and had him buried in the cemetery near his own residence. Surely he can hardly have been thinking as far ahead as Napoleon's eventual death and a French desire to have his body brought home to France. As we shall see, when at last this natural desire was gratified, Napoleon's coffin was opened and its occupant was instantly recognised as the Emperor. No one has alleged that Cipriani closely resembled Napoleon, and, although his body, without the elaborate protection which had delayed decomposition in Napoleon's body, would certainly have decomposed, Napoleon's old companions at his exhumation could hardly have been so deceived.

There is no possible reason to suspect that when they stated that the Emperor's appearance was virtually unchanged by the passage of nearly twenty years, they were not telling the truth, or that they were helping to compound some curious British felony, belatedly dreamed up by a French journalist almost a hundred and thirty years later. Unless we are to suppose that a British Government was capable of acting like a pack of practical jokers with a perverse sense of humour it is hard to see what they had to gain by any such elaborate hoax. I think that our reply to M. Rétif de la Bretonne's appeal can be monosyllabic and not over-polite.[7]

The British Government had in fact from the first shown no reluctance about returning Napoleon's body to the French.

Madame Mère had written to Bertrand to say that she would ask for her son's ashes unless he had expressly asked to be buried in St Helena. Since Napoleon had wanted his body to be interred by the Seine, Bertrand and Montholon sent his mother's request to King George IV through Lord Liverpool, the Prime Minister. The British Ambassador to France sent for Montholon on 2nd December 1821 and told him that he was instructed to say that His Majesty's Government would return the body if the French Government asked for it. However King Louis XVIII turned a deaf ear to the proposal. It was Louis' prerogative to be magnanimous and, if his advisers considered that the time had not yet come for such a gesture, our country must not be blamed for following normal diplomatic procedure.

When at last in 1840 King Louis Philippe, probably seeking to bolster up his failing popularity by a noble gesture to placate the Bonapartists, did ask for Napoleon's body, the British Government cordially granted the request.

Napoleon himself, a master of the theatrical staging of events both great and small, could hardly have faulted the profoundly moving ceremonies by which Louis Philippe gratified the Emperor's desire that his ashes should be placed by the banks of the Seine. Perhaps he could have chosen a vessel with a more fitting name than that of the frigate in which the Prince de Joinville sailed to St Helena to bring back the precious cargo. Surely our Royal Navy would have selected some noble name — *Invincible* – *Indefatigable*; the French sent *La Belle Poule*. Rather French perhaps; but somehow strangely inappropriate.[8]

Accompanying the Prince de Joinville were several survivors of the days of exile — Bertrand, Gourgaud, young Emmanuel de las Cases, and Arthur Bertrand, born in St Helena and presented to Napoleon by his mother as 'the first French visitor to arrive in St Helena without Lord Bathurst's permission'. The Service were represented by Marchand, Saint Denis, Noverraz, Pierron and Archambault. In the nineteen years since they had left the Emperor in his tomb they had aged; and none more than the grizzled Bertrand who, even at the peak of his career, had always looked older than his years.

The coffin was opened and they gazed down upon the Emperor, exactly as they had known him, lying there in the familiar old green uniform which had always become him so much better than any ornate court dress. Napoleon's face, the placid features refined by death to the classic nobility which we can see in the death mask, was virtually unchanged.[9] They were all nearly twenty years older; he was fifty-one for ever. Surely in that solemn moment Bertrand forgot the secret dislike, the bitterly candid reading of the true nature of this impossible master, which still lay locked in his undeciphered journal, and became again 'The Faithful Bertrand', incarnation of true loyalty, which was how the world still saw him.

If Napoleon's body had not yet begun 'a'mouldering in the grave' his soul, his Legend, was already marching on. France was united, superficially at any rate, in a tumultuous welcome to the national hero. Napoleon's journey to Paris, in that bitterly cold December of 1840, was more of a triumph than a funeral. Over Paris itself the guns boomed out in salute just as they had done when the wonderful little man had returned after his great victories. In a sense this was his last and greatest victory; his most majestic and triumphal procession through his capital — *his* capital again, then and ever since. For, when at last the doors of the Invalides were thrown open and the waiting throng inside — the King of the French and his Ministers; the Princes, nobles and élite of the nation — rose to their feet in silent spontaneous tribute, it was in response to the loud ringing voice of a chamberlain proclaiming *'The Emperor'*.

Following his coffin walked his surviving companions of St Helena. Bertrand laid Napoleon's sword upon the pall.

How Napoleon himself would have loved that wonderful scene in the Invalides. But perhaps it was as well that he could be there only in the spirit and in his coffin. His flair for theatricality combined with a simple compelling dignity was complemented by a genius for 'debunking' a solemn occasion, impishly assuming the personality of the simple soldier to whom all the ceremony was meaningless posturing. Before his Coronation he had said to his brother Joseph: 'If our father could see us now'; and he had personally designed much of the service to emphasise that he was taking his place among the anointed ones, chosen by God to rule over the French. Yet, at a solemn moment, he attracted Cardinal Fesch's attention by a good nudge in the ribs with his sceptre.

Napoleon's industrious re-moulding and gilding of the Napoleonic Legend whilst he was in St Helena was unquestionably directed, not only to his own glorification or self-justification, but to paving the way for a restoration of the Bonaparte dynasty in the person

P

of his son. These aspirations must have received welcome encouragement from the religious, popular and military overtones of the *Retour des Cendres* — the English version 'Return of the Ashes', sounds an inappropriately cricketing note.

One hundred and fifty thousand soldiers took part in the ceremonies, which were watched by over a million people, many of whom must have felt a resurgence of hope for a Bonaparte restoration. Survivors of the Emperor's army, marching in the funeral procession each wore in his buttonhole a sprig of laurel from the wreaths on the coffin. None of the Emperor's relatives were present, for they were still proscribed, in exile or in prison. Louis Napoleon, 'The Man of December', had been sent to life imprisonment in the Fortress of Ham earlier in the month. Only eight years later, again in December, he became Prince President of the French Republic, after the abdication of Louis Philippe. Four years after that, on December 2nd, 1852, he proclaimed himself Emperor, hoping to restore the glory of the great days. He may have been a pale shadow of the great Napoleon; he may not have been a real Bonaparte at all; but he was a true Frenchman and probably loved the French people more sincerely than his Corsican predecessor had ever done.

The French, who had flocked in masochistic fervour to make further sacrifices for Napoleon I after every reverse, cast off Napoleon III after Sedan. In defeat he did not blame his soldiers, nor complain that the French people were an unworthy instrument of his genius, as the great Corsican had done in calm reflective moments as well as in the bitterness of defeat.

Napoleon was a man of moods and no doubt he was completely convinced of his sincerity when he directed in his will that his ashes should rest by the banks of the Seine in the midst of the French people whom he had loved so well. He judged them well in relying on them to welcome him back to their hearts. There can have been few on that emotional day in December 1840 who remembered anything but the glory. It was the supremely fitting climax to the wonderful story, blotting out, at least for a time, the sad and rather sordid end in Longwood House, which is where most biographers take leave of him.

When did he really die?

Thirty-nine years of brooding in some forgotten monastery may seem as appropriate sequel to the strange mystical life of the enigmatic Tsar Alexander I. A Scarlet Pimpernel rescue may help to salve the conscience of all those French and British admirers who long to believe that the splendid Michel Ney escaped the firing squad.

In the case of Napoleon the question is irrelevant. He is the archetypal old soldier who will never die — nor will his Legend fade away.

# Notes to the Text

# NOTES

## Chapter I

### THE NAPOLEONIC LEGEND

1. Several of the Questions and Answers in this extraordinary catechism can be read in J.M. Thompson's *Napoleon Bonaparte. His Rise and Fall*. Mr Thompson points out that in ousting St Roch from the calendar Napoleon also expressed his displeasure with the curé of Saint-Roch, who had recently refused to give Catholic burial to Mlle Chameroy, a dancer at the Opera. Perhaps St Roch was in any case not too pleased with Napoleon, for it was on the steps of his church that General Bonaparte had mowed down many Royalist rebels in the *Vendémiare* rising.

2. Kléber and Desaix could hold their own with Napoleon as generals but lacked his flair for intrigue and publicity, and his pushfulness. Louis Antoine Desaix de Veygoux, a member of the old minor nobility, a fine straightforward soldier dedicated to his profession, served Napoleon unselfishly until he died for him at Marengo. He disliked the ruthless, unscrupulous, selfish qualities which he discerned in Napoleon. Kléber's dislike was more openly expressed, and according to J.C. Herold he is said to have commented as follows on Napoleon's abandonment of his army: 'That b...r has left us with his breeches full of s...t. We'll go back to Europe and rub them in his face.' Jean Baptiste Kléber, the son of a mason, was a fine soldier and popular, although a strict disciplinarian. A man of imposing appearance he easily dominated those around him, when they did not include the sallow Corsican scarecrow, whose tricks of cultivated personal magnetism the robustly straightforward Alsatian despised. The enmity between them was well-known, and each had his faction in the army. Some generals, like Menou, with the caution bred by the Revolution, waited to see which way the cat would jump. The bolder General Sarrazin dared to denounce Napoleon as early as 1811, but significantly his book was published in London.

3. One of the marshals succeeded, where Napoleon failed, in establishing a permanent dynasty, and his descendants occupy the throne of Sweden today. Jean Baptiste Jules Bernadotte, the son of an attorney in Pau in the Lower Pyrenees, was a regular soldier and a sergeant in 1789, after which his promotion was rapid. It may have been with an eye on Napoleon's protection that the Swedes asked Bernadotte to be their Crown Prince in 1810; though Napoleon was not too well pleased. Perhaps because Bernadotte had

married his old sweetheart Desirée Clary he did not press his opposition. But at the time of Napoleon's return from Egypt Bernadotte had been prominent among those who wanted him to be tried by court martial and probably shot, for leaving his command without permission. Napoleon's triumph in the *Coup de Brumaire* ended any hopes Bernadotte may have had of becoming the leading man in France; but in 1814 the Allied Powers considered offering the throne of France to Bernadotte, who in 1813 had led his Swedish troops against his old master and his native land.

The only other marshal to become a king also joined Napoleon's enemies at the end, and his defection was most contemptible for it was partly urged on him by his wife Caroline — Napoleon's own sister. Joachim Murat, the son of a Périgord innkeeper, became King of Naples, but the dashing cavalry leader was a most ineffective king. His unpleasant wife Caroline Bonaparte may have pushed him into his final treachery, but his own dislike of Napoleon and his belief that what one general had done another could do, had flared out openly in 1812, when, following Napoleon's example, he abandoned the retreating army. He openly denounced Napoleon in a council of officers in Posen, saying that if he had accepted advances made to him by England he could have become a real monarch. He wrote to Napoleon, describing his régime as 'criminal', and tactlessly referring to himself as 'the reanimator of your lost courage on the 18th Brumaire'. But in the end he proved unable to stand on his own feet without his powerful brother-in-law and, after failing to re-establish his former régime in Naples, was shot by a firing squad in 1815.

4. Attempts have been made to compute the 'butcher's bill' of Napoleon's campaigns, but the figures, however staggering, hardly convey the misery and suffering inflicted upon Europe by his aggression. The casualties in battles which hardly made the headlines of history ran into thousands, and any Napoleonic battlefield presented a scene more horrible than any in the First World War, which in turn greatly exceeded anything seen in the Second World War. Dead and dying soldiers were often heaped so thickly that no ground could be seen; and in some battles the corpses and any wounded men who could not crawl away were incinerated by the fires started by the gunfire, in long dry grass, as at Talavera. The hopelessly overworked surgeons could lop off a leg in a couple of minutes, for there were no anaesthetics. An abdominal wound was normally fatal. Men grew hardened to the horrors. Writing of Waterloo, a famous anonymous diarist of the 71st Regiment, having described the field of battle covered and heaped with bodies, ends:

> The wounded crawling along the rows of dead was a horrible spectacle; yet I looked on with less concern . . . than I have felt at an accident when in quarters. I looked over the field of Waterloo as a matter of course — a matter of no concern.

But the French never grew hardened to the mental agony of marching away, disengaging themselves from the despairing grasp of wounded comrades pleading to be taken with them, knowing that once the army had gone their throats would be cut and their bodies stripped by plundering carrion peasants.

5. Marmont's treachery had to be insisted upon to divert blame from where it really belonged. General

Count Yorck von Wartenburg says that Marmont's action spurred Napoleon to this outburst: 'If the Emperor has despised men, as people have reproached him with doing, the world will now recognise that he had reasons which justified this contempt.' Wellington said that the accusation of treachery was 'a great mistake . . . All that Marmont did was this — the French marshals and troops being quartered from Fontainebleau to Paris all began to treat, and Marmont being nearest to Paris treated first. That was all.'

6. *Napoleon's attempted suicide.*
After the publication in 1937 of the memoirs of General de Caulaincourt, Duke of Vicenza, a faithful and intimate friend of the Emperor, Napoleon's attempt to poison himself could not be dismissed as a rumour, based only on the memoirs of the valet Constant, who had deserted his master and was eager to justify his conduct. Caulaincourt dates the attempt as the night of 12th/13th April 1814. In the closing stages of the 1814 campaign Napoleon had written to his secretary telling him to be prepared for anything, 'even the Emperor's death'; and he told Caulaincourt that when he thought of what the invaders might do to France he could not bear to live. But on the night of the attempt Caulaincourt begged Napoleon to let him fetch a doctor, only to be ordered by Napoleon 'as a final service', not to thwart him, for the indignities, attempted assassination or insults which he foresaw would be worse than death. He gave Caulaincourt a loving letter for the Empress and said, 'soon I shall exist no more'.

When his condition grew worse and Caulaincourt tried to slip out to get assistance, Napoleon clung to him with all his strength. He was clenching his teeth to avoid vomiting. Between spasms he gave Caulaincourt presents and messages for relatives. When Napoleon was prostrate Caulaincourt succeeded in fetching Dr Yvan, from whom Napoleon demanded a stronger dose of opium, complaining that the poison was taking so long to kill him. When he finally recovered he said, 'I shall live, since death cares as little for me in my bed as it does on the battlefield.' In the following days he spoke of his regret at failing to kill himself and said, 'If they have me assassinated along the way or if they put me through humiliating experiences, you will have to blame it on yourself, Caulaincourt.' On questioning Constant and Roustam, Caulaincourt learned that for some time Napoleon's 'whole talk had been of nothing except ways to commit suicide'. Yvan's son, Alexandre Napoléon Yvan, said that his father had fled from the Palace for fear that he might be accused of having poisoned the Emperor. This is quoted, from a paper by Yvan's son, in an article *Yvan Chirurgien de Napoléon*, by Médécin Lieutenant Colonel J.M. des Cilleuls. In that article Yvan's initials, in a reference to an article written by him, are shown as A.U. No biographical dictionary even mentions Yvan, and in every book in which he is mentioned it is simply as Dr Yvan. Any document which he signed shows only 'Yvan', 'Citoyen Yvan' or 'Baron Yvan' — whatever A.U. may have stood for is not revealed.

7. Benjamin Constant's *Esprit de Conquête*, published in January 1814, was a powerful denunciation of military dictatorship and of war itself; and it ended with an appeal to Napoleon 'to cease robbing the world

of its inheritance'. So it was not only his infatuation with the beautiful empty-headed Juliette Récamier which led him to risk his life by openly denouncing Napoleon after his return to France. Constant did not recant, but attached himself to the new Imperial team through honest hope that this time Napoleon genuinely wanted to be shown how to become a constitutional monarch, which Constant, who suffered from a lifelong itch to instruct, felt himself well qualified to attempt, as he had studied the subject in England. Napoleon being constitutionally incapable of learning to be a constitutional monarch, Constant was naturally regarded as a turncoat. The academician Claude Manceron observes, 'It is a great misfortune for men of letters that they cannot betray in silence like a soldier or a civil servant.'

8. 'Up Guards and at 'em' — part of the 'Wellington Legend', is as impossible and out of character as is the suggestion that the rather dreamy violin-playing Etonian learned anything much on the playing fields. 'Stand up Guards', are the words given by, for example, Richard Aldington, Sir Charles Petrie, Sir Arthur Bryant, and the official Netherlands History, where they are given in English. Sir Arthur Bryant writes that, just before these words, 'The Commander-in-Chief's voice rang out "Now Maitland, now's your time" '. Wellington himself believed that he spoke these words, to Major General Maitland, commanding the Guards Brigade, in a quiet voice. Rejecting the 'Up Guards and at 'em' myth, the Duke said to John Wilson Croker, 'What I must have said, and possibly did say, was "Stand up, Guards!" and then gave the commanding officers the order to attack.'

*The Croker Papers. Vol. II, p. 469.*

9. During his voyage to St Helena on H.M.S. *Northumberland*, Napoleon was more specific about the 'ill-disposed persons'. He told Admiral Sir George Cockburn that they were 'disaffected officers'. Memories of Waterloo and of his last days as Emperor of the French were still in the forefront of his mind. He contradicted General Gourgaud, who had told Sir George that Napoleon had mistaken the Prussians for Grouchy's army, and assured the admiral that 'he knew early in the day the Prussians were closing on his flank; that this, however, gave him little or no uneasiness as he depended on General Grouchy also closing with him at the same time, and he had ordered a sufficient force to oppose the Prussians, who were in fact already checked.' This may explain, though hardly condone, his attempt to deceive his soldiers. He spoke warmly to the admiral about 'the lower order of people in France', but said that 'in proportion as you rose in class of people in France, the character became worse, and above the bourgeois they were too fickle and too volatile to be depended upon . . . and he attributed solely to the disaffected officers of his army his Waterloo disasters.'

Extract from *A Diary of Rear Admiral Sir George Cockburn, With particular reference to General Napoleon Buonaparte*, London, Simpkin Marshall & Co., 1888.

## Chapter II
### THE CORSICAN, THE FRENCH AND THE ENGLISH

1. The late General Sir Frank Messervy in a letter giving me permission to tell this story, commented as follows:

It is appalling how cruel and inhuman men can be even today in part of the UK, Northern Ireland. But on the whole I think the Englishman is tolerant and kindhearted both to other men and to animals. Of course, as far as I am concerned you can publish the story of the men of the 24 Anti-tank Regiment and the Jap prisoner. Most of the men of this regiment were cockneys, many of them bus or taxi drivers. The Cockney, in my opinion, with his sense of humour and his humanity is probably more tolerant and humane than most people. All our young soldiers in Ulster have certainly shown marvellous restraint in very difficult circumstances. It makes one very proud of the British Army today and shows that our young generation are basically sound if properly trained and well-led.

2. Theodore Stephan von Neuhof (1694-1756) a Westphalian baron, was a page to the Duchess of Orleans from the age of 14 to 17, served as a young officer in the Régiment d'Alsace and the Bavarian Hussars, and lost his commission on account of gambling debts. Debts complicated his life to the end and he went to prison with monotonous regularity, mostly for debt. His career after leaving the army was hardly that of a soldier of fortune; he was too careful to avoid combat. 'Gentleman-adventurer' has been used. He had an unusual share of adventure and was certainly born a gentleman; but 'confidence trickster' is nearer the mark, though perhaps he did anticipate that curious modern career of professional fund-raiser. He worked for a time for the cause of the exiled Royal Stuarts, but less from affection for James III or his son Charles Edward, than from a desire to line his own pockets from the contributions of loyal Jacobites. Seeing a chance of profiting from the intense desire of the Corsicans for

freedom from the yoke of Genoa, he persuaded the Jews and Greeks of Tunis that he could guarantee them the trading rights in Corsica only if he became king.

He was never really a king. Crowned with a diadem of laurels, after one of chestnut twigs had been deemed 'unseemly', he failed to eject the Genoese, and spent most of his time skulking in the mountains, often paying for board and lodging by the award of titles such as Illustrious Knight and Excellent Commander, in the Order of Liberation which he founded. Men were ready then, as now, to pay for a piece of green ribbon. He foolishly incurred a vendetta by having a minor Corsican chieftain shot for treason — treason to whom one might ask. Even after his ignominious flight many Corsicans still hoped he might provide a focus for resistance, but he merely hung limply around the courts of Europe, drawing the dole from any who would pay it, waiting for an opportunity to combine profit with a minimum of risk. A promising rebellion, clandestinely backed by Britain, in 1745 'flickered out through clan dissensions like Prince Charlie's affair in Scotland' (Vallance); but Theodore had not the guts, like Charles Edward Stuart, to put it to the touch in person. England and other European countries kept Corsica in mind as a possible naval base, or as a thorn in the flanks of their enemies. If the island was a mere pawn in the political game Theodore was something even less valuable than a pawn.

His story, much of it admittedly guess-work, was told by the late Aylmer Vallance, in a book *The Summer King*, which is of interest chiefly for the insight it affords into the complexities of Corsican politics; and for the brief appearance at

Theodore's headquarters of a little boy, Pasquale Paoli, accompanying his father Giacinto Paoli, who quickly became disillusioned with King Theodore, who later made his banishment one of the conditions on which he would consent to return to his loving subjects. No one sang 'Will ye no' come back again' and the Paolis stayed in Corsica.

3. Another very good judge of a soldier did not think much of what he saw of the Corsicans. General Sir John Moore took part in the Corsican campaign and brief occupation of the island (1794-1796). He commented upon Paoli's 'complete ignorance of military matters'; and had this to say of his Corsican troops:

> Instead of the active warlike people I took them to be, zealous in the cause of liberty, they have proved to be a poor, idle, mean set, incapable of any action which requires steadiness or resolution and have been absolutely of no use to us since we landed.

## Chapter III
## BRITAIN'S TASK

1. Having ventured to describe Commandant Lachouque's idea of Maitland using French prisoners to snatch Napoleon before his admiral's arrival as 'laughable', I may as well refer to some curious errors in his book. A knighthood is conferred on John Wilson Croker, Secretary to the Admiralty; Wellington's brother is called Baron Marlborough (instead of Maryborough); Viscount Ebrington becomes Elsington. His translator, who might have kept him straight on such English matters, scores some odd mis-translations. Ney is called the Prince of Moscow (instead of the Moskowa, the French name for the

Battle of Borodino); the raft in the Niemen on which Napoleon met Alexander I, has become a bridge; and surely 'Old Baldy' cannot be right for Napoleon's nickname '*Le Petit Tondu*' — I have yet to meet a Frenchman who likes it.

2. Franklin D. Roosevelt did not live to see the birth of the minor European state of Wilsonia, to the conception of which he, with our wartime enemy Joseph Kennedy, and John Foster Dulles, had contributed a gentle push or two. Feelings about colonial expansion depend on who is expanding. The inhabitants of the sub-continent of India, whom we can no longer simply call 'Indians', had some causes for hatred of British rule, but many more reasons for gratitude than had the Indians of North America or Mexico. Lord Palmerston's cynical comment 'Mexico was destined to be devoured by the Anglo-Saxon race before it disappeared altogether as the Redskins did before the white man', perhaps explained, but hardly justified the grabbing, between 1837 and 1849, by the United States, of over a million and a half square miles of Mexican territory, including Texas, New Mexico and Southern California. Pierre Salinger, reviewing Dee Brown's book *Bury my Heart at Wounded Knee*, said that the United States' treatment of American Indians 'ranks high in the list of History's attempted extinction of one race by another'. At least *we* have not flooded the world with 'Easterns', to match all those epic Westerns, differing from one another only in the names of the tribes whose Redskins bite the dust, on our TV screens, week after weary week.

3. Admiral Sir Alexander Cochrane had brought a case for libel against

Anthony Mackenrot, who had accused him of negligence in failing to attack a French squadron under Admiral Willaumez in 1806. Mackenrot proposed to call as witnesses for the defence Jerome Bonaparte, who had served in Willaumez' squadron, and Napoleon, who was to give evidence about the state of the French fleet at the time. This somewhat transparent plot to delay Napoleon's embarkation for St Helena could succeed only if a subpoena could be served on Lord Keith in person.

4. Hitler made a similar threat to bury the world beneath the ruins of his Third Reich; but he meant it, which Napoleon obviously did not. As the Allies advanced through the terrible ruins of German towns the Public Relations Department began to sow the seeds of de-Nazification by displaying in some of the most devastated areas large notices bearing a quotation from one of Hitler's pronouncements: *'Give me five years and you will not recognise Germany.'* [*Gebt mir fünf Jahre und ihr werdet Deutschland nicht wiedererkennen.*]

5. One American Bonaparte family would not have welcomed Napoleon. Whilst Napoleon's youngest brother was serving in the French Navy he had met and married a young society beauty of Baltimore, Betsy Patterson. Napoleon, furious with this tiresome young brother for marrying beneath him, compelled him to abandon his pregnant wife, and later married him to Princess Catherine of Württemberg, who made a splendid loyal wife to the inconstant playboy King of Westphalia. Betsy Patterson Bonaparte came to England, gave birth to her son in Camberwell and named him Jerome Bonaparte. One of his descendants became Secretary to the United States Navy. The American Bonapartes rightly insisted on the legality of Betsy's marriage, which was solemnised by the Roman Catholic bishop of Baltimore. The Pope refused to annul it, or to recognise Jerome's second marriage, from which the present Pretender to the Bonaparte crown of France is descended.

6. One of the best of the fine American naval officers was the country's hero, Stephen Decatur, who had gained the highest praise from Nelson himself. Decatur boarded and burned the United States frigate *Philadelphia*, which had been surrendered by Captain William Bainbridge when she ran aground off Tripoli in 1803. Nelson called this 'the most daring act of the age'.

Bonapartist swords were available for ventures in Canada. William Lyon Mackenzie (1795-1861) a native of Dundee, who led 800 men to Toronto in 1837 to protest against various abuses, was aided by a Bonapartist officer, Van Egmond. Mackenzie fled to the USA where he was imprisoned for twelve months for breach of the neutrality laws. The establishment of responsible government in Canada has, however, been said to have been largely due to Mackenzie's efforts.

## Chapter IV
## MEDICAL BOARD

1. Opposing viewpoints on Napoleon were represented in the first number of *Blackwood's Magazine* after news of his death reached Britain — July 1821.

On the first page, in a long declamatory poem in the slushy style then prevalent, a French veteran was portrayed weeping for the lost leader.

It is no shame that he should sigh,
His heart is like to break.

Napoleon could have had only one fault to find — scansion required the Italianate pronunciation of his name, given as Buonaparte. But the magazine ended with a vitriolic exposure of Napoleon's crimes by a regular contributor, George Croly, an Irish divine, who clearly did not feel inhibited by the kindly Christian principle — *De mortuis nil nisi bonum*. Among the murders attributed to his agency was the death of Admiral Villeneuve, usually thought to have been due to suicide. Alleging that he was murdered, Mr Croly said that he had 'three mortal wounds in his *back*'. By way of summing up he wrote as follows:—

Napoleon is now beyond the power of disturbing the world; he ought to receive the measure of lenity which belongs to a man beyond the power of defending himself. But it would be gross injustice to human nature, to attribute his guilt to mere common weaknesses. He was selfish, perfidious, bloody. He had no value for any life but his own — to secure that life he spared no crime. He never had an object of suspicion whom he did not make away with, and that privately. . . . With the power of good and evil, he chose evil. There is not on record a single act of his clemency, or generosity, or public spirit. He crushed the hope of freedom in France, and would have crushed it through the world. He was a tyrant in the darkest sense of the name. . . . His seizure of the English families travelling under his own passports, was an unheard of perfidy, still more cruel than the imprisonment of his military captives. Of those 12,000 English not more than one-third ever returned. . . . His private life was the fitting root for his public enormities. His conduct to Josephine was of the most heartless ingratitude; he was an adulterer and an apostate. Passion has with some men served as a

feeble excuse for the one, and prejudice for the other; with him, the cause of both crimes was selfishness, and his punishment came from his selfishness. It made him shrink, when to shrink was to be undone; and finally, it sent him, stripped of empire, fame, and public commiseration, from a hopeless dungeon to a dishonoured grave. If his oath could have been believed by any power, he might have sat free and prosperous to the last, but his perfidy extinguished all compromise. He was felt to be that enemy of mankind, whom no faith could bind — to have suffered him on a throne would have been only to prepare new misfortunes for the earth. He was declared an outlaw by the hearts of all nations, before he was by their lips; and after having run the career of a villain, he died the death of a slave.

## CHAPTER V
## ST HELENA AND SIR HUDSON

1. Las Cases tried to teach Napoleon English but without success, though Napoleon could be heard in Longwood ardently practising English sentences. Napoleon was no linguist. Italian was his native tongue and he spoke and wrote poor French. German was a barbarous tongue to him and his friendship with Goethe had to survive his inability to get nearer to the pronunciation of his name than 'M. Goat'. His attempt to learn English ended with this despairing letter.

Count Lascases,
Since six weeks y learn the English and y do no any progress. Six weeks do fourty and two day. If might have learn fivty word, for day, i could know it two thousand and two hundred. It is in dictionary more of fourty thousand; even he could most twenty bot much of tens. For know it or hundred and twenty week, which do more two years. After this you shall agree that

the study one tongue is a great labour, who it must do into the young aged.

2. Napoleon and the Bonapartes were the victims of many literary forgers. The most prolific, who was not unveiled for years, was Charles Doris of Bourges, most of whose scurrilous pamphlets were published under the name of Le Baron de B.... The list of his works given in *Supercheries Litéraires Devoilés*, M. Querard, Paris 1870, includes a book '*Chagrins Domestiques de Napoléon Bonaparte à Sainte Hélène*, purporting to be a collection by E. Santiné, of private letters and documents in Napoleon's own hand. It was published in Paris in 1821.

First in the field was the well-known *Manuscript of Saint Helena*, 1818. Supposed to be written by Napoleon it deceived many people because of its authentic ring, and it was later attributed to various writers who had known Napoleon; among them Benjamin Constant and Mme de Staël. It was finally established as the work of a Swiss writer, Jacob Fréderic Lullin de Chateauvieux.

## Chapter VI
## TWO STIFF SURGEONS

1. Dear Sir, November 5th 1814. The attention and meritorious conduct of Mr Barry O'Meara, while surgeon with me in the Goliath, calls upon me as an act of justice to him and of benefit to the service, to state that during the fifteen years I have commanded some one of his majesty's ships, I have never had the pleasure of sailing with an officer in his situation who so fully answered my expectations. Not being a judge of his professional abilities, though I have every reason to believe them of the first class, and I know that to be

the opinion of some of the oldest and most respectable surgeons in the navy, I shall only state that during a period of very bad weather, which occasioned Goliath to be extremely sickly, his attention and tenderness to the men was such as to call forth my warmest approbation, and the grateful affection of both officers and men. Were it probable that I should soon obtain another appointment, I know of no man in the service I should wish to have as surgeon so much as Mr O'Meara. As, however, in the present state of the war that is not likely, I trust you will do me the favour of giving him an appointment, as an encouragement to young men of his description, and believe me,

Dear Sir &c &c &c

Frederick L. Maitland.

To Dr Harness, &c. &c. &c.
Transport Board.

2. In the Medical Annual of 1937 on page 23, an authority on tropical diseases, Dr, later Sir Philip Manson-Bahr, reporting an epidemic of amoebiasis in Chicago, wrote that 1049 carriers of *E. histolytica*, were found in Chicago alone; whilst on page 273 Mr A. Rendle Short wrote that 'a good many amoebic abscesses of the liver are seen in the Southern States of America'. No doubt the second world war, from which thousands of men returned to their home countries from service in tropical countries, has led to a further increase in amoebiasis in places where it was formerly uncommon. Writing in the British Medical Journal, 17 iii 73, Dr R.G. Hendrickse of the School of Tropical Medicine, Liverpool, remarking that *E. histolytica* has a global distribution, calls intestinal amoebiasis 'one of the most perplexing entities in clinical practice'.

3.   The anonymous pamphlet *Facts Illustrative of the Treatment of Napoleon Buonaparte in St Helena*, later republished under Theodore Hook's name, was reproduced in *Napoleon in His Own Defence* in 1910, by Clement Shorter, who described the pamphlet as rare.

Hook was a noted punster and a wit. He is described as 'partly educated at Harrow'; but it is not clear if he said this himself, in the same vein as Sir Osbert Sitwell's entry in *Who's Who*, that he was educated 'during the holidays from Eton'. It is believed that the aim of his pamphlet was to ingratiate himself in Government circles, where he was in bad odour. His two day visit to St Helena was en route to England to be tried for peculation as Accountant General and Treasurer in Mauritius. 'I hope you are not going home for your health, Mr Hook', asked someone. 'Why,' said Hook, 'they think there is something wrong in the chest.' He visited Longwood House, but there is no evidence that he saw Napoleon.

4.   O'Meara was twice married. In 1823 he became the second husband of Theodosia, the aged widow of Sir Egerton Leigh, Bart. She had been first married to a Captain Donellan, whom the Scottish surgeon John Hunter unsuccessfully tried to save from the hangman, after he was condemned for the murder of his wife's brother, Sir Theodosius Allesly Boughton. O'Meara died from erysipelas of the face at the age of 50.

5.   Carefully worded attempts to enlist Dr Verling as Napoleon's man were resolutely and repeatedly refused. He said that he was an officer on military duty at Longwood. He was once offered 12,000 fr if he would 'lean rather to an augmentation than a diminution of the

disease'. Verling ultimately rose to become Inspector General of Sanitation to the Army. His diary is in the National Archives of France. A typewritten copy, by A.E. Ross, is in the Bodleian Library, where I read it, through the kindness of Miss Rosemary Dunhill.

6.   The Reverend Richard Boys, Chaplain to the Honourable East India Company delighted in denouncing evil living wherever he saw it, and he saw plenty in St Helena. He was greatly liked by many Servicemen, but those who have been chastened by the Pakenham-Whitehouse whips may be thankful that they know not the scorpions of 'the terrible Mr Boys'. He kept it up to the end, and on July 8th, 1821, a few days before Sir Hudson Lowe and his staff sailed for England, they had to sit through Mr Boys' last sermon as he thundered away about publicans and harlots.

7.   *Charges against Dr John Stokoe.*
1st. For having on or about the 17th January last, when permitted or odered by Rear-Admiral Plampin, Commander-in-Chief of His Majesty's Ships and Vessels at the Cape of Good Hope and the seas adjacent, etc, to visit Longwood for the purpose of affording medical assistance to General Buonaparte, then represented as being dangerously ill, communicated with the said General or his attendants upon subjects not at all connected with medical advice, contrary to standing orders in force for the governance of His Majesty's naval officers at St Helena.

2nd. For having on or about the same day, on receiving communication both in writing and verbally from some of the French prisoners at Longwood, taken notice of and given an answer to such communications previous to making the same known to the Commander-in-Chief, contrary to the said standing orders.

3rd. For having in pursuance of such unauthorised communication signed a paper purporting to be a bulletin of General Buonaparte's health, and delivering the same to the said General or his attendants, contrary to the said orders, and to his duty as a British naval officer.

4th. For having in such bulletin stated facts relative to the health of General Buonaparte which did not fall under his, the said Mr John Stokoe's, own observation, and which he afterwards confessed were dictated or suggested to him by the said General or his attendants, and for having signed the same as if he himself had witnessed the said facts, which was not the truth and was inconsistent with his character and duty as a British naval officer.

5th. For having in the said bulletin inserted the following paragraph: 'The more alarming symptom is that which was experienced in the night of 16th instant, a recurrence of which may soon prove fatal, particularly if medical attendance is not at hand', intending thereby contrary to the character and duty of a British officer to create a false impression or belief that General Buonaparte was in imminent or considerable danger, and that no medical assistance was at hand, he, the said Mr John Stokoe, not having witnessed any such symptom, and knowing that the state of the patient was so little urgent that he was four hours at Longwood before he was admitted to see him, and further knowing that Dr Verling was at hand, ready to attend if required in any such emergency.

6th. For having, contrary to his duty,

communicated to General Buonaparte or his attendants information relative to certain books, letters and papers said to have been sent from Europe for the said persons, and which had been intercepted by the Governor of St Helena, and for having conveyed to the said General or his attendants, some information respecting their money concerns, contrary to his duty, which was to afford medical advice only.

7th. For having contrary to his duty and to the character of a British naval officer, communicated to the said General Buonaparte or his attendants an infamous and calumnious imputation cast upon Lieutenant-General Sir Hudson Lowe, Governor of St Helena, by Barry O'Meara, late surgeon in the Royal Navy, implying that Sir Hudson Lowe had practised to put an end to the existence of the said General Buonaparte.

8th. For having disobeyed the positive command of his superior officer in not returning from Longwood on or about the 21st of January aforesaid at the hour especially prescribed to him by the Rear-Admiral, there being no justifiable cause for his disobeying such command.

9th. For having knowingly and willingly designated General Buonaparte in the said bulletin in a manner different from that in which he is designated in the Act of Parliament for the better custody of his person, and contrary to the practice of His Majesty's Government, of the Lieutenant General, Governor of the island, and of the said Rear-Admiral, and for having done so at the especial instance and request of the said General Buonaparte or his attendants, though he, Mr John Stokoe, well knew that the mode of designation was a point in dispute

Q

between the said General Buonaparte and Lieutenant-General Sir Hudson Lowe and the British Government, and that by acceding to the wish of the said General Buonaparte he, the said Mr John Stokoe, was acting in opposition to the wish and practice of his own superior officers, and to the respect which he owed them, under the general printed instructions.

10th. For having in the whole of his conduct in the aforesaid transactions evinced a disposition to thwart the intentions and regulations of the said Rear-Admiral, and to further the views of the said French prisoners in furnishing them with false or colourable pretences for complaint, contrary to the respect which he owed to his superior officers, and to his own duty as an officer in His Majesty's Royal Navy.

8. Madame Mère, Cardinal Fesch and Louis Bonaparte (still calling himself King Louis) gave Stokoe money in gratitude 'for the services he had rendered to the Emperor'. Joseph Bonaparte engaged Stokoe as medical attendant to his younger daughter on her voyage to join him in America at the end of 1821. Further missions of the same sort came Stokoe's way in 1823 and 1824, and he kept up a friendly correspondence with Joseph, until the ex-King of Spain died in 1843. Edith S. Stokoe, the great grandniece who translated Frémeaux's book about Stokoe, contributed two articles about him to the *British Medical Journal*, Volume 1 of 1905. Stokoe was born at Ferry Hill near Durham in 1775. He was apprenticed to his uncle Dr Robert Stokoe, a retired naval surgeon, in 1788. After his uncle re-joined the navy Stokoe himself became a surgeon's mate in

the navy. By attending medical classes in London he completed his medical education which his uncle had rather neglected; and was gazetted full surgeon at the age of 23. He spoke several languages, including Russian. He married late in life, and his wife and two children died before his own sudden death, after a stroke on September 13th, 1852.

## Chapter VII
### ANTOMMARCHI AND ARNOTT

1. Bertrand has been granted a belated and unintended revenge for all the insults. His home in Chateauroux is now the *Musée Bertrand*, in which may be seen relics of his time in St Helena, including his faded Grand Marshal's court dress. In one room are some sketches of Napoleon made at Saint Cloud in 1812, by Girodet Troison, which show a chubby Emperor as, one might imagine, he would least like to be remembered. One of these, a perfect representation of a gynandromorphic or eunuchoid individual, is reproduced in three books by doctors in which this effect of pituitary dysplasia in Napoleon's case is described — those of Brice, Sokoloff, and myself.

2. Bertrand records Napoleon's attempt to get rid of Antommarchi, in these words: *Eh bien, qu'il passe tout son temps avec ses catins; qu'il les foute par devant, par derrière, par la bouche et les oreilles. Mais débarassez-moi de cet homme-la qui est bête, ignorant, fat, sans honneur. Je désire que vous fassiez appeler Arnott pour me soigner à l'avenir.*]

## Chapter VIII
### CORONOR'S INQUEST

1. The first two years of my life as

a doctor gave me opportunities of comparing the two systems. As a house surgeon in the Royal Infirmary of Edinburgh I gave evidence before the Procurator Fiscal of Edinburgh, a kindly bearded figure, intent on putting young doctors at their ease, protecting them if necessary from lawyers who tried to confuse them; and thus, as I realise in retrospect, protecting our Hospital from the sort of journalistic sniping to which hospitals are sometimes subjected today. Things were very different in the court of the Coroner of Westminster, in which I appeared as a brand-new Lieutenant R.A.M.C. A soldier had died from an unusual condition, aneurysm of the heart, resulting from the lodging of a 0.22 bullet in the pericardium (the covering around the heart) following the accidental discharge, in India a year before, of the cantonment dogshooter's rifle. Sniffing out the shooting, the coroner questioned me aggressively, seeming to imply that the Army was hiding something. Rather nettled, I unwisely answered one question a bit curtly; Q: 'What is a dog-shooter?' A: 'A man who shoots dogs.' Although the accident had been fully investigated at the time, I was told to stand down, and a senior officer was sent for, who explained the duties of a cantonment dog-shooter. By this time the parents of the victim were plainly suspicious of something not quite straightforward, and a trustful sympathetic friendship, formed during their son's last illness was somehow tarnished. When I was finally handed thirty shillings, in open court, it felt like blood-money (and to make it worse I had to hand it in to my unit's imprest account).

## 2.    THE FIVE REPORTS

(a) The official report, dated 6th May 1821, signed by Drs Shortt, Arnott, Burton and Mitchell.

(b) Shortt's copy, showing the deletions ordered by the Governor.

(c) Antommarchi's report, dated 8th May, 1821; the only one accepted by the French.

(d) Henry's report, written in Ireland in 1823.

(e) Antommarchi's second report, in his book *Les Derniers Moments de Napoléon* 1825.

(a), (d) and (e) can conveniently be studied in James Kemble's book *Napoleon Immortal*. (c) is reproduced in the Memoirs of Marchand and of De Montholon. It is quite a short report, though longer than the official report. The paragraphs which deal with the stomach and liver are as follows:—

*Translation of Articles 7 to 15 of Antommarchi's Second Report.*

7.  The upper convex surface of the left lobe of the liver was adherent to the corresponding part of the concave surface of the diaphragm.

8.  The lower surface of the above-mentioned lobe was strongly adherent to the anterior surface of the lesser curvature of the stomach, and also to the lesser omentum.

9.  Having carefully detached, using the scalpel as well as the fingers, the above-mentioned adhesions, I observed that the adhesion to the left lobe of the liver formed a hole about three lines* in diameter in the anterior surface of the stomach close to its right extremity.

10. Having opened the stomach behind the greater curvature I observed that it was partly filled by a blackish liquid substance with a pungent and unpleasant smell.

11. Having removed this liquid I

observed a very extensive cancerous ulcer occupying particularly the upper part of the internal surface of the stomach, and stretching from the cardiac orifice to about one inch (*pouce**) from the pylorus.

12. At the edge of this ulcer, near the pylorus, I saw the above-mentioned hole (paragraph 9) caused by the perforation by the ulcer of the coats of the stomach.

13. The ulcerated coats of the stomach were considerably swollen and indurated.

14. Between the ulcer and the pylorus and close to the ulcer I observed a swelling and scirrhous induration several lines* in extent which encircled the right extremity of the stomach.

15. The liver was congested and larger than normal.
*Mémoires de Marchand*, pp. 1952-1955.

3. George Henry Rutledge was one of the two doctors present at the autopsy who were debarred from signing because they were only assistant surgeons. The other, Walter Henry, about a year younger than Rutledge, was ordered to take notes, and it is possible that Rutledge was told to help Antommarchi. In Volume 3 of W. Forsyth's *History of the Captivity of Napoleon*, pp. 291-292, can be read Rutledge's description of the disposal of the heart and stomach. The heart, sealed with a silver coin of George III in a silver vessel surmounted by an eagle, and the stomach in a silver pepper-box, without any preservatives, were

* The *pied de roi*, the French unit of measurement then in use, was subdivided into twelve *pouces*, and the *pouce* consisted of twelve *lignes*.

finally placed in the coffin together with a silver dinner plate, knife, fork and spoon etc, twelve pieces of gold and twelve of silver coins, and a plate with Rutledge's address, as the last British officer who had seen Napoleon's body. This little touch of exhibitionism might incline one to side with those who have doubted the veracity of Rutledge's report. He further wrote that before the stomach was sealed up Mme Bertrand 'actually introduced the point of her little finger through the cancerated hole'.

Lieutenant Duncan Darroch, in a letter to his mother, which was published in *The Sunday Times*, 22nd and 30th December 1934, described how one of the doctors showed him the stomach and heart, in a silver urn beside the body – '. . . they were covered with fat -- in his stomach I was shown the hole that had caused his death – a hole that I could have put my little finger into.'

He described the grave as follows:

The grave was dug interior capacity was 12 ft deep, 8 ft long and 6 ft wide, surrounded by a wall about 3 ft thick all the way down and plastered with Roman cement. About 2 ft from the bottom and resting on blocks of stone. The stone coffin was constructed like a large stone box with the lid open and the lid resting on one of its edges.

Into this stone box the wooden coffin was lowered.

4. Arnott is believed by many to have used his opportunity to make a death mask of Napoleon, possibly at the request of Napoleon's brother Jerome, who subsequently bought it and left it to Napoleon III. The peregrinations of this mask are related in *The Illustrated London News*, April 1855; and in papers kindly shown to me by Arnott's

great-grand-niece, Mrs Donald Sinclair of Edinburgh. In a privately printed family history *The House of Arnot*, Edinburgh 1918, Mrs Sinclair's father Surgeon Lieutenant Colonel James Arnott, observing that Dr Archibald Arnott always denied having made a mask, speculated that this disclaimer could have been dictated by prudence, since the mask, if made, was made without the Governor's knowledge or permission.

The question of the authenticity of the Arnott mask will be discussed in two chapters of the book now being prepared by Baron de Veauce.

5. Photographs of the specimens can be seen in the following (see bibliography) Lord Brock's book, and the articles by Keith, de Mets and Proger. An article in Charles Dickens' magazine *Household Words*, 14th December 1850 (page 281) describing a visit to the Hunterian Museum, where the specimens were on view, relates the following scene:

> One day a perfect scene occurred –
> '*Perfide Albion*' shrieked a wild Gaul, whose enthusiasm seemed as though it had been fed upon Cognac. '*Perfide Albion!*' again and more loudly rang through the usually quiet hall. 'Not sufficient to have your Vaterloo Bridge, your Vaterloo Place, your Vaterloo boots, but you put violent hands on de grand Empereur himself. '*Perfide! Perfide! Perfide!*' he yelled again, and had he not been restrained would have run a Gallic muck among the bones and bottles that would have been recollected for many a day. From that time the pathological record of Napoleon's fatal malady has been unmarked and – to the million – unrecognisable.

C.K. Shorter, in *The Sphere*, 1st February, 1913, noting that the specimens lay beside 'the internal workings of Lord Liverpool and William IV', remarked on the odd fact that they were thus next to Napoleon's 'head gaoler, the Prime Minister of the time.' This implies that in 1913, when Keith described them, they were again on view; but when Lord Moynihan showed them to the Frenchman, Professor René Leriche, after a public dinner in 1927, according to Leriche they went to a private room, where Lord Moynihan explained that the specimens had been entrusted by the Government to the President of the Royal College of Surgeons of England, who had to keep them locked up, the key always on his person. The conversation was interrupted because the Prime Minister was feeling ill, (allegedly after viewing other pathological specimens) and Lord Moynihan had to conduct him to his carriage. Leriche wrote his book a quarter of a century after this experience, and his memory of the unusual after-dinner entertainment was possibly hazy.

6. After the publication of my first book, in which I speculated about the effect which hypogonadism might have had upon Napoleon's character, I received a letter from an old friend, Major W.A. Spowers, late the Grenadier Guards, and now a Director of Christie, Manson and Woods, in which he said: 'I cannot remember if I discussed with you the occasion when I had to offer at sale here Napoleon's private parts, mounted in a velvet Cartier box.' In the catalogue of the sale on 29th October, 1969, of the Vignali Collection of Napoleonic Relics, this particular item is described as follows:—

> A small dried-up object, genteelly described as a mummified tendon, taken from his body during the post-mortem. [The authenticity of the macabre relic has been confirmed by the publication in the *Revue des Mondes* of a post-

humous memoir by St Denis, in which he expressly states that he and Vignali took away small pieces of Napoleon's corpse during the autopsy.]

The reference should presumably be to the *Revue des Deux Mondes*, but I have been unable to find the memoir referred to. Ali's memoirs were published in 1922, and on p. 280 he describes Antommarchi taking two small pieces of rib.

Major Spowers informs me that this relic was sold by the Vignali family after the war to Maggs Brothers of Berkeley Square, London. They sold it to Rosenbach in New York, a firm which was later taken over by a dealer named Fleming, from whom it was bought by an American Donald Hyde, who eventually sold it back to Fleming. Fleming then sold it to the anonymous dealers who bought it as a speculation and sold it in partnership at Christies, who, Major Spowers tells me, were mystified by the fact that one of the partners bought it, either for a client or for his own sole interest. Mr Allan Lazarus, for over thirty years a student of Napoleon's captivity, informs me that the buyer was named Gimelson and that the relic is still on offer by Flayderman, a well-known dealer in the United States.

Another correspondent, Dr Norman T. Gridgman, a biomathematician of Ottawa, informs me that this relic was described in the *New York Herald Tribune* in 1954 or 1955; and he enclosed 'a xerox of pp. 114 and 115 of *The Ms Girls*, a sex book by Cheryl Nash, a Dell paperback New York 1972. If this is anything to go by the organ is in medical hands anyway.'

In the Library of The Wellcome Institute of the History of Medicine there is a single page from a French illustrated paper, (un-identified and undated, but thought by Mr Robin Price, assistant librarian, to be 1966) with an article *Un Morceau d'Empereur*, in which the specimen is described as '*une pièce anatomique parfaitement identifiable dont il est impossible de préciser la nature sans offenser la décence.*'

Mr Lazarus believes that 'Dr Rosenbach, the great American dealer in books . . . invented the penis/tendon as a "talking point".' Understandably he cannot believe that such desecration of the Emperor's body could have been perpetrated by devoted Frenchmen, though they may have taken some sort of sacred relic to France. It is easier and kinder all round to accept this sane theory; but I might comment that, devoted though Ali may have been, I would not trust Antommarchi or Vignali to have been swayed by feelings of respect or even of human dignity; and it remains a fact that dealers, not normally easily hoaxed, have paid up to £18,000 for the curious relic. I have been informed by the distinguished English writer, Cecil Roberts now living in Rome, that Napoleon's foreskin is to be seen in the Napoleonic Museum in Rome (1 Via Zasardelli). It seems that the perpetrators of this reprehensible act of desecration deserve condemnation also for the cupidity which led them to dispose of their trophy in two "lots".

7. In his book *The Crime Explosion* Peter Gladstone Smith explains that when the victim had had small doses of arsenic administered to him over a long period, doctors were encouraged to prescribe tartar emetic and calomel for the resultant symptoms; and 'when calomel was combined with Orgeat, a common invalid drink at the time, it formed soluble mercury salts, which are toxic, corrosive and deadly' (p. 134).

Napoleon unquestionably consumed quantities of tartar emetic, calomel and orgeat.

8. There is evidence that amoebic dysentery was known to Hippocrates. The use of ipecacuanha in its treatment was first mentioned in Purchas's Pilgrims (1625) and it was used as a secret remedy against dysentery in Paris about 1680. It was purchased by the French Government in 1688, for 20,000 francs. (*Medical Bibliography*, L.T. Morton, 1970).

Emetine, the curative principle in ipecacuanha, was first used in 1911, and stovarsol ten years later.

E. histolytica was described in a case of dysentery in Russia in 1875 (Lösch); associated definitely with the disease in 1886; and differentiated from the relatively harmless E. coli by Schaudinn in 1903.

9. Bearer of a name famous in Corsican military history, Dr Abbatucci's full name is Count Jacques Pierre Louis Savarin Abbatucci. In his books and articles he uses the name Dr S. Abbatucci. A letter to *La Presse Médicale*, p. 1757, Vol. 42, 1934, is signed 'Abbatucci'. In Surgeon Lieutenant General Brice's book he is referred to as Medécin Major Abbatucci; and in Dr Ganière's book as a general. Dr A. de Mets served in the first World War and also ran a clandestine organisation helping young Belgians to escape and join King Albert's army. When the organisation was discovered by the Germans in 1918 forty six members were shot and de Mets himself was condemned to perpetual hard labour.

10. Dr Hillemand, wrongly stating that John Hunter founded the Hunterian Museum, (which was founded by Sir Astley Cooper) mentions that Hunter believed the Napoleonic specimens to be genuine. Hunter died twenty eight years before Napoleon. He quotes a Latin sentence with which Walter Henry in his memoirs veiled his description of Napoleon's genital organs; the sentence is quoted twice by Hillemand — on pages 103 and 210, each time differently and each time wrongly. The bibliography, which is messy and misspells many English words, cites as authorities two works which are not genuine sources. One of these — *Chagrins Domestiques de Napoléon Bonaparte à l'isle de Sainte Hélène*, by E. Santiné, Paris 1821, purported to be by Santini, a footman at Longwood, but has been known for well over a hundred years to be a forgery. In *Les Supercheries Littéraires Dévoilées*, M. Quérard. Paris 1870, it is attributed to a most assiduous literary forger, Charles Doris of Bourges, who under various names, wrote books and pamphlets designed to denigrate the Bonapartes. *Le Journal Intime de Napoléon*, by G. di Lo Duca, is in a different category; an entertaining, well-researched book, pretending to be Napoleon's private diary. A curious theme running through it is Napoleon's belief that Jomini, the Swiss tactician was his *alter ego*. In one entry Napoleon is made to refer to 'Wellington', on a date long before he had been awarded that title, chosen for him almost at random by his brother William, and consequently, on the date in question, unknown not only to Napoleon but to Arthur Wellesley himself.

11. Walter Henry's memoirs were recently reprinted as *Surgeon Henry's Trifles*, edited by Pat Hayward, Chatto & Windus, 1970. Henry put in a good word for Hudson Lowe, writing that his generosity and acts of kindness to the French after

Napoleon's death 'shew that Sir Hudson Lowe was a very different man from what he was represented by his enemies at the time, and what the world still believes him to be'. He also tells a curious story of Mme Bertrand telling Lowe of 'the Emperor's last request that the past might be forgotten, and that a reconciliation should take place between the parties.'

Neither of the two principal medical officers left memoirs, though Mrs Shortt is said to have written a brief memoir, perhaps for family circulation.

*Alexander Baxter* (1777-1841) Principal Medical Officer, 1816-1819. Graduate of Edinburgh University; appointed Assistant surgeon 1799; saw some active service before being appointed Surgeon to the Corsican Rangers under Lowe's command in April 1805. Present when Lowe surrendered Capri. Later was at Battles of Albuera, 1811, Blandensburg and Baltimore, 1814. In 1816 accompanied Lowe to St Helena; after leaving the island in 1819 returned to Edinburgh, proceeded M.D., with a thesis on remittent fevers. Later served in Barbados.

*Thomas Shortt* (1758-1843) Principal Medical Officer 1819-1821. Graduate of Edinburgh University; appointed Assistant Surgeon 1806; served in Italy, Sicily and Egypt. Had retired from the army and was in civilian medical practice in Edinburgh when he reluctantly accepted the appointment in St Helena. After Napoleon's death he resumed his practice in Edinburgh; became a Member of the College of Physicians of Edinburgh; Physician to Royal Infirmary of Edinburgh and lecturer in Medicine in Edinburgh University, 1828.

These and other public appointments enabled him to decline further military service when an attempt was made to recall him.

### Epilogue

1. John Montgomery's book *Toll for the Brave* supports the belief that the charges against Sir Hector Macdonald were concerned with homosexual conduct, and dismisses the idea that Kitchener might have helped to discredit Macdonald, 'for Kitchener was in no position to arraign anyone on such charges', as his own conduct was notorious. The Mackensen story was revived in an article in *Blackwood's Magazine* – 'Two Lives or One' by A.M.G. June 1962; pp. 481-491; as a result of which Edgar Lustgarten made a detailed study of the evidence for *The Sunday Express*.

2. This strange woman qualified for many pages in French and German dictionaries of biography, in which her maiden name is given in various forms – e.g. Barbara Julie von Wietinghoff; Julienne Vietinghoff; Julie de Wietinghoff.

3. The only 'English lord' associated by rumour with Alexander's supposed flight from Russia was the Scottish nobleman, Lord Cathcart (10th Baron Cathcart in the Scottish peerage and 1st Viscount and Earl Cathcart in the English peerage) who knew the Tsar well. He had lived in St Petersburg for 2 years, after leaving Eton, his father being ambassador there; a position which he himself held from 1812-1820, after a distinguished military career. In a personal letter his descendant Major General the Earl Cathcart has told me that he cannot believe the rumour about his distinguished ancestor's involvement in any such

plot, adding '... the 10th Lord Cathcart was a disciplined soldier for more than 46 years and thereafter the holder of many responsible posts, added to which he was 70 in 1825. Not much Pimpernel about him.' Lord Cathcart, a keen and experienced yachtsman, which the 10th Lord Cathcart apparently was not, points out that even to charter a yacht for such a venture as this expedition to the Black Sea in midwinter would have been a formidable undertaking for a man of 70, and an unlikely one for a peer who at the time was an active member of the House of Lords, a privy councillor, a full General and Lord Lieutenant of Clackmannanshire.

4. Another king who was popularly believed to have ended his life as a hermit was the unfortunate Edward II of England, who, after being deposed in favour of his son Edward III, and imprisoned, certainly escaped once. His death was considered essential to the stability of the throne and it has been assumed that he was recaptured and done to death in Berkely Castle. His robust frame resisted severe privations and hardships, even torture, his shrieks being audible well beyond the confines of the castle. To avoid external evidence of murder he was finally killed in a particularly horrid manner, by a red-hot poker thrust into his rectum. Rumours of his escape were supported by a letter sent to his son Edward III by a Genoese priest, Manuel Fieschi, breaking the secrecy of the confessional. This related that Edward had murdered a porter, taken his keys and escaped; the porter's body being passed off as that of the king. Edward took refuge in Corfe Castle, going thence to Ireland, Flanders and Languedoc. In Avignon he had an interview with Pope John

XXII. Later, travelling from one hermit cell to another, he ended up in Italy where he died. *The Conspiracy of Thomas Dunheved 1327*, F.J. Tanquerey, *Eng-Hist. Rev.* XXXI, pp. 119-24, 1916, and *The Captivity and Death of Edward of Carnarvon*, T.F. Tout, Manchester 1920 (reprint from The Bulletin of the John Ryland's Library. Vol. 6, No. 1, 1920).

5. The Vignali Collection, sold at Christies on 29 x 69 (see Note 6, Chapter 7) included Ange Paul Vignali's diploma of Rome University as Doctor of Medicine, his diploma of Theology, and a Faculty to permit Vignali to practise Medicine and Surgery in St Helena.

6. Thomas, Lord Cochrane, 10th Earl of Dundonald (1775-1860) nephew of Admiral Sir Alexander Cochrane (Note 3 to Chapter 3) specialised, during a long and distinguished career in the Royal Navy, in daring and irregular operations. He found it easy to fall out with higher authority. Whilst an M.P. he was unjustly accused of involvement in a Stock Exchange fraud; expelled from the House of Commons and sent to prison, whence he escaped, was recaptured and finally released on payment of a fine of £1,000; which he made with a banknote preserved in the Bank of England, on which he had written — 'My health having suffered by long and close confinement and my oppressors being resolved to deprive me of property or life, I submit to robbery to protect myself from murder, in the hope that I shall live to bring the delinquents to justice'. He continued to oppose the Government, embittered by a sense of injustice, and was again imprisoned for the original offence of breaking out of prison. This time his

fine was paid by public subscription. In May 1817 he accepted command of the navy of Chile and, after further adventures joined the Brazilian Navy and later the Greek Navy. His constant aim was re-instatement in the Royal Navy, which he achieved, together with a free pardon, in 1832. Cochrane, who had many of the qualities of C.S. Forester's Horatio Hornblower, might have helped in a rescue attempt, to spite the Government; but Napoleon was in no mood for adventures. He had 'several times evaded offers of rescue' is how David Stacton puts it in his book 'The Bonapartes'; which, despite an American journalistic style and a few errors, is entertaining, not least for some memorable sentences — e.g. his remark that Napoleon III and the Prince Imperial both had 'the stubby, scuttling Bonaparte legs'. Apart from Bonapartists, the only man who might have welcomed Napoleon's escape was the old warrior Blücher, who had half seriously suggested to Wellington that they might connive at the attempted escape in order to have another trial of strength with the old enemy.

7. *Anglais,. Rendez nous Napoleon.* Although England is accused of the 'odious crime', some accomplices are also in the dock. Bertrand, Montholon and Marchand, thinking that Napoleon's death mask made by Dr Burton should be suppressed because it made him look old and fat, purloined it and sent it to his mother who gave it to Cardinal Fesch to be locked away, and never shown to Napoleon's son. A death mask of Cipriani, made by O'Meara in 1818, was substituted, and, when Cipriani's face had thus been accepted as the face of Napoleon, it was easy for the British, to whom the deception was

betrayed by O'Meara, to substitute Cipriani's body for that of Napoleon. They secretly exhumed the real Napoleon, brought his body to England, concealing it in Westminster Abbey, and into his tomb in St Helena put the body of Cipriani, dressed in Napoleon's uniform, taken after Waterloo. Not expecting that the French would ever ask for the coffin to be opened, they were care-less over some minor details. The emotion shown by Napoleon's old fellow-exiles when the coffin was opened was really due to chagrin at being unable to expose the fraud.

Demanding that the sarcophagus be opened, Georges Rétif de la Bretonne says that even if Britain is not shamed into making a second, and genuine, *Retour des Cendres*, the French could cast out Cipriani — 'The Traitor beneath the Dome'; who, says the author, was a double agent in Capri, Elba and St Helena; and committed suicide by taking arsenic when his treachery was exposed. The hairs from which Forshufvud and others diagnosed arsenical poisoning were not Napoleon's but Cipriani's; the speci-mens in the Hunterian Museum were from Cipriani's body; and the excel-lent state of preservation of the exhumed body was due to the massive amount of arsenic which it contained. An entertaining essay in crime fiction.

8. I am indebted to Mr Peter Minchener, a former naval officer, living in Jersey, for some interesting facts about *La Belle Poule.* After I had remarked in *Blackwood's Magazine* (Feb. 1974) that *The Pretty Chicken* seemed an unsuitable name for the frigate chosen for so sacred a burden, he wrote to tell me that, whilst that may be a direct translation, some such name as

'Lively Lady' would be nearer the mark. He warned me that *poule* is a term which the English should avoid in French conversation. One dictionary gives not only 'chicken' but 'girl, bird, skirt, tart, mistress', so the name may not be too inappropriate in connection with the Napoleon of Guy Breton's book *Napoleon and His Ladies*, with his preoccupation with 'shapely rumps . . . which set his palms itching' — the hero of my first book, bisexual and probably sterile.

Mr Minchener points out that the name has a long history in the French navy. One ship of the name was captured by the British; the one which went to St Helena is the subject of a long chapter in *Les Grands Voiliers du XV au XX Siècle; sous la Direction de Joseph Jobé*: printed in Lausanne. The present bearer of the name is a training schooner attached to the Naval College at Brest, and of its title the book says (Mr Minchener's translation):

At the launching ceremony of the present vessel it seemed relevant to explain the origin of the name, thought by some of the cadets' families to be unsuitable. (*incongru*) It was therefore officially stated that this name hallowed the memory of a young woman who, in her day, was famous for her beauty as well as for her virtue and her demeanour, Paule de Viguier. Daughter of a noble family of the Languedoc, she was chosen in 1533, aged 15 years, by the Councillors of Toulouse to read the address of welcome to Francois I on the occasion of his visit to that city. The King was entirely captivated by her charm and christened her 'La Belle Paule'. But the imprecise orthography of the period, allied to local pronunciation, developed the name *La Belle Poule*.

9. A doctor named Guillard had accompanied the party and was allowed about two minutes to examine the body, but contrived to prepare a fairly full report, which Dr Arnold Chaplin reprinted as Appendix III in his book *The Illness and Death of Napoleon Bonaparte*, 1913. Guillard described the position of the body in some detail, noted that the two silver vessels containing the heart and stomach were still in position, and that the Emperor's boots had come unstitched, the last four toes being visible on each side.

The beard appeared to have grown after death; the cheeks were full and the skin of the face felt soft and supple. . . . The features of the Emperor were so little changed that his face was instantly recognised by those who had known him when alive, and his entire person presented the appearance of one recently interred.

The vessels containing the heart and stomach were left sealed in the coffin and the last chance of examining the alleged cancer was lost. Perhaps it would have been too late; but when a later movement was set on foot to have the coffin opened it was not for the purpose of examining the stomach, but in order to X-ray the skull, to see if the *sella turcica* was enlarged, which would have supported the view that the changes in his body, attributed to pituitary dysplasia, had been due to a tumour of the pituitary body. (P. Ganière, *Napoléon à Sainte Hélène Vol. 3, p. 345-346*. Dr Guillard attributed the perfect state of preservation of the body, which some recent writers have suggested might have been produced by arsenic, to mummification, a process to which the method of burial and the climate could well have contributed. A world-famous forensic pathologist, Sir Sydney Smith who had long experience in hot countries, wrote as follows: 'Mummification is extremely common in the tropics. In such conditions the features often remain recognisable; and bodies often retain their appearance so well that identification is possible after considerable periods.' *Forensic Medicine*, Sir Sydney Smith & F.S. Fiddes. 1949, p. 36 and p. 630.

# Bibliography

## Books

Abbatucci, S. & De Mets, A., '*Napoléon Les Derniers Moments*', Antwerp, 1938

Anonymous, *Journal of a Soldier of the Seventy First Regiment*, Edinburgh, 1822

Antommarchi, F., *The Last Days of the Emperor Napoleon*, London, 1825

Arnott, A., *An Account of the Last Illness, Decease and Post mortem appearance of Napoleon Bonaparte*, London, 1822

Arnott, J., *The House of Arnot*, Edinburgh, 1918

Aronson, T., *Queen Victoria and the Bonapartes*, London, 1972

Aubry, O., tr. A. Livingstone, *St Helena*, London, 1937

Aubry, O., tr. M. Crosland & S. Road, *Napoleon*, London, 1964

Bailey, J.W., *The Curious Story of Dr Marshall*, Cambridge, Mass., 1930

Bainville, J., *Napoléon*, Paris, 1931

Balmain, Count, *see* Park, J.

Bertrand, H.G., ed. P.F. de Langle, '*Cahiers de Sainte Hélène*', Paris, 1944-59 (1816-1817: pub. 1951, 1818-1819: 1959, 1821 Jan-May: 1949)

Boyd, W., *A Textbook of Pathology*, London, 1961

Bretonne, Commandant Retif de la et son fils Georges, '*La Verité sur le lit de Mort de Napoléon*', Monte Carlo, 1960

Bretonne, G. Rétif de la, '*Anglais Rendez Nous Napoléon*', Paris, 1969

Brice, R., tr. B. Creighton, *The Riddle of Napoleon*, London, 1937

Brock, R.C. (later Lord Brock), *The Life and Work of Astley Cooper*, London, 1952

Brookes, M., *The St Helena Story*, London, 1961

Bryant, A., *The Great Duke*, London, 1971

Cabanes, A., '*Au Chevet de l'Empereur*', Paris, 1924
Cabanes, A., '*Dans l'Intimité de l'Empereur*', Paris, 1932
Castellot, A. et al., '*Le Livre de la Famille Impériale*', Paris, 1969
Cecil, A., *Metternich*, London, 1933
Chaboulon, F. de, '*Mémoires*', Paris, 1901
Chaplin, T.H.A., *The Illness and Death of Napoleon Bonaparte*, London, 1913
Chaplin, T.H.A., *Thomas Shortt*, London, 1914
Chaplin, T.H.A., *St Helena Who's Who*, London, 1919
Chaptal, J.A.C., '*Mes Souvenirs sur Napoléon*', Paris, 1893
Clough, A.H., *Poems*, London, 1888
Cockburn, Admiral Sir G., *Napoleon's Last Voyage.* (Cockburn's Diary) London, 1888
Connelly, O., *The Epoch of Napoleon*, New York, 1972
Constant, *see* Wairy
Conybeare, Sir J. & Mann, W.N., *Textbook of Medicine* (12th Edn.), London, 1957
Costello, E., *Adventures of a Soldier*, London, 1841
Cronin, V., *Napoleon*, London, 1971

Dale, P.M., *Medical Biographies*, Norman, Oklahoma, 1952
Davidson, Sir S., *The Principles and Practice of Medicine*, London, 1966
Dible, J.H., *Napoleon's Surgeon*, London, 1970
Duhamel, J., tr. R.A. Hall, *The Fifty Days*, London, 1969
Dunbar, F., *Emotions and Bodily Changes*, New York, 1954

Emerson, R.W., *Representative Men*, London, 1900

Firmin-Didot, G., '*La Captivité de Sainte Hélène d'après les rapports du M. de Montchenu*', Paris, 1894
Forshufvud, S., *Who Killed Napoleon?* London, 1961
Foy, General M.S., '*Histoire Générale de la Guerre de La Péninsule*', Paris, 1828
Frémeaux, P., tr. E.S. Stokoe, *With Napoleon at St Helena*, London, 1902
Frémeaux, P., '*Les Derniers jours de l'Empereur*', Paris, 1908
French, H., *Index of Differential Diagnosis*, London, 1967

Ganière, P., '*Corvisart: Médecin de Napoléon*', Paris, 1951

Ganière, P., *'Napoléon à Sainte Hélène'*, 1957, *'Le Dernier Voyage de l'Empereur de Malmaison à Longwood*, Paris, *'La Lutte Contre Hudson Lowe'*, Paris, 1960. *'La Mort de l'Empereur: L'Apothéose'*, Paris, 1962

Geer, W., *Napoleon and His Family*, (3 vols), London, 1929

Godlewski, G., *'Aux confins de la vie et de la mort'*, Paris, 1950

Gorrequer, *see* Kemble

Gourgaud, G., tr. S. Gillard, *The St Helena Journal of General Baron Gourgaud*, London, 1932

Guillemin, H., *'Napoléon tel quel'*, Paris, 1969


Henry, W., *Trifles from my Portfolio*, (by a Staff Surgeon), Quebec, 1839

Henry, W., *Events of a Military Life*, (2 vols), London, 1939

Henry, W., ed. P. Hayward, *Surgeon Henry's Trifles*, London, 1970

Herbert, A.P., *Why Waterloo?* London, 1953

Hereau, J., *'Napoleon à Sainte Hélène'*, Paris, 1829

Herold, J.C., *Bonaparte in Egypt*, London, 1962

Hillemand, P., *'Pathologie de Napoléon'*, Paris, 1970

Home, G., *Memoirs of an Aristocrat*, London, 1838


Jackson, B., *Notes and Reminiscences of a Staff Officer*, (first published privately in 1877), London, 1903

James, M.E.C., *I was Monty's Double*, London, 1954


Kemble, J., *Napoleon Immortal*, London, 1959

Kemble, J., *St Helena during Napoleon's Exile*, (Gorrequer's Diary) London, 1969

Korngold, R., *The Last Days of Napoleon*, London, 1960


Lachouque, H. tr. L.F. Edwards, *The Last Days of Napoleon's Empire*, London, 1966

Larrey, D.J., *'Mémoires de Chérurgerie Militaire et Campagnes'*, Paris, 1812

Larrey, F.H., *'Madame Mère': 'Napoleonis Mater'*, Paris, 1892

Leriche, R., *Souvenirs de ma vie morte*, Paris, 1956

Ludwig, E., tr. E. and C. Paul, *Napoleon*, London, 1927


MacLaurin, C., *Post mortem*, London, 1923

Malcolm, C., (Lady), *A Diary of St Helena*, London, 1899

Manceron, C., tr. J. Richardson, *Which Way to Turn*, London, 1961

Manceron, C. tr. G. Unwin, *Napoleon Recaptures Paris*, London, 1968

Manson-Bahr, Dr P.H., *The Dysenteric Disorders*, London, 1939

Manson-Bahr, Sir P.H., *Manson's Tropical Diseases*, London, 1950

Marchand, L., *Mémoires*, Paris, 1952

Markham, F., *Napoleon*, London, 1963

Martineau, G., tr. F. Partridge, *Napoleon's St Helena*, London, 1968

Martineau, G., tr. F. Partridge, *Napoleon Surrenders*, London, 1971

Masson, F., tr. L.B. Frewen, *Napoleon at St Helena*, Oxford, 1949

Mellis, J.C., *St Helena*, London, 1875

Meynell, H., *Conversations with Napoleon at St Helena*, London, 1911

Montchenu, *see* Firmin-Didot

Montgomery, J., *Toll for the Brave*, London, 1963

Montholon, General Count, *History of the Captivity of Napoleon*, London, 1847

Nicolson, H., *Benjamin Constant*, London, 1949

O'Meara, B.E., *Napoleon in Exile*, London, 1882

Paléologue, M., tr. E. and W. Muir, *The Enigmatic Czar*, London, 1938

Park, J., *Napoleon in Captivity*, (Count Balmain's Memoirs), London, 1928

Pasquier, E.D., tr. D. Garman, *The Memoirs of Chancellor Pasquier*, London, 1967

Petrie, Sir C., *Wellington*, London, 1956

Peyre, H. et al., *The Myth of Napoleon*, (Yale French Studies No. 26), New Haven Connecticut, 1950

Pillans, T.D., *The Real Martyr of St Helena*, London, 1913

Pradt, Abbé D. de, *'Histoire de l'Ambassade dans le Duché de Varsovie en 1812'*, Paris, 1815

Price, F.W., *Text Book of Medicine*, London, 1966

Reynier, General Count J.L.E., *De l'Egypte après la bataille à Héliopolis*, Paris, 1802

Richardson, F.M., *Napoleon: Bisexual Emperor*, London, 1972

Robbins, S.L., *Pathology*, Philadelphia, 1967

Rosebery, Fifth Earl of, *Napoleon: The Last Phase*, London, 1900

Saint Denis, L.E., *Napoleon from the Tuileries to St Helena*, London, 1922

Saint Denis, L.E., '*Souvenir du Mameluk Ali*', Paris, 1926

Sarrazin, General, '*Confession du Général Buonaparte*', Londres, 1811

Schiff, L., *Diseases of the Liver*, Philadelphia, 1963

Seaton, R.C., *Sir Hudson Lowe and Napoleon*, London, 1898

Ségur, General Count de, tr. H.A. Patchett Martin, *An Aide de Camp of Napoleon*, London, 1895

Shorter, C.K., *Napoleon and his Fellow Travellers*, London, 1908

Smith, P. Gladstone, *The Crime Explosion*, London, 1970

Sokoloff, B., *Napoleon: A Doctor's Biography*, New York, 1937

Sokoloff, B., *Napoleon: A Medical Approach*, London, 1938

Soubiran, A., '*Le Baron Larrey*', Paris 1966

Stacton, D., *The Bonapartes*, London, 1967

Stanhope, P.H. Fifth Earl, *Notes of Conversations with the Duke of Wellington*, London, 1888

Stevenson, R.S., *Famous Illnesses in History*, London, 1962


Thompson, J.M., *Napoleon Bonaparte: His Rise and Fall*, London, 1963

Thornton, M.J., *Napoleon after Waterloo, England and the St Helena Decision*, Stratford Univ. Press, California, 1968

Treue, W., tr. F. Fawcett, *Doctor at Court* London, 1958

Triaire, P., *Dominique Larrey*, Tours, 1902


Vallance, A., *The Summer King*, London, 1956

Vandal, Comte A., *Avènement de Bonaparte*, Paris, 1910

Vox, M., tr. M. Thornton, *Napoleon*, London, 1960


Wairy, L.C., tr. P. Pinkerton, *Memoirs*, London, 1896

Wartenburg, Count Yorck von, *Napoleon as a General*, London, 1902

Watson, G.L. de St M., *A Polish Exile with Napoleon*, London, 1912

Willis, Professor R.A., *Pathology of Tumours*, London, 1967


Xenophon, *Anabasis*, Book III Ch 4:47-49, (Soteridas the Sicyonian), 4th Century B.C.

# Bibliography

## Articles

(Abbreviations in accordance with *World Medical Periodicals*, 1961)

Abbatucci, S., *'L'Hépatite suppurée de N.Ier à Sainte Hélène'*, Presse Med., 1934, 42, 2, 1269.
Abbatucci, S., *'A propos de la dernière maladie de Napoleon Ier'*, Presse Med., 1934, 42, 2, 1757
Abbatucci, S., *'Autour de la mort de Napoleon Ier'*, Presse Med., 1937, 45, 1, 461-62
Andrews, E., *The Diseases, Death and Autopsy of Napoleon I*, J. Amer.Med. Ass., 1895, 25, 1081-85
Ayer, W.D., *Napoleon Buonaparte and Schistosomiasis*, J.Amer. Ass., 1966, 196, 1, 802
Ayer, W.D., *Napoleon Buonaparte and Schistosomiasis or Bilharziasis*, N.Y., St., J.Med., 1966, 2295-2301

Baclen, J., *'La Position du Docteur O'Meara à Ste Hélène'*, Presse Med., 1969, 77, 51, 1911-1912
Baudouin, M., *Le Docteur Stokoe et la maladie de Napoleon Ier'*, Gaz.med., Paris, 1901, 69-70
Baudouin, M., *'Remarques cliniques sur la dernière maladie de Napoleon Ier'*, Gaz.med, Paris, 1901, 81-84
Bertaut, J., *'Le Docteur O'Meara à Ste Hélène'*, Hist.Med., 1957, 7, 6, 57-64
Binger, V., *'A propos de la dernière maladie de Napoleon Ier'*, Presse Med., 1934, 42 1638
Bradley, C.D., *Craven and O'Meara, Medical Boswells to Jefferson Davis and Napoleon Bonaparte*, Bull.Hist.Med., 1952, 26, 141-152
Brewis, A., *John Stokoe, Proc.Soc.Ant. Newc.*, 4 ser., Vol. 1, 164-168
Broadbent, Sir W.H., *Clinical Thermometry in the Case of the First Napoleon, Brit.Med.J.*, 1903, 1, 813

Cawadias, A.P. et al., *Correspondence about Napoleon's death*, Lancet, 1962, 1, 101; 272; 428; 749; 914; 1128

Chevalier, A.G., *Napoleon's Maladies and Death, Ciba Symp.*, New Jersey, 1941

Cilleuls, J.M. de, *Yvan, Chirurgeon de Napoléon. Arch.Méd. Pharm.milit.*, 1935, (Dec)

David, P., '*Antommarchi, dernière médecin de l'Empereur*', *J. Sci.Med.*, Lille, 1936, 36 232-244

Dryburgh, D.C., *Napoleon and his Doctors, Pulse*, Woking, 1972 (Nov)

Forshufvud, S. et al., *Arsenic Content of Napoleon I's Hair probably taken immediately after his death, Nature*, London, 1961, **243**, 103-105

Ganière, P., '*De Quoi est mort Napoleon?* ' *Presse Méd.*, 1963, 71, 2262-63

Godlewski, G., *Napoleon's Last Illness, Ciba Symp.*, New Jersey, 1957

Goldstein, H.I., *Cancer of the Stomach with some notes on the case of Napoleon Bonaparte, Rev. Gastroent*, 1941, 8, 205-206

Gridgeman, N.S., *Uncle Sam Bonapartes, Dalhousie Review*, 1971, 51, 3

Groen, J.J., '*La Dernière Maladie et la cause de mort de Napoléon*', *Janus*, Leiden, 1963

Haddad, F.S., *Three Famous Autopsies in History*, J. Palest, *Arab.Med.Ass.*, 1948, 48, No. 3, 55-70

Henderson, R.J. and Hill, D.M., *Subclinical Brucella Infection in Man, Brit.Med.J.*, 1972, 3, 154-156

Hendrickse, R.G., *Dysentery including Amoebiasis, Brit.Med.J.*, 1973, 1, 669-72

Kalima, T., '*De quelle maladie est mort Napoleon Ier?* ' *Acta chir.scand.*, 1932, 72, 1-17

Keith, Sir A., *The History and Nature of certain specimens alleged to have been obtained at the Post Mortem on Napoleon the Great, Brit.Med.J.*, 1913, 1, 53-58

Keith, Sir A., *History and Nature of the Napoleonic specimens in the Museum of the Royal College of Surgeons of England, Lancet*, 1913, 1, 187-189

Knott, J., *The Fatal Illness and Death of Napoleon the Great*, *J.Irish Med.Ass.*, 1913, **135**, 119-134

Mets, A. de, '*Comment mourut Napoleon, Revue de la Corse Ancienne et Moderne*', Antwerp, Jun. 1931

Mitchell, C.A., *Walter Henry and the Autopsy of Emperor Napoleon Ist, Univ. Ottawa Med.J.*, 1965, **9**, 3

*Napoleon's Death*, Leading article, *Lancet*, 1961, **2**, 1395-96

O'Meara, B.E., *Note on O'Meara*, J.Irish Med.Ass., 1963, **53**, (313) 3

Proger, L.W., *A Napoleonic Relic, Ann.Roy.Coll.Surg.*, Eng., 1960, **26**, **1**, 57-62

Rosebery, Fifth Earl of, *The Coming of Bonaparte, Fortnightly Review*, 1912, D.XVII, July

Tailhefer, A., '*La Maladie de Napoléon Ier à Sainte Hélène*', *Presse Med.*, 1941, **49**, 19-22

*Vaccination in St Helena*, Note in *Brit.Med.J.*, 1903, 2 445

Viel Castel, Count L. de, '*Sir Hudson Lowe et la Captivité de Saint Hélène*', *Rev. des Deux Mondes*, 1855

Wallace, D.C., *How did Napoleon die? Med.J.Aust.*, 1964, **1**, 13, 494-495

Warren, R. de, *Un Bonaparte, Ministre de la Marine Americaine, Rev. de Def. Nationale*, 1969

Wolff, G., '*Die letzte Krankheit Napoleons I*', *Med. Mschr.* 1963, **7**, 443-447

# Index

# INDEX

**DATE DUE**

| | | | |
|---|---|---|---|
| ~~MAY 5 77~~ | | | |
| MAR 3 1983 | | | |
| MAR 2 4 1983 | | | |
| APR 7 1983 | | | |
| JAN 2 4 1985 | | | |
| OCT 1 7 1985 | | | |
| 5-13-87 ILL: 3320507 Alma College | | | |
| | | | |
| | | | |
| | | | |
| | | | |
| | | | |
| | | | |
| | | | |
| | | | |